TERRORISM IN INDIAN OCEAN REGION

TERRORISM IN INDIAN OCEAN REGION

Editor

Dhruv C Katoch

INDIA FOUNDATION
Analysis • Advocacy • Awareness

PENTAGON PRESS

Terrorism in Indian Ocean Region
Editor: Dhruv C Katoch

ISBN 978-93-86618-38-2

First Published in 2018

Published by
PENTAGON PRESS
206, Peacock Lane, Shahpur Jat
New Delhi-110049
Phones: 011-64706243, 26491568
Telefax: 011-26490600
email: rajan@pentagonpress.in
website: www.pentagonpress.in

Printed at Aegean Offset Printers, Greater Noida, U.P.

Contents

Introduction

Dhruv C Katoch

Counter Terrorism has been the flavour of the season ever since the dastardly attacks on the United States took place on 11 September 2001, now referred to as 9/11 in popular jargon. In response, the United States launched its Global War on Terror (GWOT), which continues till date. The word terrorism itself dates from the eighteenth century, but it was only after 9/11 that the term acquired its present salience. In India, the security forces in general and the Indian Army in particular have been waging a relentless battle against terrorists and insurgents for over six decades, and for the most part, this has been a lonely battle. The world awoke to the threat of terrorism, when, post the 9/11 attacks, the realisation set in that acts of terror can take place in any part of the globe and that cooperative efforts were required to stem the growth of the phenomenon.

This book presents the proceedings of the Third Counter Terrorism Conference (CTC)—an annual feature of India Foundation which first started in 2015, drawing upon political leaders as well as professionals in the field of counter terrorism from all across the globe. The first two conference were held in Jaipur, in partnership with the government of Rajasthan and the third was held in Delhi in partnership with the Government of Haryana. All the conferences have been supported by the Ministry of Home Affairs, Government of India.

After CTC 2016, which was focussed on Global Terrorism, CTC 2017 held in Delhi had as its focus, the Indian Ocean Region. This region and its immediate neighbourhood is most impacted by terrorism, particularly the Af-Pak region, West Asia and the East coast of Africa. India, Bangladesh and the ASEAN countries too have been impacted by terrorism in various degrees.

The Indian Ocean is also a hot spot for piracy, and considering the large volume of international trade that passes through its waters, the importance of stability in the IOR gets further highlighted.

Why do people pick up the gun against the state? The answer to this question is the first step towards formulating an appropriate response strategy. The Vice President of India, Shri Hamid Ansari spoke of four main factors, namely ideological differences, ethno-political issues, politico-religious dissonance and cross border terrorism as motivating factors. All these factors have been adequately highlighted by various speakers along with what needs to be done to formulate a suitable response. Along with this, the issue of governance was also discussed with Mr ESL Narasimhan highlighting what the term meant. But good governance by itself cannot be a panacea to counter terrorism, though admittedly it does form a very important constituent. Where terrorism is promoted from across the border by regimes as 'war by other means' on their neighbours, then obviously, the governance factor loses much of its relevance.

Within the four broad parameters stated above, there will be a great deal of overlapping with respect to the motivation for terrorism and insurgencies, and any of the above factors can have varying shades of the others embodied within its structure. In terms of Kautilyan statecraft, terrorism and insurgencies referred to above could have three variants. The first is externally sponsored and supported, in furtherance to the designs of a hostile power. Next is where internal factors have led to the onset of terrorism and insurgency, which thereafter has received external support. The third is when the causes are internal but the insurgency or terrorism does not receive external support.

A response strategy to terrorism which is externally sponsored and supported must of necessity deal with the external actor. It is different to those insurgencies that have internal causes and may or may not be supported by external actors. The former is part of an adversary's attempt to use terrorism as a part of state policy. Pakistan's use of terrorism, in creating instability in Jammu and Kashmir and also in other parts of India is an apt example of state support to terrorism. Obviously, in such cases, the external actor has to be addressed if peace and stability are to be brought about. Here, Pakistan has a well thought out and craftily enunciated strategy to "bleed India with a thousand cuts". Not much headway has been made by India in addressing this threat, primarily because the response was reactive. To prevent attacks, a defensive mindset came into operation, with more and more walls and fences being constructed around high profile targets. This reduced the number of attacks but did not resolve the problem, leading some scribes to describe Indian reactions as 'survival by a thousand bandages'. India undertook no punitive action when its parliament was attacked, when the Akshardham attack took place or even after the 2008 bloody Mumbai attacks.

There appears to be a change in stance in Indian response patterns post the 2014 elections, when the BJP led NDA government came to power. The surgical strikes of 28 September 2016 following the killing of 19 soldiers in an attack on an army base on 18 September was perhaps the most visible signal of a likely end to the era of Indian inaction and putting the Pakistani military establishment on notice. While the surgical strike has done little to change the fundamentals of India's strategic dynamic with Pakistan, their political, psychological, diplomatic and strategic benefits have been greater than the tactical military gains. Pakistan stands virtually isolated in the region, and is largely being recognised by the world community as a sponsor of terrorism.

While three years is too short a time to assess the effectiveness of the change in Indian strategy, it remains an incontrovertible truism that peace cannot result unless the sponsors of terror are appropriately addressed. There perhaps is a need to increase the level of deterrence against such rogue states, to force them to sever ties with terrorist groups, whom they use as their strategic assets. Realising this objective calls not for overt belligerence or brinkmanship but for a silent war, employing multiple tools of leverage and coercion, for, however, long it takes to bring those states to heel, who sponsor terrorist groups.

The role of governance and its importance in preventing the seeds of terrorism to germinate was extensively deliberated upon. What was highlighted was the need to distinguish between foreign sponsored terrorism and home grown militancies and insurgencies, which have now blossomed into terrorism. While governance is an important and vital component in conflict resolution of the latter, in the case of foreign sponsored terrorism, the argument of governance becomes somewhat irrelevant. It remains important, but it is not the answer to the resolution of the imported species of terrorism.

The United Nations has based its counter-terrorism strategy on four pillars, which find universal applicability. These four pillars are:

- Addressing the conditions conducive to the spread of terrorism;
- Preventing and combatting terrorism;
- Building capacity; and
- Ensuring human rights and the rule of law.

We find here that governance plays a critical role as a preventive strategy. It is a composite term encompassing within its ambit a vast array of institutions—the executive, the legislature, the judiciary, the media, human rights organisations, civil societies, etc. Weak institutions, large scale corruption and lack of justice delivery mechanisms provide fertile soil for the growth of terrorist movements. Denial of justice is a prime motivator which impels people to take the law into their own hands. The growth and spread of Left Wing Extremism in India can to some extent be attributed to the fact that justice to a large group of people was denied. This is one of the reasons why the movement still exists, over 50 years after the first violent attack took place in 1967. Governance structures need to look into accountability, periodic audit of performance and transparency. This is not easy to achieve as there will always be a great deal of institutional resistance to reform.

Another issue highlighted during the conference was that good governance by itself may not be an adequate safeguard against terrorism and violent extremism. As an example, one of the speakers stated that North Korea, Zimbabwe and Haiti are three countries which have poor governance, yet remain free from acts of terrorism. Contrarily, if you look at France, Australia and Canada you see three countries which despite having good governance are indeed suffering from terrorism. This was attributed to the phenomenon of radicalisation as manifested in Islamism.

Factors such as anger at injustice, moral superiority, a sense of identity and purpose, the promise of adventure and becoming a hero have all been implicated in case studies of radicalisation. Religion and ideology serve as vehicles for an "us versus them" mentality and as the justification for violence against those who represent "the enemy," but they are not the drivers of radicalisation. India, as indeed the world, is confronted today by Islamism, by which is meant a certain kind of understanding of Islam, namely, the application of Islamic law in its severity and in its entirety. To many in the Muslim world, there is this belief that they would be strong, if Muslims return to full application of the Sharia. Trend lines here are the growth of ISIS, al Qaeda, Boko Haram, al-Shabab, and closer home, the radicalisation of a section of Muslims in Kashmir.

When we view Islamism, we are looking at an attraction to an idea—a very powerful idea. Just as communism was a radical utopian ideology that held great attraction for many people, particularly the educated, as did fascism, now it is the turn of Islamism. There is this great attraction to an idea that seeks to strengthen the Ummah by going back and applying Islamic law. Within this construct, jihadi violence is not about governance; it is not about personal status—being rich or poor, employed or unemployed, educated or not. It is about attraction to this idea, and results from this deep sense that the Muslim community, the Ummah, has not done well in the modern era.

An interesting aspect of CTC 2017 was the first hand experiences of people who had given up the gun for the ballot. Mr Sajad Lone very eloquently explained why he chose the path of the ballot, crediting his change of stance to the behaviour of two officials. Mr Mohilary also gave out his reasons for opting for the ballot, but put in a caveat. He said that his experience of democracy and the federal structure of the Constitution show that conflict can be resolved through dialogue. However, he put in a word of caution, by quoting from the speech of Malcolm X, where he advised African-Americans to judiciously exercise their right to vote, but if they continued to face discrimination, then it might be necessary to once again pick up the gun. In essence, what was highlighted was the need for justice for all people.

As part of strategy formulation to counter terrorism, a vast array of ideas were discussed. The experience of Singapore in controlling radicalism and in empowering its citizenry was revealing. The importance of appropriate legislation to combat terrorism also received a lot of emphasis. Some of the speakers, while alluding to strategy formulation, emphasised the need to deal with causative factors, preferably before they erupted into violence on the streets. Besides effective institutions, it was highlighted that civil society and a free and unbiased media had an important role to play. As a long term preventive strategy, education remains the key, with thrust on appropriate syllabus content. Alongside, the dire necessity of addressing corruption in public life was given out as a core priority to restore faith in the system.

The spread of communication technology and the availability of modern weapons have made the terrorist networks truly global in nature. Detecting and combatting terrorism would hence involve a whole of government approach and detailed cooperation at the bilateral, multilateral and global level. The role of the United Nations in the global war on terror was highlighted, especially in terms of a number of UN Conventions on the subject which have been endorsed by most countries. The fact which is of relevance is that the basket of conventions, 19 international instruments in all, can be considered collectively as a comprehensive approach to countering terrorism. They include conventions such as the Convention on Terrorist Bombings, International Convention for the Financing of Terrorism and the Convention on Nuclear Terrorism. Since

2006, the UN has had a global counter-terrorism strategy, adopted by the General Assembly, which is currently under review. Pursuant to that strategy, it also has a counter-terrorism implementation task force which brings together around 39 different agencies that have many and varied roles in tackling terrorism. In addition, certain measures adopted by the Security Council, under Chapter VII of the UN Charter, makes them legally binding on all the member-states. They include the 1267 Regime that was first adopted in 1999 by which the Security Council imposes sanctions on individuals and entities linked to al-Qaeda or Daesh (ISIS). It also includes the 1373 Regime which is a business and counter-terrorism committee and which expects member-states to impose national sanctions against individuals and entities linked to terrorism including, but not confined to, al-Qaeda and Daesh. All this goes to show that a very solid legal base for action exists.

Indian legal instruments to counter terrorism are considered weak by some, after the repeal of the Prevention ofTerrorism Act (POTA) in September 2004. Its place has been taken by the earlier The Unlawful Activities (Prevention) Act, 1967 (UAPA), with some amendments, to give a legal base to prosecute terror cases. There is a view that the repeal of POTA has debilitated India's anti terrorism effort, especially as the onus to prove guilt now rests on the police and not on the accused to prove his or her innocence. There would be a requirement for a stricter law, but it is unlikely to come about in the present political climate.

India's intelligence agencies are well geared for the task at hand, and now with the formation of the National Investigative Agency, we have a dedicated investigative agency as well. The fact that terrorist related incidents have registered a steep fall in the country testifies to the effectiveness of the agencies. In terms of kinetic effort, adequate security forces exist to counter the threat. In terms of public response to terrorism, much however still needs to be done. There is also a lack of a counter narrative to prevent the radicalisation of minds. This includes counter-narrative from the state as well as counter-narrative from civil society, where the former holds greater traction.

The battle against terrorism will be long and the road to be traversed is difficult. But it is a battle that India and indeed the world must win, for the sake of humanity.

PART I

REGIONAL VIEWPOINTS

1

State-Sponsored Terrorism: War by Other Means

M Hamid Ansari

In recent years, nothing has caused greater pain, disruption and inconvenience to societies, governments and individuals than the phenomenon of terrorism. Its manifestation in any shape or form anywhere in the world is disruptive of normal life and therefore has to be condemned and countered. A UN panel on 17 March 2005, described terrorism as an act 'intended to cause death or serious bodily harm to civilians or non-combatants with the purpose of intimidating a population or compelling a government to or an international organisation to do or abstain from doing any act.'

Notwithstanding this, governments of the world continue to argue about the precise import of the term. One reason is the antiquity of the expression and its uses down the ages. Kautilya classified terrorising as 'secret war.' The 'Zealots' of the Roman period and the 'Assassins' of the Middle Ages used violence to terrorise their adversaries. It was used in the 'Reign of Terror' period of the French Revolution and its agents were officially depicted as 'terrorists.'

The number of terrorist groups proliferated in the 19th and 20th centuries and this trend continues today. A Google search produces a list of 38 non-state right-wing and left-wing groups accused of terrorism from 1978 to 2003; it indicates the period of their activity, targets and tactics, and governments viewed as adversaries as well as those who sponsored or supported them. More names can be added to it today. The stated motivation in each case related to addressing grievances of a political nature, very often embedded in and seeking empowerment from ethnic, nationalist or religious sources. Modern weapons and easy access to lethal devices have added to the efficacy of terror tactics; so has globalisation and information technology.

Modern terrorism is global in its dimensions. My focus in this paper is on the Indian Ocean Rim, which has 26 littoral states and is home to some 2.3 billion people. It has emerged as one of the most dynamic regions of the world. It has about 65 percent of the world's oil reserves, its ports handle about 30 percent of global trade and half of the world's container traffic passes through this ocean. This region is also culturally diverse with a variety of languages, religions, traditions and cultures. The countries of the Indian Ocean littoral and its immediate hinterland vary in terms of their geographies, populations, levels of economic development and political structures.

Security in the Indian Ocean region is capricious on account of a complex set of problems inherited from its recent past. These pose a widespread complex set for policymakers, especially since many of the issues are transnational and groups have resorted to using force to further demands for national self-determination, separatism and militant religious extremism.

The fragility of institutions of new political systems in the region has often allowed political violence to prevail. In addition, militant groups have exploited local grievances and have drawn upon international events to promote radical and extremist causes. The objective of these groups remains the capture of state power and the transformation of the system of governance to one that conforms to their worldview.

An overarching approach to the menace found expression most recently in the declaration emanating from the 20th Anniversary meeting of the Indian Ocean Rim Association (IORA) on 7 March 2017, that denounced 'terrorism and violent extremism in all its forms and manifestations' and 'resolved to stand together' in preventing and countering it.

The typology of terrorism in the Indian Ocean Rim indicates the following:

- Left-wing violence carried out by groups seeking to overthrow existing governments;
- Ethno-political violence carried out by groups motivated along ethnic lines;

- Politico-religious violence carried out by religiously motivated groups; and
- Cross-border terrorism promoted by regimes as 'war by other means' on their neighbours.

Of these, the last is perhaps the most abhorrent of the kind we in India have had to suffer for a number of years. Such terrorism is sustained by external agencies and states. There is now wider recognition that this is the type of terrorism which creates conditions for growth of terrorist networks into massive conglomerates with international operations. Conflicts beyond the Indian Ocean Rim, including those in Afghanistan–Pakistan and Syria–Iraq in Asia, also overflow and impact the wider region. Neither pious denunciations nor generalised prescriptions are sufficient to combat terrorism in all its manifestations. A beginning has to be made in each case by understanding its operational philosophy, strategy and tactics, its targets and support systems.

It has been suggested that 'human insecurity provides the enabling conditions for terrorism to flourish.' Certain conditions provide a social environment and widespread grievances that, when combined with certain percipient factors, result in the emergence of terrorist violence. These conditions could include poverty, demographic factors, social inequality and exclusion and dispossession.

Terrorism and violent extremism in Indian Ocean Rim countries, therefore, has to be examined against the historical roots of militancy in these countries to provide the context for assessing the degree to which local agendas are either subsumed within a broader ideological framework or shaped by the extremist movements. For convenience of analysis, the background and situation of the region can be considered in five segments: South Asia, southern Arabian Peninsula, Horn of Africa, East Africa and the ASEAN region.

Colonial rule and the neo-colonial policy of creating or aggravating religious, ethnic or linguistic fissures lies at the root of many of the present-day conflicts and tensions. External interventions motivated by geopolitical considerations have exacerbated them. The resulting unsettled and volatile social conditions, thus, provide fertile ground for extremists to seek political change by violence. This, in turn, creates a social, economic and political situation that encourages parochialism along with the rise of religious and sectarian extremism, often using violent and terrorist tactics to promote their creed.

Since unprovoked violence is inimical to human nature, groups and individuals resorting to terrorism or violent extremism seek to cloak their acts in motivations premised on value systems – secular, ethical or faith-based – that could be cited in justification. The record shows its consistency. This notwithstanding, the political temptation to attribute it to individual creeds is often overwhelming and for the same reason, must be resisted if strategies and tactics to counter-terrorism are to be both credible and productive. Nor can state conduct in such situations be beyond scrutiny. In recent and not-so-recent history, instances exist of states resorting to the financing, training and equipping of individuals and groups resorting to acts resulting in the killing of innocent, non-partisan civilians.

In recent times, the rise of the ISIS or Daesh, in Syria-Iraq has caught the attention of the world. Yet, even a cursory study of the factors that led to the rapid rise of such dangerous forces reveals that the very actors, who now claim to be threatened by it, have been responsible for creating the conditions – directly or indirectly – that led to its rise. The repeated attempts at regime change by force and with utter disregard for local ramifications and fall-outs had led to the quagmire, whether it be in Syria-Iraq that led to the ISIS, or Afghanistan which led to Taliban/al-Qaida, or Libya that led to al-Jama'a. The removal of existing, often moderate, regimes and the subsequent breakdown of governance, resulted in extremist groups capturing the political initiative, exploiting the resentment and anger of the local populations and carrying out terrorist acts with impunity. The so-called "War on Terror" has bred its own brand of deprivation and suffering with hundreds of people being killed or injured, even if they were not related to terrorist activities. This has led to anger and a desire to seek justice by any means, resulting in extremist action and terrorist violence.

In the aftermath of wars, the impacted communities are caught in a vicious circle of population pressures, resource stress, popular discontent and political instability, making them susceptible to a pervasive extremist culture. Weak or dysfunctional states are more likely to host terrorist groups that target not only their host states, but also carry out transnational attacks. The availability of financial resources are critical to the success of these extremist groups. A misplaced sense of charity, or religious duty, on the part of citizens, contributes to it. Linked to it is the misuse of institutions intended to impart faith-based education. Instances of it abound in Pakistan and Bangladesh and in other countries of the Indian Ocean littoral. These misinterpreted religious texts induce intolerance which, in turn, promotes a narrow and bigoted approach that is conducive to the use of violence. However, the most virulent factor fuelling terrorism is state sponsorship of, and collusion with terrorists. Such terrorists, some promoted by regimes and some operating with the connivance of elements within national militaries and intelligence organisations, have employed religious, ethnic and sectarian aspirations to justify their acts of cross-border terror.

A case in point is Pakistan's use of extremist groups as an instrument of foreign policy, that is well documented, with the U.S. State Department's Country Report on Terrorism for 2015 stating that some United Nations-designated terrorist organisations continue 'to operate within Pakistan, employing economic resources under their control and fundraising openly'. Essentially, the Pakistani military has reared 'good' terrorists for cross-border missions while battling 'bad' militants that fail to toe its line.

The association of criminal and terrorist organisations – as most terrorist groups are funded by the proceeds of different types of transnational crime and illegal money flows – makes them even more destructive. The piracy off the coast of Somalia, the illegal oil extraction in Iraq, the drug and human trafficking in South East Asia or poppy cultivation in Afghanistan, are all controlled and run by the operating terrorist networks to generate additional finances. In many cases, the lucrative criminal activity becomes the sole reason for terrorist groups seeking political control by destabilising existing regimes. Such terror groups receive support from external actors who seek quick profits. The latest research of the United Nations Office on Drugs and Crime puts the global value of transnational crime at a staggering USD 1 trillion per year, on par with some G20 economies.

How do we, then, deal with the problem of terrorism in the region? It is not sustainable for countries to continue to address terrorism or transnational crime from a narrow national interest perspective, nor can development be viewed as a stand alone endeavour independent from security. Globalisation and integration processes make it apparent that trade, development and security agendas are interrelated. A fundamental change is needed in the way we approach these challenges.

The first challenge is to the national rule of law because terrorism is an abnormal activity to which societies can only adapt with difficulties. Making a society resilient to the potential threat of terrorism may come at a high price with regard to other fundamental values in society, such as civil rights. The lack of understanding about the nature and manifestation of terrorism, and the absence of a coherent response mechanism result in sporadic and knee-jerk reactions to dealing with this threat. The introduction of extraordinary, usually draconian, laws to address terrorism, in a bid to seek quick solutions, more often than not, prove detrimental and can even exacerbate the terrorism problem. Use of indiscriminate force and heavy-handed action debases the protection of human rights and can lead to an institutionalisation of oppression, fostering a culture of impunity within state security forces and agencies. At the same time, countries being taken by a surprise terrorist attack face the problem of responding swiftly without causing economic and societal disruptions.

The second challenge comes as international, or transnational, terrorism involves more than one country and multiple legal frameworks at the national and international level. This becomes most obvious in the context of the well-known saying, 'one man's terrorist is another man's freedom fighter'. While the saying is without much meaning since freedom is an end while terror is a means, it points to the problem that the national legal perceptions of groups may not coincide. What is more, national legislation may induce terrorism spillovers to other countries, as there are no generally accepted norms in international law that help to avoid this problem. This calls for international coordination and ultimately for norms in international law that help to harmonise cross-border externalities.

To provide a comprehensive answer to the threats posed by transnational crime and terrorism in the Indian Ocean Region, regional security and development agendas need to be connected and coordinated. Forums like BIMSTEC, SAARC, ASEAN, the IORA and the UN have a direct interest, and the responsibility to ensure that related efforts are comprehensive and have the resources necessary to respond quickly to the threat of terrorism. What is needed to curb and eliminate the scourge of terrorism is for the countries in the region to unite and fight it in all its forms and manifestations. States sponsoring terrorism must be isolated by the international community and forced to abandon the use of terrorism as a tool of state policy. Nations must not distinguish between friends and foes when it comes to identifying terror-sponsoring states.

We need a flexible framework of security that respects the diversity of security perspectives and developmental choices of member states and is based on a clear renunciation by all parties, of the threat or use of force against any other state, aimed at promoting connectivity in accordance with international law to promote and protect the well-being of all the peoples who inhabit the Indian Ocean region.

2

The Threat From Non-State Actors

Ranil Wickremesinghe

The Indian Ocean Rim Association (IORA) Summit was held in Jakarta from 5-7 March 2017. The Jakarta Accord, arrived at in the meeting, has committed IORA to countering terrorism in the region and establishing an IORA working group on maritime safety and security.

I need not describe in length the growing geopolitical, geo-strategic and geo-economic importance of the Indian Ocean Region (IOR). To many, the future of Asia lies in the Indian Ocean, which is a rising giant, home to 3 billion people. Half the world's container ships travel through the Indian Ocean. It is the vital energy link between the Middle East and Asia. It is also the main shipping route between Asia and Europe. Therefore, the global economy depends on the free flow of Indian Ocean traffic. Hence, the security of the Indian Ocean is of concern to all.

The greatest challenge the security of the region faces today comes from non-state actors who engage in terrorism, both on land and at sea. We are witnesses to terrorist activities from the East African coast to South East Asia. Terrorist groups are either engaged in battle or are attacking civilian and other targets. During the last one and a half decades, this threat has spread to the maritime domain. It is a real threat in the Indian Ocean. Maritime terrorism is not at par with land-based terrorism. Maritime terrorism also has the capacity to disrupt the global economy. The Indian Ocean is well known for its choke points and disruption in two choke points simultaneously will have far-reaching consequences throughout the world. We in Sri Lanka have been the victims of terrorism. We have faced terrorist attacks on our cities, conventional fighting in the North and in the East and maritime terrorism. Thankfully, we have finally brought terrorism to an end.

We know how powerful non-state actors can be. Since the end of Sri Lanka's terrorism, the technology used by terrorists has been upgraded, and the number of non-state actors has multiplied. We are all familiar with the nature of the terrorist threat on land. We must also recognise the importance of the threat to maritime security. These non-state actors use the most modern technology in their attacks, a recent example being a small unmanned remote controlled boat used on a Saudi Arabian warship by Yemeni militants.

Terrorists have also attacked maritime infrastructure. In the future, logistic hubs and maritime infrastructure may face more frequent attacks. The possibility of non-state actors hiding among the civilian maritime traffic is a nightmare that we prefer not to think of. The complexity of maritime threats requires navies to rethink their role and how we can respond effectively and adequately against these non-state actors. Systems disruptions and the potential for deploying digital systematic terror is another growing threat in the Indian Ocean Region Commons. The digital sector is an emerging threat that needs careful study and smart solutions, whether it be in traditional terror financing or the encryption of messaging technology emerging as tools for terrorist organisations.

Furthermore, the processing of global financial transactions, especially the billions of diaspora and global remittance transactions to their home countries around the Indian Ocean, are replete with the vulnerabilities of the electronic payment systems and their operators. Analysis demonstrates that these digital networks are beyond national control and are easily deployed for digitally enabled disruption associated with weapons of terror.

Counter-terrorism therefore, needs close cooperation by all the states. One man's terrorist cannot be treated as another man's liberator. IORAs declaration, on preventing and countering terrorism and violent extremism is a good start. The resolution requires the states to support each others' efforts to counter the threat of terrorism and violent extremism, including the enhancing of cooperation and coordination of effort, dialogue and sharing of information, expertise, best practices and lessons learnt, including stemming the financing of terrorism within the framework of the UN Resolution on Terrorism, ASEAN Convention on Counter-Terrorism and the SAARC Regional Convention on the Suppression of Terrorism. Close cooperation between regional countries is the only way in which counter-terrorism measures can succeed.

3

Need For a Definition

Manohar Lal Khattar

India has been and remains a victim of international terrorism. In fact, India became a victim long before the menace bared its global fangs and posed a grave threat to peace and security in a large number of countries. Today, it has snowballed into a full blown, multi-dimensional and multi-headed global security threat.

My State, Haryana, suffered the brunt of terrorism during the days of militancy in Punjab. Not that the threat has blown away – since Haryana surrounds the national capital, Delhi, from three sides – the threat looms. We thus need to put our heads together and work out strategies to counter terrorist activities, both effectively and decisively.

Indians and Indian culture emphasise the philosophy of 'Vasudhaiva Kutumbakam,' which means the whole world is one family. It was in the spirit of this message given by Lord Krishna in the Bhagwad Gita that India proposed the Comprehensive Convention on International Terrorism (CCIT) in 1996.

The aim was to secure the global community against the scourge of terrorism and let people breathe in the air of liberty, safety and security. Our Prime Minister, Shri Narendra Modi, at the G20 summit held in Antalya in Turkey, gave a call to the global community to unite against terrorism without making any distinction between individuals and nations, and to adopt the convention proposed by India in 1996. Our External Affairs Minister, Smt. Sushma Swaraj, in her speech at the UN General Assembly in September

2016 also made an appeal to the world to adopt the convention. I am of the firm conviction that if the convention is adopted, it would make the world a terrain hostile to terrorists and more habitable for the people. It would lay the ground for the signatories to coordinate and calibrate their actions to deny terrorist groups' access to weapons, funds, manpower and safe havens.

The need for this can hardly be overemphasised, as life, growth and prosperity hinge on peace, safety and security, something that terrorists all over the world, are put up to disrupt. It is indeed an irony and a matter of grave concern that even though no corner of the world today is free from the curse of terrorism; the international community does not appear close to evolving a united stand and strategy against terrorist activities. We have failed to make cross-border terrorism an extraditable offence worldwide, which has made several countries safe havens for terrorists. We have also not been able to agree on banning all groups and shut down terror attempts. Some countries are still allowing terrorist sanctuaries on their soil. They use terrorism as an instrument of state policy. What is most unfortunate is that some of us are still busy debating what is good and what is bad terrorism, so much so that we have not been able to work out and agree on a universally accepted definition of terrorism. All these issues need to be considered with thorough deliberation and meeting of minds so that an effective global counter-terrorist strategy can be developed and accepted. We thus need to define terrorism in comprehensive and universally acceptable terms.

International terrorism has many dimensions. Gone are the days when terrorism could be defined neatly in terms of acts of violence and mass murder. Today the world is facing terrorist threats in the form of cyber terrorism, terrorism through social media, terrorism in outer space and issues related to maritime security. The list goes on and on. We need to work together to identify these challenges and devise protocols and norms to take them head on. We should not stop short of bringing all the countries on the same page and show a strong resolve to combat terrorist activities in a collaborative and coordinated manner.

A lot of factors are fuelling global terrorism. They include religious fundamentalism, poverty, historical baggage, policies of socio-economic exploitation, desire to colonise economic resources, unemployment, unprincipled use of social media, unethical practices in cyberspace, sectarian interests of different kinds and quest for political hegemony. Youth that feel alienated on account of one reason or the other from mainstream society get radicalised easily and bite the bait thrown by the protagonists of terrorist ideology. We need to figure out the root causes of international terrorism and, while doing so, let us not forget that terrorism breeds terrorism. We need to brainstorm and devise a comprehensive counter-terrorism strategy that would make the world an inhospitable place for the sinister practitioners of terrorism in all forms. In the words of Prime Minister Narendra Modi, "We need to rise above politics, divisions, discriminations, and distinctions between good and bad terrorists and need to adopt the Comprehensive Convention on International Terrorism, proposed by India."

4

The Concerns of Nepal

H.E. Bimalendra Nidhi

Terrorism, in all its forms and manifestations, is a serious threat to humanity, irrespective of geographical boundaries. In today's globalised world, terrorism has become the greatest security concern. It is not confined to one country, one region or one continent. Terrorist activities are detrimental to the values of liberty, humanity, freedom and universal brotherhood. Terrorism not only causes loss of precious lives of innocent people, but also disrupts the progress of society and the development of the country. It undermines the overarching value of 'Vasudhaiva Kutumbakam' on which our civilisation was founded. This is a Sanskrit phrase found in Hindu texts such as the Maha Upanishad which means "the world is one family" (Mahopanishad VI.71-73). These words incidentally are also engraved in the entrance hall of the Parliament of India.

We have experienced great consequences of terrorism in our region. As the number of terrorist outfits and their sophistication and technology rises, threats of terrorist attacks on any given day become all the more possible. In today's inter-connected world, terrorism does not have any boundaries. Incidents of terrorist violence in our region over the past decade have made us vulnerable and this calls for our united action in countering this menace.

The activities of large networks of terrorist organisations on the global scale and their reported expansion in the Asia Pacific region provide us a reason to be extra vigilant, to counter the threats and ensure the security of our people. Terrorist networks are trying to spread their wings, but we must be able to nab and dismantle them.

Acts of terrorism cannot be condoned. No pretext, be it political, ideological or any other can justify such senseless and horrific acts. It is of the utmost importance for law enforcement machineries in all countries, to cooperate and collaborate in identifying terrorists and defeat terrorism. We all must be united and in an unreserved manner, demonstrate commitment at the highest level to stop terrorist acts and bring the perpetrators to justice.

The world is shrinking day-by-day due to technological advancements, especially in communications and in mobility. We cannot protect our citizens unless we work together, to strengthen our national, regional and global security environment. In this age of inevitable interconnectedness, mobility of people around the world is a reality. The safety, security and welfare of every individual is our common responsibility. Humanity is a common culture. Killings and brutality are today unacceptable acts that have to be condemned in the strongest possible terms and countered with all resolute measures.

I recall with a heavy heart, that in 2004 twelve Nepalis seeking employment in Iraq were captured and brutally killed by terrorists. In 2016, thirty Nepalis were killed when suicide bombers attacked a minibus carrying Nepali security guards in Kabul. Such heart-rending acts of terrorism have led to the demise of thousands of innocent peoples in one way or the other within their national boundaries as well as across them.

The transnational nature of terrorism should be recognised and countered with national, regional and global perspectives and capabilities. Every country should therefore formulate counter-terrorism strategies by detecting the sources of radicalisation, possible recruitment for foreign terrorist fighters (FTF), exploitation of the internet and various social media platforms by terrorist organisations.

Misuse of borders, terrorist financing and forged identity documents and radicalisation through social media is a rising threat. We need to enhance our capacity to monitor and counter such activities. Each measure should be complemented by a stringent legislative framework to deter and disrupt all kinds of terrorist activities. Between governments and law enforcement agencies, close co-ordination and co-operation must be ensured including all intelligence and technology sharing to enhance counter-terrorism capability. Needless to say, terrorism anywhere is a serious threat to peace, security and development.

Terrorism is a shared security concern not only of the national authorities but also of the international community. Nepal unequivocally condemns terrorism in all its forms and manifestations, wherever, whenever and for whatever purposes it occurs, and whosoever commits terrorist acts. Nepal calls for resolute international action in the fight against terrorism.

Nepal never allows her land to be exploited by any group which tries to carry out terrorist activities in our region or beyond. We have underscored time and again that terrorism should never be used as a means to achieve a goal. It is also important that we never allow propagation of terrorism in our region. As a member of UN, SAARC and BIMSTEC, we have signed several international conventions on counter-terrorism including on aircraft safety, maritime safety and against taking hostages, as well as the UN Security Council Resolutions. Nepal remains fully committed to implementing them despite the constraint of resources and technical capabilities.

In terms of national capability, Nepal has enhanced her security infrastructure and fully-trained security personnel are prepared to meet the emerging security demands including prevention of any form of terrorist attack. Nepal remains committed to work in concert with the international community in realising a world free from the evils of terrorism. Nepal will resolutely join hands with all countries in countering the scourge of senseless acts of terrorism.

5

Need For Shared Security

MJ Akbar

The world or at least the United Nations has for long been searching for a definition of terrorism that will have wide acceptance. Over 20 years have elapsed, and the world body still appears to be groping to define the most important war that we have faced in our lifetime. If you can't define a war, how can you fight it? While many eminent personalities have given splendid definitions of terrorism which were clear and unambiguous and which encompassed terrorism in all its multi-faceted dimensions, worldwide acceptance remains hard to come by. We must understand that there is no binary definition of terrorism. There is no good and there is no bad terrorism. Evil is evil and evil is a menace.

A matter of considerable importance is the need to discuss the true impact of terrorism. In my view, the most deleterious impact of terrorism is the manner in which it poisons plural societies with the phantom of fear. Terrorism uses this fear to divide people from one another – people who have lived together as fellow human beings for thousands of years, despite their differences. But they are being divided, and we can see the impact of this in behaviour patterns all across the world.

We are proud that in India we have been able to meet this challenge and confront it, and in a sense, keep the impact of terrorism beyond our borders. This is not a small achievement. It has not come about easily, but is the result of the whole country and all its people sharing a certain united philosophy –

a philosophy of humanism that is the true way in which we can keep this danger from being a bigger menace than what it could be. It is not just death which is the consequence, it is the consequences of the fear of death which is really beginning to impact minds.

On another note, why do we believe that terrorism is the biggest danger that we are facing in our lifetime and in the future? After all, war is not a new phenomenon. In the 20th century, more havoc was created by wars than ever before. We lost about 120 million people, young men and women, in the two World Wars in Europe alone. We are not even counting the numbers who died on unknown battlefields in anonymous areas. So, we have seen devastation of an unparalleled kind, and sometimes when I use the word 'humanity,' I wonder if I am using the right word because human beings have it in themselves, not only to rise to great heights, but also to sink to unfathomable depths.

The fear of death remains a prime consequence of terrorism, but we can overcome this challenge. When seen in perspective, the 19th century can be considered as the end of the age of empires, and the 20th century as the end of the age of colonialism. It is my belief that the 21st century is the one in which humanity has the opportunity to create something really unprecedented – shared prosperity.

The rise of democratisation – not simply the structure of democracy but also the spirit of democracy – and on a parallel line, the tremendous explosion, the revolutionary explosion of technology, which is not merely at the service of the elites, but also at the service of the poor in villages – the same technology is creating revolutions today; and one of the greatest things that Prime Minister Shri Narendra Modi has done is taking this technology to the poor. This, I think, will be the subject of more books than perhaps anything else.

However, this shared prosperity is threatened by the menace of death and the menace of terrorism. To achieve shared prosperity, we need shared security. We need to find the capacities and the ways in which we can keep aside our differences and move towards a shared security architecture for the good of our people.

6

Indonesia's War Against Terror

Wiranto

No single country, including those in South East Asia and the countries of the Indian Ocean Region (IOR), is immune to terrorist threats. And no single country can overcome them alone. The threats that we are facing and are likely to face in the future are now getting more serious. In 2016 alone, there were over 160 terrorist attacks across the world. The first attack of 2016 took place in Jakarta on 13 January 2016 and the last attack of the year was in Berlin on 19 December 2016. Again, on 1 January 2017, Istanbul was rocked by a terrorist attack and we continue to face such attacks all across the world. In India, on 7 March 2017, a blast took place on the Bhopal-Ujjain passenger train in Shajapur, Madhya Pradesh that left eight people injured. This was but one of the numerous attacks that India has faced over the years. The threat from terrorism is hence becoming more insidious and more imminent since the terrorists, whether they operate in groups or as 'lone wolves', continue to develop their strategy and tactics such as expanding the radical narrative and utilising more sophisticated cyber technology for their pernicious propaganda and for capability enhancement. It is therefore necessary to remain prepared at all times, continually improve our level of preparedness and plan necessary measures to prevent and combat these extraordinary crimes. We have to increase our capacity on early warning and early detection mechanisms, as well as capability to respond quickly.

An analysis of the terrorist networks that operate across the world indicate that the situation in Iraq and Syria is serious and demands our attention. The

Islamic State (Daesh) and its affiliates remain active in parts of Syria and Iraq. This region has become more than just a melting pot of radicals, extremists and terrorists; it also provides training grounds, protection and resources to spread terrorism across its borders. Despite the trend indicating that the terrorists have started losing ground in Syria's, Aleppo and Iraq's Mosul, the corresponding threats have not necessarily declined. As the situation stabilises in Iraq and Syria, the cross-border terrorist fighters in these areas may return to their respective countries or may move to new operational bases. Information is available which indicates that some of these fighters are opting for moving their operational base or region as a part of their agenda to enforce the so-called 'mission terror' under the command of Abu Bakr al Baghdadi to whom they have sworn allegiance. There is also strong evidence that they have established networks with various terrorist groups in South-East Asia. This development indeed requires our focused attention and cannot be taken lightly.

Indonesia is blessed with peace and stability, despite the fact that the country encounters grave security challenges. The resilience of the people remains Indonesia's strength in its fight against terrorism, especially during difficult times. On the part of the government and its security forces, the security threat is never underestimated, especially the threat from terrorist groups both within and outside the country. Indonesia's response to these threats takes a dual approach through the application of both hard and soft power.

In the hard power approach, the security forces and law enforcement agencies target terrorists and their organisations focussing on dismantling terror networks and to enforce the law of the land. As a result of this approach, many senior leaders of terrorist groups have been eliminated by the security forces. These include Dr. Azahari bin Husin, who was believed to be the technical mastermind behind the 2002 Bali bombing. He was killed by security forces in November 2005. In September 2009, Noordin Mohammad Top, a Malaysian Muslim extremist, who was a key bomb-maker and financier for Jemaah Islamiyah (JI) was eliminated. More recently, Indonesia's most-wanted terrorist, Santoso, also known as Abu Wardah, was shot dead in the jungles of Central Sulawesi province. He was the leader of the East Indonesia Mujahidin (MIT) and had pledged his allegiance to the Islamic State (IS) in 2014. Santoso had taken part in the Muslim-Christian conflict that racked Poso from 1998 to 2001. The above are but some of the concrete examples that show that the Government of Indonesia is focused in its war on terror and is committed to pursue all terrorist groups that operate within its borders.

The government, however, applies a softer line to terrorists who have been captured or who have surrendered. Such individuals are put through de-radicalisation and counter radicalisation programmes run by the Indonesian National Counter Terrorism Agency. This approach also follows an understanding that there is a need to address pockets of poverty, economic disparity and social injustice which are the causative factors for the spread of radicalism. Indonesia is, however, conscious of the fact that in the short to medium term, terrorist groups and networks will continue to pose a threat to the country. To tackle the networks, there is a need to further strengthen cooperation with other countries to fight terrorism. Towards this purpose, at the national level, a number of measures have been put in place by the government. Indonesia is also cooperating with other countries, at the bilateral, regional and global levels in this war against terror, as without such cooperation it would be well nigh impossible to win such a war.

As part of this international cooperative effort, Indonesia, in August 2016, co-hosted two international events simultaneously with Australia in Bali. These were the second International Meeting on Counter Terrorism (IMCT) and the second Counter-Terrorism Financing (CTF) Summit. It was commonly accepted at this conference that terrorist threats continue to grow in line with increasing incidences of cross-border terrorism and increases in the numbers of Foreign Terrorist Fighters (FTF). The conference also delved on the increase in cyber terrorism propaganda, techniques, strategy and tactics as well as mobilisation of finances.

In the above-mentioned conference, the participants acknowledged that the return of FTF from Syria and Iraq to their respective countries of origin has posed new threats. They also realised the importance of strengthening joint efforts of international communities with respective governments, the private sector and civil society and were cognisant of the challenges ahead to implement measures such as strengthening of law enforcement, border control, intelligence exchange among countries of origin, transit and destination. There was unanimity on the need to enhance joint efforts in formulating an effective counter-narrative against the extreme propaganda of the terrorist groups as well as on de-radicalisation and counter-radicalisation programmes. It was also appreciated that effective measures needed to be put in place to prevent terrorists from gaining more access to cyber technology and to terrorist financing. On a global level, we have financing institutions of the United Nations that are encouraged to take leading roles in combating terrorism and addressing its root causes. The need for cooperation among the de-radicalisation centres that have been established in a number of countries in the region was also emphasised.

Regional cooperation on counter-terrorism was also highlighted during the Indonesia-Australia Ministerial Council Meeting on Law and Security in Jakarta on 2 February 2017. The participants agreed to increase cooperation on intelligence-sharing and law enforcement, especially in countering the growing effect of FTF in the region and in strengthening cooperation on countering financing of terrorism, especially in the field of the Financial Action Task Force.

During the IORA Conference in Jakarta in March 2017, the ministers reiterated the importance of countering political terrorism and violent extremism through the following measures, amongst others:

- Promote collaboration to rehabilitate those who have been radicalised;
- Promote social cohesion amongst the radicalised elements; and
- Promote cooperation amongst regional institutions, specialising in preventing and countering terrorism and violent extremism.

Countering terrorism in the IOR cannot be separated from national maritime security issues. Indonesia, Malaysia and the Philippines are still encountering challenges in sanitising the areas that have significant ISIS influence. In 2016, 22 Indonesians were taken hostage by the Abu Sayyaf group. With the assistance and support of the Philippines' authorities, most of the hostages have since been released, but six are still in the hands of the group. It is alarming that such actions relate to terrorist financing.

Within the IOR, we need to continue with our focus on de-radicalisation and counter radicalisation. Here, we need to include and empower the moderate religious and community leaders, former terrorists, terrorist victims, NGOs and also utilise social media. Indonesia welcomes friends and partners to use the capacity of Jakarta Centre of Law Enforcement in deepening our cooperation in countering violent extremism. In addition, we also welcome expertise and good practices from other countries which will enhance our efforts in this direction. The Centre will introduce identification, rehabilitation and education programmes. For the integration programmes, they will be provided with technical assistance, nation building, teaching materials, discussions and moderation in religion and entrepreneurship. They will also be introduced to those people who were radicalised and who have now successfully returned to normal living in the community.

To conclude, the IOR is not likely to be rid of the scourge of terrorism any time soon. Indonesia is cognisant of this challenge and its government, law enforcement agencies and security forces are geared up to meet the challenge. With dedication and a cooperative framework, we can, through concrete action, win the war against terrorism.

7

Afghanistan: Facing the Brunt

Hekmat Khalil Karzai

Before I begin this paper, I wish to quote a couplet, which very much expresses my feelings toward India and the people of India:

Haadsa Banke Koi Khawab Bikhar Jaye To Kya Ho,
Waqt Jazbaat Ko Tabdeel Nahi Kar Sakta
Dur Ho Jane Se Ehsaas Nahi Mar Sakta
Ye Mohabbat Hai Dilo Ka Rishta
Ye Mohabbat Hai Dilo Ka Rishta
Aisa Rishta Jo Zameeno Ki Tarah
Sarhado Mai Kabhi Taqseem Nahi Ho Sakta

An English translation of the above is difficult, but the stanza below, while not a literal translation, captures to an extent the thought behind the poem:

Life's slings and arrows may shatter dreams
But neither passage of time nor distance
Can dull my senses or quench my thoughts
For this is love my friend, this is love
Unlike a boundary which can divide the land
This is love, where none can divide us.

India is very close to my heart and, as the poet says, boundaries cannot divide us. However, in this paper I will dwell on my homeland, Afghanistan – a region where terrorism is still a major challenge and a major threat. I will focus on three issues:

- Defining the environment and the threat that we face in Afghanistan;
- An analysis of how we have responded to the threat; and
- A peep into what could possibly be the way forward and what are some of the key policy recommendations that we would have to, at least as a policy maker, put forth for other colleagues.

First, I want to propose and start with a very simple question: what is the historic and particularly the current context of Afghanistan in the light of terrorism and why is Afghanistan important today? Let us understand that terrorism did not come into the region with the dastardly attacks on the USA on 11 September 2001 (9/11). For those who have automatically become terrorism experts after 9/11, there was a reality before 9/11 and it was the Afghan people who suffered and who were the prime victims of that terrorism.

Before 9/11, the former Soviet Union invaded Afghanistan and it was in Afghanistan that the former Soviet Union was defeated. It collapsed because of the engagement in Afghanistan. One may argue that there may be several reasons as to why the former Soviet Union collapsed, but most militants will tell you that it was because of them. Al-Qaeda will tell you that because God was on their side, they were able to defeat the former Soviet Union. That stark reality exists today also. There are militant groups operating in the Afghanistan-Pakistan (Af-Pak) region who also believe that there is another super power that they can defeat in the Af-Pak region. Historically, there is also this resonance.

But let us look at today. Why is Afghanistan important? It is important because we have in the Af-Pak region the highest concentration of terrorist groups. These groups do not see Afghanistan as the end state. They use Afghanistan and the region as a launch pad to conduct attacks against the world.

I will begin by describing the four circles of threats that we face. These are the key threats that we face particularly from the key groups operating in our region. First, are the Afghan groups. They start with the Taliban. The Taliban, at one point, was the government. After 9/11 they went into sanctuary, recruited from various madrasas and now putting forth a very aggressive campaign of toppling the government. Similarly, joining the Taliban is the Haqqani network.

This is a ruthless group that has conducted attacks against many, including against our Indian colleagues and on various different diplomatic facilities.

The second grouping that we face a threat from, the second circle, are the Pakistani groups. Here, mention is made of the Tehrik-e-Taliban Pakistan (TTP). We are also talking about Lashkar-e-Jhangvi (LeJ), Lashkar-e-Taiba (LeT) and the most recent phenomenon of Jamaat-ul-Ahrar (JuA), which has been responsible for quite a few devastating attacks. Many of these groups have conducted attacks, particularly against Pakistani targets.

The third circle, or the third threat, comes from regional groups. Here, we have groups like ETIM (East Turkistan Islamic Movement). This is the group that heavily focuses on China, but at the same time operates in the Af-Pak region. It was provided with an enormous amount of training in Waziristan and in many other areas. Now, joining them, there are developing groups and old groups such as IMU (Islamic Movement of Uzbekistan) and Jundallah, which has a heavy focus on Central Asia. The fourth circle comes from international groups. These are groups such as al-Qaeda and Daesh, the latter also going by the name of Islamic State.

One could well ask another question: after 15 years of international engagement in Afghanistan, where at one point of time 150,000 foreign troops were deployed to deal with these issues and to destroy these various groups, why are we still facing this problem? There are four reasons which come to mind. First and foremost is because there are states in our region that support terrorist groups. These states use terrorism as an instrument of their foreign policy. Such states provide terrorists with infrastructure, sanctuaries and the wherewithal to conduct a long and bitter guerrilla war.

Second, many of these groups also benefit from the proceeds of narcotics and they have a symbiotic relationship with drug traffickers. Terrorists provide security while the drug traffickers provide the resources. If you look at the drug trade that is taking place in the region, there is an enormous amount of wealth. Some estimate this trade to be over USD 4 billion.

Third, many of these elements also receive, at the lower level, an enormous amount of benefit from illegal mining, taxation and from criminal activities which range from kidnapping to extortion.

Fourth, we still see individual funding coming from the Middle East to different groups. We have not been able to deal with the problem of terrorist financing. As a consequence, these groups are being able to survive.

Over the years, in terms of terrorist evolution or in terms of individuals, there has been a lot of change. One thing we have seen in our own region is how the dynamics have evolved. An old friend of mine, Brian Jenkins, was one of the key premier thinkers on terrorism. It was Jenkins who said, "Terrorists want lots of people watching but not many people dying." This was a very famous saying in terrorism, but al-Qaeda changed that narrative with the 9/11 attacks they conducted and with various other attacks where many people were killed. Daesh, however, has taken that narrative to a different level. Today, terrorist groups like Daesh don't just want people dead; they want them killed with an enormous amount of barbarity. This barbarity was reflected in the attack on the Sufi shrine, Lal Shahbaz Qalandar, in Pakistan. It was reflected very recently in Kabul where terrorists went into hospitals and killed innocent children and doctors who were treating people. So, the evolution has taken place and at different levels where the thin line between killing a soldier and killing an innocent person has become blurred and that, quite unfortunately, is a development that governments all over the world have to deal with.

In our region, technology has always been prevalent, but now technology is used at the village level to recruit not just the foot soldier but qualified people such as doctors and engineers, who can actually deliver sophisticated capabilities to them. Consequently, we have very educated people (not just in our region, but also in Europe) joining Daesh and other groups and this has become a very serious challenge for many of us.

Many of the groups that now operate in our region do not operate in isolation but support one another through their established networks. If one provides a safe environment, the other provides technical assistance. So, there is this synergy that has developed between terrorist groups, where one benefits from the other. Sadly for us, collectively as a region, our response at best can be categorised as weak.

Why do I say this? A successful counter-terrorism approach needs two elements. The first is the tactical element which includes the use of military, security, intelligence and law enforcement. The second is the strategic element which deals with the ideological battle.

The fact is that the likes of bin-Laden have always argued that we are facing a clash of civilisations. This is the classical argument that Huntington put forth. But are we really facing a clash of civilisations? In any case, this is for us Muslims to argue and not the job of the West to argue for us. It is the job of Muslims to put forward this argument if we are really dealing with the clash of civilisations or otherwise.

We also have to deal with the socio-economic grievances of people. In many instances, people do not join a militant group because they are ideologically motivated, but because they are financially motivated. There is an argument in the West that all terrorists are educated. This may be true in the case of those who hijacked the planes on 9/11, and a few others like them, but it is not true at the gross root level. There are families which have several kinds of grievances, they also join terrorist groups for specific reasons. They are taking revenge because their members were sent to Guantanamo Bay detention camp, or because of ethnic and tribal reasons. So, it is also extremely important to understand the context of identity in this regard.

I personally feel that our approach was very much focused on tactics. We have not really employed the strategic context, particularly we Muslims, and particularly the people who understand this region, and that is what I am going to argue for. So, the way forward against terrorism, the defining challenge for our generation, is to win the ideological war. This is not something that we are going to deal with for one year. It is something that is going to be with us for a long time.

We also need a sincere and, I emphasise the word 'sincere', collaboration between states and policy-makers. Secondly, Afghanistan, as I mentioned, is fighting on behalf of the region. We have an enormous number of threats from groups that represent a large part of the world and they are operating in Afghanistan. We are dealing with them and we are fighting against them. This is a huge task and in terms of capability we need huge support and a much greater collaborative effort.

The third component is rather crucial. We need to make sure that we see a terrorist as a terrorist. We cannot distinguish between a good and a bad terrorist. The logic that 'those who attack me are bad terrorists and those who attack my enemies are good terrorists,' is inherently flawed. The same terrorist who has been propped up will, over time, attack the very hand that fed it. We have already seen that some of the states that have nurtured terrorists have now become victims themselves, with no one to blame but themselves.

Also, being a citizen of South Asia, good governance is something that we lack and it is something that we must deliver, particularly to our citizens. We need far better delivery of services. This is something crucial as not everyone in our region joins a terrorist group because of ideological reasons. There are so many other reasons that one looks at. Finally, under the Heart of Asia Istanbul Process, Afghanistan has put forth a regional counter-terrorism strategy. We feel that this is a shared threat that requires a collective response. We live in an environment where our capabilities and particularly our actions must be intertwined. If different militant groups are able to collaborate, then we are beholden as states to do so likewise, to win the war against terror.

8

Bangladesh: Proactive Engagement Against Terrorism

Assaduzzaman Khan

Bangladesh is a peace-loving country. While a majority of its population is Muslim, people of different faiths and various ethnic minority groups have lived here in harmony for centuries. The social and economic environment of the country is also not at all conducive for the breeding and spread of terrorism and violent extremism. Reiterating the zero tolerance policy of the government, the Prime Minister of Bangladesh, Sheikh Hasina, has already made it clear that Bangladesh is against all types of terrorism and violent extremism. Despite this, Bangladesh has experienced acts of extremism and has been the target of terrorist attacks, despite the 'zero tolerance' policy of the government. Due to the relentless efforts of law enforcement agencies and with the active cooperation of the people, Bangladesh has, however, arrested the situation and brought terrorism under total control.

The policy of the Government of Bangladesh is that it will not allow its soil to be used as a launching ground for any kind of terrorist activity against any part of the globe, let alone our neighbours. Regretfully, in the last few years, Bangladesh has experienced a series of terrorist attacks on different foreign and local targets. The entire nation was shaken by the carnage that took place when terrorists attacked the Holey Artisan Bakery in Gulshan Thana, claiming 29 lives. The killed included 22 civilians, five terrorists and two police officers. Amongst the civilians killed, there were 17 foreigners, of which nine were

Italians, seven Japanese and one Indian. The Indian was Ms Tarishi Jain, a young talented girl. Of the five Bangladeshi civilians who were killed, one was Faraaz Hossain, a young Bangladeshi Muslim. This boy was given the option of leaving by the terrorists, but the 20-year-old decided to stay to protect his friends. Two courageous police officers gave their lives during the first wave of resistance. Later, commandos from different law enforcement agencies promptly launched their operation, code-named Operation Thunderbolt and rescued 13 people, including foreigners. In this hour of grief, the people as well as the Government of India stood by us which is a manifestation of the depth of the relations of our two friendly countries.

One of the most serious security challenges that has emerged after the Cold War is undoubtedly terrorism, which represents a transnational form of violent extremism led by non-state actors. We have seen how the 9/11 terrorist attack on the United States of America in 2001 became a watershed event in the shaping of the global security agenda. The USA orchestrated Global War on Terror (GWOT) and actively sought to counter-terrorism in different parts of the world. Asia was no exception. Soon after the Bali bombing in 2002, the region was alarmed by the terrorist threat posed by an extreme ideology that had developed an underground network of violent extremism throughout the region. The trail of carnage that followed was also seen in India, where we witnessed the 2008 terror attack in Mumbai claiming 164 innocent lives. In Bangladesh, we have some home-grown groups who have been radicalised. These elements are acting to destabilise the country to hinder through terror, the current rapid socio-economic development taking place in the country. In some cases, this is being done in connivance with a few radical political affiliations. Moreover, we have also unveiled the unholy nexus between these groups and those who are against the trial of the anti-liberation war actors and perpetrators in the international crime tribunal. Against this backdrop, Bangladesh has a comprehensive four-pronged strategy to counter-terrorism. The four pillars of this strategy are:

- Prevention,
- Disruption,
- Capacity building, and
- Upholding human rights.

Strengthening of the measures being taken by law enforcement agencies against those who are involved in terrorist activities is being pursued according to the law of the land. Different law enforcement agencies, including the Bangladesh Police, Rapid Action Battalion and different intelligence agencies are working round-the-clock in this regard. As part of capacity building, we are equipping law-enforcing agencies and training them on countering and deterring terrorism, both at home and abroad and to include the use of sophisticated hardware. While doing so, Bangladesh has maintained a high benchmark with respect to the upholding of human rights in compliance with the UN Convention on Human Rights. The total anti-terrorism drives initiated by the different law enforcement agencies and the ministries are being coordinated by some high-level national committees like the Cabinet Committee on Law and Order headed by a cabinet minister, and the National Committee on Militancy Resistance and Prevention, of which I am the head.

The Bangladesh Government is strengthening its efforts to bring anti-terrorism financing and terrorism-related legislative regimes in line with UN international counter-terrorism initiatives. We have some powerful legal instruments to counter-terrorism in the form of the Anti-Terrorism Act, 2009, Money Laundering Prevention Act, 2001, The Extradition Act, 1974, Information and Communication Technology Act, 2006 and the Special Power Act, 1974. The government has already proscribed seven extremist outfits in the last seven years and listed these organisations in the schedule of the Anti-Terrorism Act, 2009.

The seven proscribed extremist outfits include Jama'atul Mujahideen Bangladesh (JMB), Jagrata Muslim Janata Bangladesh (JMLB), Harkat-ul-Jihad al-Islami (HuJI-B), Hizb ut-Tahrir, Shahadat-e-al Hikma, Ansarullah Bangla Team and Ansaral-Islam. Besides, the Government of Bangladesh has already taken a series of other counter-terrorism and counter-violence extremist actions encompassing different government and semi-government organisations, NGOs, CSOs and other stakeholders from the grassroot level. A series of meetings with the heads of educational institutions and vice-chancellors of different universities have been held. Suspected educational and other institutions have been identified and are being kept under continuous surveillance. The educational curriculum is also being revisited and changes, as necessary, will be brought in.

To counter radicalisation, a consolidated 'missing youth list' has been prepared and the necessary investigation is in progress. Lists of suspected Bangladeshis staying abroad have been prepared and collection of necessary information is under way. Social media monitoring has been enhanced and has identified militant links. Social media and other online platforms are also being used as one of the ways to generate and deliver youth-based content as a counter narrative. We have arranged meetings with editors and senior media personalities and discussed these issues with them. We are also engaged with the police forces, parents and teachers, all of whom have been asked to be more caring and careful in bringing up their children. To counter the terrorist narrative, we are organising mass awareness programmes all over the country through print media, TV channels and online social networks. The counter narrative aims to negate the false propaganda of terrorist groups and informs the public of their evil designs. More than 100,000 Ulema (leaders of Muslim Umma) are now educating the public that no form of terrorism is sanctioned in Islam. To this effect, a booklet has been published which was launched by the Prime Minister of Bangladesh, Sheikh Hasina, on 11 August 2016. This is being read out before every Jumma (Friday) prayers in mosques all over the country. A series of interfaith dialogues and get-togethers have also been organised in all parts of the country.

Addressing other areas as well, the government has stepped up security measures for the diplomatic community and all foreigners. Intelligence agencies have increased their surveillances and are monitoring security measures for the whole country. Police have asked all house owners to get police verification of their tenants done. Prisoners are now under continuous surveillance and are being monitored by the government. Publicity is also being given to the government's initiative to facilitate the return of those who have joined terror groups and now wish to resume normal life. This is in line with the directions given by the Prime Minister that any person who has taken the wrong path will be forgiven if such person abandons it. As a result, a large number of people have already returned. Mothers are also bringing back their sons who had strayed and are giving assurances that their wards will no longer take up the gun. This approach has been positively received and is undoubtedly very successful. As a result, all across the country, teachers, journalists, educationalists, students, etc., are coming forward to resist and stand up against terrorists.

Terrorism and violent extremism is a phenomenon that cannot be fought alone by any country. Bangladesh is not alone in this fight against terrorism and has all sorts of engagements: bi-lateral, regional and global as a part of its commitment to fight terror. For the eventual elimination of terrorism, Bangladesh is party to all 14 United Nations conventions on combating terrorism and violent extremism. One of the major areas of cooperation on counter-terrorism and against transnational crime is in the Bay of Bengal Initiative on Multi-Sectoral Technical and Economic Cooperation (BIMSTEC), where Bangladesh is an active member of the anti-terrorism engagement.

Bangladesh, along with other member-states, signed a SAARC regional convention on suppression of terrorism. So far as bilateral engagement is concerned, we have a treaty agreement with India relating to the extradition and transfer of sentenced prisoners, on mutual legal assistance in criminal matters and in combating international terrorism, organised crime and illicit drug trafficking.

Moreover, Bangladesh signed agreements with some developed countries like the USA, UAE, Australia and others to enhance counter-terrorism cooperation between the two countries in terms of capacity building, information sharing and information exchange between law enforcement agencies. Bangladesh is committed to the eradication of terrorism and will work together with the countries in the IOR and others to bring an end to this scourge, thus ensuring a better and safer tomorrow.

9

Sri Lanka: Post-War Conflict Resolution Measures

Sagala Ratnayaka

India is not just a close neighbour but is inevitably bound to Sri Lanka in many aspects – social, cultural and economic and, in some respects, strategic too. Both India and Sri Lanka are among Asia's oldest democracies and are steeped in the principles of fundamental freedom, participatory governance and solidarity. There exists between the two countries a lasting friendship that has faced the test of time over centuries. In the contemporary world, the people of both countries aspire to the same future that is built on peace, stability and prosperity.

Sri Lanka and India, in the broader region, have not been immune to conflicts. We have had our own share of violent pasts, of varying degrees though, of conflicts which essentially arose from internal contradictions often with cross-border ramifications. These are not new to the region that we are situated in. The causes of grievances, whether real or perceived, have enmeshed with political and other factors to produce an explosive mix, which often manifests in violence and terrorism. As far as India and Sri Lanka are concerned, such situations have only helped us to understand each other better, support each other in tackling the criminal or violent part of the challenge and in addressing concerns that are found to be real. The fact that both countries are democracies and have mutual respect, goodwill and friendship towards each other goes a long way in ensuring this outcome.

The LTTE (Liberation Tigers of Tamil Eelam), which waged a war that lasted three decades against the State, was a guerrilla outfit which used acts of terrorism to supplement its fight by creating fear. In this paper, I am not going to talk about how Sri Lanka fought that war, because there are people who were involved in the strategy and fighting who can talk about it better. I will focus, hence, on the post-conflict scenario.

The 30-year war has led to Sri Lanka losing its ability to earn its rightful place in the world, struggling with the legacies of the war – debt-ridden economies, weak state institutions and a population that suffered the scourge of war and terrorism. In Sri Lanka, we now have the onerous task of rebuilding the nation by taking the people from all the communities on a journey of peace and progress, almost eight years after the armed conflict has ended. Reconciliation remains at the heart of this process which is reinforced by two of its main adjuncts, namely, re-democratisation and economic development.

The electoral office elected His Excellency, Maithripala Sirisena as President of Sri Lanka in January 2015 on a policy platform of peace building, development, democracy, rule of law and preservation of human rights. This provided a real opportunity to reunite our people, one which was within our reach immediately after May 2009, but which was, unfortunately not availed of for some reason. So, President Sirisena and Prime Minister Ranil Wickremesinghe, with the Unity Government, were tasked to put the nation through the healing process and advance along the path of progress.

For the first time since the end of armed conflict, doors were opened in 2015 for people to seek solutions to their conflict related issues. Strengthening of the Unity Government at the parliamentary elections held in August 2015, which reflected the popular will across the nation, led to the adoption of new initiatives aimed at expediting economic advancement, intensifying national cohesion and peace building. It has hardly been a month since the new cabinet was sworn in following the parliamentary elections that the government of Sri Lanka decided to co-sponsor resolution 30/1 at the UNHRC. The resolution contains the voluntary commitment undertaken by the Government of Sri Lanka in the interest of its own people. It is important to highlight that all this follows the change of tactics in Sri Lanka's outreach strategies which puts a premium on constructive engagements and dialogue with UN agencies and other organisations, including the Human Rights Council.

As of March 2017, there is another resolution under consideration at

HRC, Geneva, seeking to give adequate time to the Government of Sri Lanka to continue to make progress as part of its voluntary commitment. On one hand, this signifies the acknowledgement from different sections of the international community that Sri Lanka is making efforts in good faith to progress further. On the other, it testifies to the fact that Sri Lanka has also gained confidence in engagement with its partners and friends.

The 30 years of armed conflict had torn the people of Sri Lanka apart. Of the almost eight years of the post-conflict phase, only the last two years have witnessed national healing and reconciliation at a faster pace. It is but natural that the post-conflict priorities continue to abound today.

One of the key challenges that any peace-building enterprise encounters in the post-conflict phase is setting up of priorities covering all aspects of human endeavour. Often competing with each other for scarce resources, all priorities appear urgent at once. And all are classified as immediate needs to be fulfilled without delay. But the government, inevitably, has to work with a number of constraints to see to those priorities and needs. While attuning to those urgencies, it needs to take care not to create or contribute to inter-regional or inter-group disparities, or any other inequities.

It is important as well to ensure that when priorities and needs are catered to or facilitated, people at the local level should feel that they own them. It is imperative that people who have been affected by the conflict and the rest of the population gain confidence. The Sri Lankan government, working with its stakeholders, and in some cases donor countries and donor organisations, has introduced various reconstruction, resettlement and rehabilitation projects in both the North and East. Building of houses, schools, hospitals, etc., providing for irrigation facilities, payment of compensation, land release, education at reasonable prices and livelihood assistance are among the many programmes that have been implemented in conflict areas.

The national policy on durable solutions for conflict-affected displacement was approved by the Cabinet of Ministers on August 2016. The signing of the Galle principles for protection of civilians constitutes two important pillars in assuring the conflict-affected people the protection they deserve. Terrorism, as in armed conflict, and psychological factors completely disorient people and make them lose confidence in themselves. The environment they live in is of fear. Fearing the context of conflict, terrorism or violent extremism is manifest in different ways; internal disturbance, suspicion of others, loss of self-confidence, sexual or other forms of abuse, hopelessness for justice, self-restriction on movement, etc. Many people have lost their near and dear ones, and have themselves been wounded or harmed. Some have faced sexual violence and some of them have even been denied access to relief and redress to justice. All this needs to be addressed with seriousness in the post-conflict situation.

It is not only the victims who always demand post-conflict justice. In some instances, it is also sought by those who are reported to have committed excesses, claiming that they themselves had been victims to policies and command orders. Even in such situations, it is important to note that it is fear or some other psychological factor that drives them to such excesses. For both, it is important to address all types of fear and provide access to justice to ensure non-recurrence of the same in the future. The record of the National Unity Government is self-evident in this context since it has put in place a number of legal and other frameworks to address these challenges. First and foremost, we have commenced the process of drafting a new constitution, having converted the whole house of parliament into a Constitution Assembly. Minority rights, central peripheral relationships, decentralisation and devolution are some of the issues that are being discussed extensively.

One of the key questions that the framers constantly have in mind is how to manage the root causes of conflict. In the meantime, the 19th Amendment of the Constitution, enacted by Parliament in 2015, aimed to address the issue of fear, by making national institutions independent and bringing in several democratic safeguards to government. It is seen, more often than not, how aggressively these institutions uphold their independence. Secondly, the Right to Information Act serves as an effective tool to obtain information about persons or things that are within the knowledge of ministries and agencies of the Government. Thirdly, the Victim and Witness Protection Act protects a victim or witness in a criminal case from being threatened or harmed by a party to the case and prescribes specific punishments for those who violate the provisions of law. Fourthly, the Office on Missing Persons (OMP) Act enables the tracing of missing or disappeared persons, and provides the OMP the powers to search without a warrant any place where a person is suspected to be detained or has been previously detained. This is one of the important pillars of the reconciliation right-to-justice architecture that is currently being designed.

Besides, there are several law instruments in varying stages of drafting before being enacted by the Parliament. Placed in the order paper of Parliament, the Prevention of Persons from Enforced Disappearance Act produces provisions which will hold criminally responsible, not only those who engage in disappearance, but also those who exercise command responsibility as well. If adopted, it will be one of the most comprehensive pieces of legislation in Sri Lanka to prevent deprivation of liberty. Similarly, an amendment to the Criminal Procedure Code Act has also been drafted to allow lawyers access to suspects in police custody. The Prevention of Terrorism Act has earned notoriety as one of the most draconian pieces of legislation. The Government has developed policies and a legal framework for a new Counter Terrorism Act which will comply with international human rights norms. All these policies and legal measures, as well as other initiatives, redefine Sri Lanka's legal regime and access to justice in such a manner that accountability remains an entrenched feature in the rule of law. We will also ensure that prevention and non-recurrence will be the overarching principle of justice in the governance of Sri Lanka. All these will go a long way in assuring that fear has no place in the life of any person in Sri Lanka. At present, we are concentrating on converting the fruits of peace to tangible outcomes for the people. Development of destroyed infrastructure, livelihood opportunities and linkages to market and national and international value chains are the prioritised areas. Access to credit and capital is also being facilitated.

We also have the enormous challenge of re-organising our security sector. We have to deal with an army of battle-hardened young people who, after the war, find themselves without purpose, without work and, more importantly, without the necessary skill set to integrate with the post-war peacetime economy. We have initiated rapid training for police officers to serve in this conflict mindset and to prepare them for the current day security challenges. We have also managed to rehabilitate approximately 12,000 ex-LTTE combatants, many of whom have now been integrated into mainstream employment. With a group, we are currently taking steps to form a political party to contest the upcoming Sri Lankan elections.

Sri Lanka was, is and will continue to be, a multi-ethnic country, rich in diversity and rich in tradition. The forces of language, religion, caste and ethnicity will continue to have their interplay as they should. Our challenge, hence, is to think of ways to manage such interplays within the nation and its people, and not allow the ugly head of competition to rise again. What we have to do now, more than anything else, is to build confidence in all people that their government is doing what is right for them and that it will help safeguard the country from conflict. Sri Lanka is firmly committed to fight international terrorism and will cooperate with all countries in the region in this endeavour.

10

The Terrorist and the State

K Shanmugam

What is it that terrorists want? After the Malaysian security forces arrested some people, owing allegiance to the Islamic State, this is what they said:

> *'If you catch us, we will only increase in number. But if you let us be, we will be closer to our goal of bringing back the rule of the Khilafat (Caliphate). We will never bow down to the democratic system of governance as we will follow only Allah's rules.'*

What terrorists want is to sweep away the Constitution, the democratic system of government. They want to replace it with what they firmly believe is the right way to do, a right way of governance to replace the existing systems of government, not just in Afghanistan or any other place, but throughout the world. That is the danger that we are facing.

Today, when we talk about terrorism, we focus on topics that deal with Islamic terrorism. Terrorism, however, is not linked or restricted to any particular religion. For example, in India, the State also faces threats from Maoists, Naxalites and others. However, the single-most dangerous situation that is facing the world today is perhaps terror based on a perversion of Islam. And inevitably, that's what we start focusing on. The epicentre of that war is in Iraq and Syria, and it is sweeping through Central Asia to South Asia and to South East Asia. And in due course, it will fan out to other parts of the world as well. We must remember, that before the rise of Europe, the centre of the world was Central Asia – a part of the 'Silk Route'. What happens here influences the rest of the world. And it will rely on the Internet to seek to brainwash people, radicalise the populace, overthrow the government, cause mayhem and disrupt civil society.

The war in the Middle East may end, but terror is not going to disappear. The following description of terrorism appears apt.

'You take a big blob of Mercury, you bang it hard, what happens? You get hundreds of little globules.'

That is what happens in the war against terror. Those who haven't been killed will disperse. Those from this region will come back here and those from South East Asia will go back to their region. And we can already see what is happening in South East Asia. The ISIS has focused on the Muslim population using emotive videos, newspapers in Malay and encouraging people to take up arms. They have issued edicts stating: '*If you can't get weapons use anything. Use a knife. If you have a vehicle, use a vehicle to drive and kill people and throw them over the parapet*'. Entire societies cannot be turned into garrisons, especially free societies. That is the challenge which has to be overcome.

There is some evidence that the southern Philippines has become an area of focus by ISIS, with the stated intention of setting up a Caliphate. Returnees are gathering there. Radicals within the region may also go there, get trained and then come back. The fact that we are all so interconnected makes these things possible. In February 2017, a German hostage was beheaded in the southern Philippines. In mid March, front page news in Singapore's national newspaper reported that Malaysia had announced the arrest of several people, at least one of whom was an immigration officer – a lady. She had let militants get into Saba, which is in eastern Malaysia, without travel documents, so that they could travel to the southern Philippines, link up with others, train and then obviously come back. East Malaysia shares a very long porous border with Indonesia. Malaysia also announced the arrest of commandos, police officers, civil servants, technicians who are servicing VIP aircraft, in fact, all sorts of people. We have had that experience. Indonesia has been active in arresting people. It is something that is growing. It is a threat to all of us because militancy knows no borders.

So what do we do about this threat, besides talking about it? There has got to be some practical concrete outcomes that we should aim for. Here, I would like to share what Singapore is doing to combat the threat. There are three aspects – The first is a direct kinetic response to the threats. The second is the strategic dimension, wherein we psychologically strengthen our population which is something I think all of us have got to do. The third is international cooperation.

For the people of Singapore, November 2015 marked a sort of inflection point. The killings that took place in Paris made it clear that the terrorists were no longer interested in taking hostages. They simply wanted to kill as many people as possible, as quickly as possible and then keep a few so that there is maximum international audience. In the coordinated attacks that took place on 13 November, 130 people were killed. The killings were done simply to get maximum exposure. To guard against such incidents, we in Singapore developed what we call Emergency Response Teams and Quick Response Teams; the difference being that quick response teams are given motorbikes so that they can travel to their destination quickly in addition to existing Special Forces. We put them on the ground all across the island. Their task is to understand buildings within their area of specificity. The security forces are expected to know the buildings in detail and arrive at a location whenever an attack takes place, within minutes. That is the kind of response we want – ready to respond, ready to take down the attackers. While there will be casualties, the attack has to be defeated quickly and must be over in a few minutes.

We are also going to put in legislation in 2017, which will require building owners to strengthen their new and existing buildings and where the minister can direct specific strengthening requirements. This is the easier part – working out logically the necessary kinetics for building security.

The second part is the psychological response of the people. When an attack occurs, what happens? What do people do? How do they react? And post attack, how do we rebound? Do we point fingers at the Muslim population or do we recognise it is the work of a small group of extremists? How do we ensure that Islamophobia is controlled? For us, we decided for an empowered citizenry comprising people who know how to react when an attack takes place. And for the psychological defence of the public, we started a major program in 2016, called SG Secure.

The SG Secure national movement is Singapore's community response to the threat of terror. It aims to sensitise, train and mobilise the community to prevent and deal with a terror attack. The intention is that over the next four years every single household in Singapore would have been visited and covered under SG Secure. There would be someone in every household who would be trained in defending, because anyone can be caught in an attack. Now, obviously, if a terrorist has a sub-machine gun, we do not expect an unarmed person to go and tackle the terrorist. But we teach people how to protect themselves and then to assist those who need help. They are also taught to notify the authorities. All of this is very challenging, so to overcome this challenge, an app was launched in Singapore which captures at one place, everything that a person needs to know and all the agencies that need to be contacted. All this can be done with a single tap. The government is now working with and encouraging telecom agencies to install this app on every mobile phone that is bought in Singapore.

People who have visited Singapore are aware of the fact that first-aid equipment is available to the public in all housing societies, in all blocks, and in all public places. Across the country, people have been trained at three levels to deal with any situation. The first level is for the people to help themselves and learn how to use first-aid equipment. The second level is for people to help others and the third is to mobilise the community. We are also putting in people with psychological training and counselling training into different parts of the population. Simultaneously, we are also trying to train various members of the population to understand psychologically what might happen and how they can react to bring the population together. If we can come together as one people, the day after an attack, the terrorists will lose and we will win. Therefore, psychological resilience in the population is extremely important. We condemn attacks and we divide the population into different segments, households, businesses, unions and schools and we take the message that we are here for peace and brotherhood everywhere. We try to inoculate the entire population, first to understand there is a threat, second, to know how to react to it, third to be psychologically prepared and fourth to look upon our 15 percent Muslim population as brothers in arms in this fight against terrorism, which, of course, they are.

The third aspect is international co-operation. No country can deal with this by itself. It can deal with it internally to a extent, but we need to develop common platforms to engage in our region. We need the regions to talk to each other from Delhi to Singapore. We need to institutionalise. We need to develop best practices and we need to end up with some concrete outcomes. We need to go beyond speeches because it is too serious and too important a topic. The determination to deal with this at the international level is crucial.

To deal with terrorism today, we need the right legislation in place. Singapore is lucky to have what we call the Internal Security Act which allows the Home Minister to order detention without trial. It is an exception to the rule of law, but there is broad public support for it as it allows us to take a zero-tolerance approach. As an example, if a person was looking at extremist websites and thinking about going to Iraq and Syria, then Singapore's intelligence agencies can approach such a person, counsel the individual and if that person chooses to continue on that path, then the Intelligence agencies have the power to detain such persons. Alternatively, they have the power to impose conditions on the movement of such individuals, while they remain free citizens.

In 2016, 14 Singaporeans were arrested under this Act. Eight of them were arrested and six were given restriction orders. As an example of how we differ, let us examine the case of the Christmas attack in Berlin. It was done by a Tunisian, Anis Amri, a truck driver, who drove his truck into a crowded Berlin Christmas market in December. This individual had served a four-year prison sentence in Sicily for several crimes including arson in 2011 and was released from prison in 2015. He arrived in Germany in July 2015 where he visited radical mosques, mingled with extremist preachers and was linked with extremist networks. German authorities had him on their radar, security services were closely observing him but their legal framework did not allow them to arrest or produce him in court. Since they could not find the evidence that was required under their system, they stopped monitoring him in September 2016. The attack took place three months later. State police said they had exhausted all legal powers to the limit to ward off potential danger. Had Anis Amri been in Singapore, he would have been arrested much earlier.

The second example that I will give is that of the UK. It is necessary to study such cases, because every country must start looking at these issues and develop the modalities to deal with them. Eventually, a balance has to be struck between the amount of tolerance for such events, the amount of risk a country is prepared to take and the amount of power the citizens are prepared to give the government. This case pertains to Jamal, a British citizen. He was picked up by American forces in Afghanistan in 2001 and detained in Guantanamo. In 2004, he was released without charge and deported to the UK. He launched a claim in the UK and was apparently awarded one million pounds. In 2014, he left the UK to join ISIS in Syria and in February 2017, he reportedly carried out a suicide bomb attack in Mosul. There is much debate and soul-searching now within the UK. It is probable that the compensation given by the UK government was used to fund the Islamic State.

While each country will take its own route to address their respective concerns, I would offer some examples that are useful for consideration. Some people might consider it to be quite a perversion that a person can initiate a claim, get paid and then use the money to kill more people. We also have to seriously consider the extent to which terrorism is filled by ideology and money from outside the country. This is a serious issue because the sources of those funds and of that ideology have neither a stake in the well-being of the country nor any interest even in the integrity of the country. What they want is that their brand of Islam flourishes. That is extremely dangerous particularly in countries like India, Singapore and others which cherish multi-cultures and promote religious pluralism and different racial identities.

Here, I would like to refer to an incident which took place in Singapore. Most countries would not consider such an incident to be serious, but in Singapore we have a different approach. We had an imam whose conduct in a mosque in Singapore was recorded. Nowadays, every phone has a camera and what was recorded inside the mosque was widely circulated. The incident occurred in February 2017 and the imam is currently under investigation. What happened was that after the imam finished his sermon, he ended with a supplication from the Quran. And then he spoke in Arabic, which translated as under:

> '*God grant us victory over the disbelievers. God grant us victory over Christians and Jews.*'

The above supplication was then repeated by the imam. We in Singapore take pride in being religiously the most diverse country in the world – a fact that is officially recognised. We can have a situation where a mosque, a temple, a synagogue and a church can exist within 10 metres of each other. However, if people going to a mosque or a place of worship are told by the imam that one of the aspects of their religion is to have victory over people who have other faiths, after a while, it has an impact on society. It is not just Islam that has these phrases. The Old Testament in the Bible has several such blood-curdling phrases too. In the context of the imam seeking victory over Christians and Jews, the origin of that particular supplication of grand victory over them comes from the Ottoman Empire. When put in context, it refers to the conflict in the Levant when the Ottomans were fighting the Christians on one side and the Jews on the other. But that context does not exist now and certainly not in South Asia. The imam is from South India and does his preaching in Tamil. What would people say if a Roman Catholic Archbishop stood up in Church and repeated what Pope Gregory said in the 13th century that all Muslims in Jerusalem were to be exterminated! The defence put up for the imam was that he was simply following tradition, but such a defence is untenable. The critical point that this incident highlights is that inevitably an area exists where governance and government authority now is coming in contact with what preachers can and cannot say. There is a requirement to ensure that preaching is done within a set framework, else it then encourages intolerance, conflict and violence. This is applicable to all religions and not to just any particular one, as all religions are capable of mindless violence.

In Singapore, such a situation was anticipated over two decades ago and to deal with it we had the 'Maintenance of Religious Harmony Act'. As we are facing such issues, we have been through this legal framework and it is being used to ensure that action is taken against such preaching. Generally, we simply sensitise the preachers and educate them on what is acceptable and what is not. But the population as a whole has to be educated on this and religious scholars have to be educated and told that their ultimate loyalty has to be to maintain peace and harmony in the entire society and within that framework, they can say as much as they please about the goodness of their religion, but they do not have the right to run somebody else down.

Another incident that warrants attention because of its crucial importance pertains to a video of a preacher who hails from India and who goes by the name of Mufti. A very charismatic man, Mufti has been to Zimbabwe and too many other countries, preaching with such great power and eloquence that would be the envy of any politician. The problem, however, lies in what he preaches. He actually tells his audience that giving gifts to Christians or greeting them on Christmas is 'haram'! This is what Mufti says in the video:

> *"I want to give a gift to this man and to that man. Can I give a gift? It is the occasion of Christmas. And I want to give a Christmas gift to my friend. And we tell them, my brother and my sister, let me explain to you logically, you have chosen to be a Muslim. Muslim means one who worships Allah alone and considers association of partnership with Allah as the highest form of blasphemy.*

> *Do you understand? So if you are a Muslim, you believe in Allah alone. And any association of partnership with Allah is the highest form of blasphemy. So it is the highest form of blasphemy, when people have considered someone as son of Allah. The Quran tells you that the skies are about to rip apart because of the statement that they have uttered. If you look at Surah Maryam, towards the end, there is a powerful verse which says, 'how could they have said that I have a son? They are insulting Allah by saying Allah has a son'. The earth would crumble and the sky would like to split because of the seriousness of their crying. Yet we want to give a gift and have a happy day with associating partners with Allah. You understand why as Muslims it would be wrong for us to take a gift? We are taking a gift and saying, my brother you have associated partners with Allah. Allah says it is the biggest blasphemy against him but take this gift, it is ok. From me. I am a Muslim. Allah hu Akbar. Can we understand and realise why we are going wrong? The same would apply if we were to give someone a gift on Diwali or tell them Happy Diwali. What we are actually telling them is I am really praying that you enjoy your day associating partners with Allah and this celebration you have of the entire association of the greatest and worst of partners with Allah. I am telling you to have a happy day, you deserve the enjoyment and here is my gift. May Allah safeguard us. Would we like to present a gift to someone upon their sin and crime"?*

We need to be careful of such preachers. What he is saying is that if you are a Muslim, and you wished someone Happy Diwali or Merry Christmas, the earth will open up and the skies will come down on you. If a Muslim does not know the Quran very well and he hears a preacher like Mufti, he can be forgiven for believing him. The consequences of such action in a multi-cultural and multi-diverse society is a fractured society. If I cannot greet you, then after a time, you will stop greeting me too. And then what do we have? Do we have a society?

Terrorists don't become terrorists overnight. Someone doesn't wake up one morning, takes up a weapon and starts shooting. It happens over a period of time, when the ground is made fertile. And it is preaching such as the one mentioned above that makes the ground fertile for terrorists. One can no longer look at such incidents as the end point. It is a kinetic action. We have got to see what makes the society readier and more fertile for extremism and we have to deal with that upfront. This was the reason why this preacher was banned from coming to Singapore. On the face of it, such preachers say that they are only preaching from the Quran. But preachers who come from overseas, although they behave themselves in Singapore, in course of time get a following and all their hate speech preaching is sadly available on the Internet. That was the reason why this preacher was banned. This also brings home the point of the fine line that has to be tread, as an interface between government and religion. This is always difficult and it has bedevilled society for thousands of years. But this is something we have to face up to now, quite seriously.

These are some of the challenges that we must confront and deal with. We must remember that in this interconnected world, what happens in Asia can happen in other parts of the world too. No part of the world can remain immune from what happens elsewhere. Each of us, therefore, will face and will have to deal with such situations. The sooner the world develops a common way of dealing with such challenges, the better it will be. As an aside, it is well to take note of an unfortunate incident that took place on Easter in 2016. A Muslim shopkeeper posted on his Facebook wall, 'Happy Easter to all my Christian friends'. The next day someone went and stabbed him to death in Glasgow, UK. If it can happen in such stable areas, it can happen anywhere. That is why, we in Singapore, focus on all these issues. While taking action against Islamic terrorists, we try to keep Islamophobia in check, because that is exactly what the terrorists want. Our focus remains on integrating all the communities and ensuring the well-being of all. We believe in spreading the message of peace while dealing with the small minority that plans to do us harm.

PART II

IMPACT AND PROGNOSIS

11

Confront the Ideology

Gen VK Singh

A great learning experience in countering terrorism comes from Israel which has been impacted by terrorism ever since the state came into existence. Over time, the state of Israel created its own responses to meet the specific threats that they faced. Whether it be the massacre in Munich or the hijacking of an Air France passenger aircraft to Entebbe in Uganda in 1976 or the various shootings and bombings that have taken place inside Israel, they have come up with their own robust responses and have learnt from each incident. This is important because if we do not learn, if we do not study, if we do not keep a repository of the knowledge that has been gained over time, then we are bound to suffer.

In India, we have had our own set of experiences. In fact, we continue to be plagued by instances of terrorism, such incidents taking place practically every month. While most such incidents are relatively low-scale attacks, much can be learnt from each of them. We have had the infamous attack on Mumbai and as terrorists tend to repeat their successes we need to be vigilant to avoid a repeat of what happened in Mumbai in November 2008. Earlier, we have seen how our former Prime Minister, Shri Rajiv Gandhi, was killed in a suicide attack carried out by the LTTE. The Indian Peace Keeping Force deployed in Sri Lanka was also subject to suicide attacks carried out by Tamil terrorist groups and while the scourge of suicide bombings and suicide attacks is not a frequent phenomenon in India, we need to understand how such situations need to be tackled. When viewed holistically, it emerges that what must be tackled is the ideology that leads people to such a path. This needs to be robustly tackled, otherwise, we will keep reacting to situations from incident to incident which will give but limited results.

What we are witnessing today is a great amount of ideological indoctrination that is taking place by various terrorist groups, especially groups such as Daesh, also called the ISIS. This phenomenon is not confined to the poorer sections of society, but includes the well-to-do and well-educated people as well those who come from rich and prosperous families. This is worrying and the world needs to sit down and work out how such people are to be tackled. When people coming from well-to-do families, people who have never seen scarcity, people who have had a good life and a good upbringing fall into this ideological trap, and start committing heinous acts, it is time to be concerned. To fight ideological battles each country needs to devise its own responses. This ideology is not just confined to the Middle East, where it originated, but has crept into many other countries, attracting people from across the globe – men, women and children, who then volunteer to fight for nebulous causes, using religion to justify their activities.

Consequently, a lot of effort now has to be put into de-radicalising campaigns, where radicalised youths can be brought back on the path of normalcy and avoid falling into the pitfall of terrorism and aiding terrorists. Just like social media networks, terror networks gain strength by creating worldwide linkages, and it is this linkage that gives it great anonymity and support. They devise their own languages and methods of communication and support each other, having little concern for the country in which they are living or the benefits they have received from it. They work as part of global networks, their focus is global and so we need to look at this threat in a much deeper manner than what we have done before. We need to keep a tab on things that are happening, otherwise the discourse in future years may well claim that Osama bin Laden was a person who came with goods laden on camels!

The fight against terrorism must thus co-opt the participation of a great number of people. The public needs to be vigilant and well informed and enabled to assist in the response that the government devises. Without the support of the people, the fight will always remain one-handed. Both the hands will never come together and this is the lesson which I think we need to imbibe.

What is needed as part of response is a very intelligent and very robust, multi layered intelligence system which works 24×7 for 365 days a year. For the counter-terrorist who wants to ensure that no terrorist attack take place, there is no option but to work and be vigilant, every day of the year, 24 hours per day. Terrorists are just looking for that small window of opportunity to launch an attack, and if we give them that chance, they will take it and achieve their nefarious intent. Therefore, a great amount of effort and resources are required to create an efficient system. Subsequently, follow-up measures are required, tie-ups are required with other countries and with their intelligence systems so that appropriate networks are created, just as the terrorists have created their own networks across the globe for their own purpose. A great deal of awareness is also required to be created among the public, which can provide useful inputs in preventing a terror attack or assisting the security forces when things go wrong. Finally, we need to have well-trained professional response teams which are able to tackle an attack that takes place, or ideally, which can prevent an attack from taking place.

Technology must be exploited in fighting terrorism, but this has to be supported by the people and a great amount of effort has to be put in. In Israel, data mining is a continuous process, in which analysts look at anything that can be classified as hate against Israel or the Jews. From this emerges leads, which at times lead to preventing an attack from happening. This is what we must do. We have been affected seriously by many terrorist attacks of various types and it is for us to draw a lesson not only from the Israeli experience, but from the experience of all countries that are fighting terror, for this is a threat in which you cannot go to sleep. It can do tremendous damage.

So far as India is concerned, our stand is very clear. There are no good or bad terrorists; there are only terrorists and that is why we always say that terrorists have got no caste, religion or colour. They are just terrorists who are only driven by one philosophy – how to create damage, how to create panic and how to get publicity for themselves to achieve their ideological goals. India has proposed the CCIT (Comprehensive Convention on International Terrorism) in the United Nations to tackle terrorism. We are hopeful that all countries will support us. Some have and some are still dithering. I sincerely hope that this dithering stops, because this is the threat which is real, which is current and which is going to affect all the countries in the world.

12

Winning the Terror War

Avi Dichter

Until about 35 years ago, countries that were fighting terrorists in the Middle East or in West Asia used to define two basic conditions in fighting against terrorists. The first condition was that the tools, whether it was a pistol, a gun, a hand grenade or a knife, and the second was the intention to use it against people. Based on these two conditions, security personnel, according to the laws in their respective countries, were allowed to open fire in order to block the terrorists, and if necessary, to kill them. In the Seventies and the Eighties, passenger aircraft were hijacked by terrorists using guns, pistols and hand grenades. In many of these cases, whether in the airport or in any other place, the attacks were foiled by counter-terrorism forces, police or other security personnel. At that time, we knew that there were very tight connections and cooperation between terrorist organisations while cooperation between countries that were fighting terrorism was not of that order. So we had cooperation between the Palestinian terror organisation at that time and the Baader Meinhof of Germany and the Red Japanese Army and in some cases under the leadership of the arch terrorist, Carlos, the Jackal, who carried out very damaging terror attacks. Since then, another dimension of terror attacks has been added to the battery of terror activities – suicide bombings.

Suicide bombings were not common in the Middle East, although we had heard about such attacks in other parts of the world, and even in the central part of Asia. This phenomenon made its appearance in West Asia only at the beginning of the Eighties. This added a new dimension to counter-terrorism activities because in the case of suicide bombers you see none of the two basic conditions. You do not see the tool because the suicide bomber is not carrying a pistol, gun, hand grenade or knife, but simply has a bomb concealed in the body, in a vest or on any other device on the body. You also do not see the intention. In my personal experience, I haven't seen even one case in which a security man has opened fire on a suicide bomber or a suspected suicide bomber because he suspected him to be one. As a matter of fact, I remember only one case, in London, in 2004, post the terror attacks in the Tube, when a Brazilian citizen came to the station and jumped over the entrance. Security policemen, thinking he was a terrorist trying to run to detonate himself, opened fire and killed him. In the event, it turned out to be a mistake.

The employment of suicide bombers in our region is very problematic. First of all, the majority of the suicide bombers, by which I mean more than 95 percent of them, are not from the hard core of the organisation. Most are recruited almost at the last minute, the majority between 17 and 24 years of age, and could be from any walk of life. They could be males or females, adults, teenagers, married, bachelors, smart people, students or illiterate people. Unlike what we thought, a suicide bomber is not necessarily a person who is miserable, it could be anyone. But all of them are very fanatic. I remember a case in which a suicide bomber ran towards a group of Israeli soldiers and civilians and tried to detonate himself with 10 kg of explosives on his back. It was fortunate that while the detonator exploded it did not set off the main charge, as a result of which only the bomber was injured and he lost consciousness. He was taken to hospital and interrogated a few hours later when he opened his eyes. The first question the interrogator asked was, "Hey man, do you know where you are?"

The bomber looked at him and said, "Yes, definitely, I am in heaven."

"You are not in heaven; you are in hospital," the interrogator told him. "Both start with an H, but it is definitely not heaven."

Then an argument ensued between the terrorist and the interrogator about the 'relocation'. Finally the interrogator said, "Allright, I will start again at the beginning". He looked at him and asked, "Who am I?"

"You, you are a bloody Israeli".

"Yes, I am an Israeli," said the interrogator. "And I am Jewish."

"But tell me," said the terrorist, "are there Jews in heaven?" He then appeared a bit nonplussed and said, "Hey man, you are right, there are no Jews in heaven so I am in hospital". Then he started to give out information.

That is the kind of thing we thought only happens to poor people, but we had a case of a student recruited to carry out a bomb attack in Jerusalem. He was to kill himself in a bus wearing a belt filled with explosives. We came to know of the plot because we had apprehended the commander of the cell. Through him, we came to know that a belt bomb had been smuggled in by a woman who had kept it in a hidden place. The student was to collect the bomb and execute his mission in a bus in Jerusalem, either on a Sunday or a Monday, but definitely not on a Tuesday. This appeared a bit odd to us, but we presumed that there must be some logic to this reasoning of which we were not aware of. A few days later we caught the student who, after a while, led us to the place where the belt bomb had been hidden. After we had exploded it, we returned to the Centre and then asked him why the bomb was to be exploded on Sunday or Monday, but not on Tuesday?

"Ah," said the student, "That is very simple. On Sundays and Mondays there is nothing special in the University. On Tuesdays, however, they have an exam." Trust me, even if you are well trained, sometimes it frustrates you, surprises you or both.

Terrorists in West Asia are not guerrilla fighters. In many cases, we hear that while they may attempt to target soldiers or policemen, they prefer to attack civilian targets as such targets are tempting, easy to find and hit, and most importantly, civilians do not respond with fire. Civilian targets also serve a dual purpose for terrorists, both in West Asia and in other parts of the world. First, civilians are an easy target, whether by a bomb, a car bomb or even rockets that Israel has been facing for the last decade. Just from the Gaza Strip, 15,000 rockets have been fired towards Israeli cities inside the Green Line. The second purpose that citizens serve, in the eyes of terrorists, is to be their human shields. We see this phenomenon in Iraq, Syria, Lebanon, the Palestine Authority and even in Yemen. Terrorists force civilians to act as human shields and the civilians comply because saying 'no' could invite instant death from the bullet of a terrorist. The first time terrorists fired on Israel, 600 people got killed in the Gaza Strip. The terrorists justified their act stating that this was a reprisal against the people for colluding with Israel. But in the

Gaza Strip, only three percent of the people have some kind of relationship with Israel which implies that 97 percent of them got killed for nothing.

Terrorists will carry out an act of terror whenever they can and whenever they consider it might pay off. While terrorists operate on their own time table, security forces all over the world have to be determined to fight terrorists all the way, all the time, 24×7. We must also remember that there is no fair play when confronting terrorists and terror attacks. Fair play does not work. The security forces must not operate according to the time table of the terrorists who use 90 percent of their time in planning and executing terror attacks and only 10 percent to survive and hide themselves. This time table must be changed, so that terrorists are forced to be on the run for 90 percent of the time due to pressure from the security forces, leaving them just ten percent of the time to plan and execute attacks. If this is achieved, that will be the first victory over the terrorist.

The second point is, there is no fair play against terrorists. People sometimes say, well there are just three terrorists hiding in a building or in the bushes who are armed with Kalashnikov rifles and hand grenades. So a group of about ten men is adequate to eliminate them. In such a scenario, at the end of the clash, two terrorists will get killed, but you might lose one or two of your own. That's why, whenever it is needed, it is authorised to fight with a F16 jet against a terrorist with an M16 rifle. It is the only way. Otherwise, if you are seeking fair play, maybe you are going to catch a terrorist or kill a terrorist, but you are going to lose your own people when there is no need to do so.

An oft-quoted phrase is that fighting a terrorist is akin to fighting a bottomless pit, or is like trying to empty the ocean with a spoon. If you have such people combating terrorists, they must, right away be moved to another job; they are not in the right position. Fighting terrorism requires commitment and belief and it cannot be a half-hearted exercise.

In 2002, we had 450 fatalities, mainly civilians, caused by suicide bombers. Another 3,000 people were injured in that year. At that time, we had a list of 400 names, all potential suicide bombers. This frustrates some people: how to find these people and take them into custody for none of them were known faces; none of them were arch terrorists. We are not speaking here about the generators of terror, or about the commanders of terror, or even about those who are manufacturing the bombs. We are just speaking of 17 and 18-year-old suicide bombers – men and women – whom we wish to detain to prevent the occurrence of a suicide bombing. Here, let me recount a true story of a woman from the Gaza Strip who was recruited to become a suicide bomber. She was suffering from cancer and had been given, as a humanitarian gesture, a special permit to go to a hospital inside Israel for radiation treatment. After two sessions of radiation, she was recruited by the terror organisation. Hamas. She was given a belt with explosives and told to detonate herself in the hospital. But she was also told to detonate herself on the spot if the metal detector at the border crossing beeped.

The woman told them that as she would be crossing with other people, all of them Palestinians from the Gaza Strip, those innocent people would be killed too, if she detonated herself at the crossing. She was told that the Hamas was prepared for such collateral damage, so long as some Israelis got killed. She then asked them why the metal detector would beep if the bomb she was to carry was filled only with explosives and had no shrapnel. They told her that she was right, but as they were unaware of the sensitivity of the Israeli metal detectors and as the detonator was made of metal, they had to take that into consideration. She then told them that she had broken her arm a few months earlier and during the surgery, a piece of metal had been placed inside to strengthen the bone. She asked if that would cause the metal detector to ring. They told her it definitely would and thereafter, took her to a clinic where the arm was opened and the metal was removed. She was told she would not require it any more.

It was fortunate that we got information about this woman and apprehended her in time, thus saving her life as also the life of Palestinians and Israelis who would have been killed had she succeeded in her mission. She is but one of the 400 names. The struggle is long, but frustration is not a characteristic of counter-terrorism personnel.

There is also a belief that it is preferable to kill terrorists whenever encountered. The slogan, "if you can't heal it, kill it," sounds good, but is not effective. A dead terrorist cannot give you any information, but it can be extracted from a detained terrorist. So, killing a terrorist is the second-best option, the best option being to keep terrorists in captivity. They can then be questioned, information can be obtained and translated into actionable activity, which, when sent to the field, can foil future plans, neutralise laboratories, unearth bomb making factories, etc. It is much easier to eliminate terrorists, but if you can take them alive and question them, there is no better way to get the whole picture about their terror infrastructure.

There are also people who say that terrorists, when captured, do not speak and most are lone wolves. But I have not met any lone wolves. I have met lone dogs. And those who speak Arabic know the difference between lone wolves and lone dogs. And that is why I think that we, as countries, must get rid of the term 'lone wolf'. The one who drove the truck in Nice and the one who drove the truck in Berlin, were dogs. I know it is not easy to target such a person – to find such individuals before they carry out their act – but that should be the aim of any counter-terrorism apparatus. It must shun the easy path, take the hard one, find the terrorist, detain him and learn from him. That's the way we can get the full picture right at the beginning itself. And from the full picture, we can thwart more and more terrorists, more and more plans, more and more generators of terror, more builders of bombs, and so on.

In security planning, basically two rings are considered. The first is intelligence so that information is available to foil an attack. But unfortunately, we know from experience that in 90 percent of the cases, we are unable to get the right information in time. That is why the second ring is required – the physical ring of security. Physical security is expensive because it entails people, guards, detectors, metal detectors, sniffers, etc. People who travel across the world know what this means, having seen aspects of physical security in airports, malls, hotels, *et al.* The physical ring is deterring, is pre-emptive and, in the eventuality of an attack, it minimises the casualties because the guards can open fire even after the attack begins and stop and block casualties in a faster time frame.

Even in the case of passenger aircraft, or any other aircraft, an additional ring is required. It has been just 16 years since the 9/11 attacks, but I am not sure that all lessons from them have been learnt. We now know that the 19 terrorists who came aboard the four passenger aircraft had clearly bad intentions. However, there is no way to analyse bad intentions and lying. To detect bad intentions in just one person can take a whole day. By using passenger aircraft as a weapon or as a bomb, we can say that the bomb was supplied by the company or perhaps even by the government. There is no way to bring down a structure like the World Trade Towers with a bomb dropped from an aircraft. The towers were brought down using the aircraft laden with fuel as the weapon – the dream of any suicide bomber, any terrorist. In such cases, if you are not a security man inside the airplane, you are irrelevant. Had we had air marshals in each of the four passenger planes that were used by the terrorists as bombs, there would have been no 9/11.

I have learnt in my life to be circumspect. I was an air marshal forty-plus years ago. My trainer was an American who put a sign above the entrance to the training centre with a very famous quote by the legendary Samuel Colt: "Fear no man, no matter size. Come to me, I'll equalise." And I trusted it. We must remember that terrorists, by habit, repeat successful terror attacks. Therefore, remember, 9/11 might repeat itself. And those countries who think in terms of saving money by not placing air marshals in passenger aircraft need to rethink this aspect. In terms of cost, a mishap will be very expensive. Remember, that the USA till date has spent trillions of dollars post 9/11, because of 9/11.

The last point I want to focus on is that terrorists are empowered by states that support terror. In the Seventies and the Eighties, when Carlos the Jackal captured 75 ministers and their delegates in Vienna, the attack was backed, supported and launched by Iraq under Saddam Hussein. The date was 21 December 1975. Thirteen years later, on 21 December 1988, Libya sent her terrorists to put a bomb in the Pan Am 103 flight that crashed above Lockerbie. Nearly 270 people were killed in that incident. In the beginning of the Eighties, another state, namely Iran, started supporting terrorist groups and it remains perhaps the only country in West Asia that continues to do so. Today, Iran runs five proxies of terror groups; Hezbollah in Lebanon and Syria, Hamas and Palestinian Islamic Jihad (PIJ) in Gaza, Houthis in Yemen and a group in Malaysia. In a significant development in 2016, 19 out of 22 Arab countries declared Hezbollah as a terror organisation, something that had never happened earlier. The three states that did not do so were Lebanon, Syria and Iraq, all three of whom are now dominated by Iran.

Those countries that fight terrorism and are committed to such a fight, must not leave any safe haven for terrorists. Terrorists being supported by Iran must know that they have to remain in Iran forever. They must know that every crossing of international borders will be monitored and prevented. For this to happen, it is essential that we share information. The more we share, the more we will have, and that will enable us to win the war against terrorism. This is a war I am sanguine that we will win.

13

Terrorism Has No Victors

Rajiv Mehrishi

An analysis of terrorism in South Asia indicates that the occurrence of such incidents in the region is perhaps one of the highest in the world, next perhaps only to Syria and Iraq, and that is a cause of worry. Incidents of terrorism in Afghanistan, Pakistan and India show a trend that is highly disconcerting and disturbing. Bangladesh too is sitting on a powder keg, though incidents of terrorism in that country are often underplayed. South Asia's thus hugely impacted by terrorism and I would like to flag a few key issues for introspection.

The first of these is the issue of states not being responsible players. In an ideal situation, states must be responsible players who do not allow cross-border terrorism and do not give shelter to individuals and organisations who sponsor terrorism anywhere. Unfortunately, we have a situation where one state in South Asia has not been very responsible in that sense and therefore we see a lot of terrorism routinely emanating from it as part of its geopolitics in international relations. In the 20th century, it was war that was seen as a continuation of politics by other means and now we have a situation in South Asia where some state players see terrorism as an instrument of state policy. This remains a worry that needs to be taken into account.

The second point is that, in this war, there are no winners. There has been no winner ever, whether you look at terrorism that started in France in the Sixties of the last century, or in later years. It is apparent that no terrorist group has ever achieved its political aim. What they have achieved is a loss at both ends, with the recipient suffering serious consequences in terms of economic and emotional costs with the very fabric of society being affected. There is a heightened sense of insecurity among citizens, but more tragically, over a period of time, the public gets inured to such acts and treats incidents of terror as the new normal. This leads to citizens becoming less sensitive to such incidents, which then do not get the level of condemnation that they should. The public only gets concerned if the incident is huge, such as the attack on Mumbai in November 2008 or the killing of school children in Peshawar in Pakistan in 2014. To combat terror, each and every incident of terrorism must attract opprobrium from the public.

An obvious counter-terrorism strategy is that the world must unite and cooperate in fighting this scourge by disrupting the financing of terror. Encouragingly, a lot of steps have been taken in this regard such as the Financial Action Task Force (FATF), an inter-governmental body established in 1989 by the ministers of its member Jurisdictions, with the objectives to set standards and promote effective implementation of legal, regulatory and operational measures to combat money laundering, terrorist financing and other related threats to the integrity of the international financial system. Whether such efforts are sufficient, it is difficult to say, but obviously such efforts over time will hopefully disrupt terror financing to quite some extent.

The next issue is minimising the effect of any radicalisation on religious grounds. This is a more difficult battle to fight because it is a battle of 'minds and hearts', and that is something which we also need to be concerned about as countries, as states and as societies. How are we going to stop and interfere with the radicalisation of our youth, ..., the consequences of which they perhaps do not fully understand, who are being misled by selective propaganda? This is a challenge which we are not, as yet, coping with very well and we will have to evolve capacities to meet this challenge also.

The fourth point I would like to highlight is about state capacity. Obviously, state capacity to meet the challenge has to increase and has to be of a high order. Terrorists would like to carry out high profile attacks in developed countries like the USA and the West to draw maximum attention, but the reason that such incidents in these countries is not much is because they have better state capacities to prevent them. Unfortunately, in this part of the world, state capacity is still not to the extent that the developed countries have achieved, whether it is in terms of the nimbleness of our intelligence agencies or the coordination capacities amongst various institutions. Our various organisations need to look at these problems, whether it is technology or whether it is commitment. We tend to be a tad insensitive to the kind of horror that terror is bringing and, therefore, perhaps, even the commitment of the people involved in fighting this menace is not of the level required. We have a system that is largely a 19th-century construct which we inherited from the British and that system more or less persists. I, too, am a symbol of that system and now, naturally, as one sees the world changing and new threats emerging, we need to look into methods of changing such systems to improve our state capacity. State capacity does not mean only the government. It also means how good our criminal justice system is, which sometimes appears to be more antiquated than our administrative systems. If someone were to study it, one would see that changes in the criminal justice system have been very slow, to the point of being almost negligible. That is a cause of worry and contributes to encouraging acts of terror.

Terror attacks actually endanger the very values that we want to adopt and live by. The damage done by terrorism to the lives that we try to choose for ourselves, which essentially, in political terms, means the democratic way of life, is huge. For example, we perhaps have greater tolerance for non-judicial settlement of some of these issues. That is not a good sign for us. We have to ensure that we live by the values that democracy has bestowed. Unfortunately, as state capacity weakens and we are unable to deal with incidents in terms of administrative capacities or effectiveness of the criminal justice system, we become more tolerant of extra-constitutional means of settling some of these issues which degrades the very foundation of democracy. The Mumbai attacks are a prime example of the failure of state capacity and the damage that accrued from the same. A lot has been written on the subject but amongst the insightful articles which point out where and how the failures took place are the articles written by Pratap Bhanu Mehta in the *Indian Express* and Robert Kagan's article in the *Washington Post*. Kagan's article speaks of the strategic motivations for the Mumbai attacks and what it implied in terms of India and Pakistan, how it almost brought about a situation where it left dilemmas not only for India and Pakistan but also for the USA. Another insightful article on the failure of state capacities was Edward Luttwak's, 'The Fatal Delay'. All these highlight the way we look at issues of governance, and the need to have a relook at the same. Ajay Shah's article, 'Look Deeper,' again highlights the same point. These articles and many others on the subject highlight the fact that while terrorism has no winners, it creates dangers for our democratic polity which we have to be very aware of. The articles also highlight the need to review our systems and enhance our state capacities, if terrorism is to be effectively tackled. Protection against terrorism begins at the level of the beat constable, and we saw in Mumbai that the beat constable and the local police were completely helpless in even cordoning off the sites of attack.

Another aspect of the lack of capacity, and I refer to India now, is that we have lost focus on some of the major issues of governance. Two issues that come to mind are education and health, where the Indian State has not delivered the kind of services that were needed to be delivered to its people. Even more important is the issue of law and order. If we cannot provide security to our citizens and a congenial atmosphere for economic activity, we are failing. Unfortunately, over the last half a century or so, governance has shifted from its core duties of health, education and law and order, to focusing on populist schemes, ostensibly in the name of the poor. Ironically, these schemes hurt the poor the most as what they really need is education, health and an environment in which they can work.

For India to confront its myriad problems, a sustained period of double digit growth is required. This is essential on the one hand, to improve our state capacities to take on these challenges and on the other, to reduce the frustration of unemployment and lack of economic opportunity for the youth, thus reducing the pool of people which terrorist organisations depend upon for recruitment to their cadre and for radicalisation.

14

The Future of Gwadar and Other Aspects of Security Within the Indian Ocean

Hein Kiessling

During my years in Islamabad in the 1990s, I had the opportunity to accompany former Pakistan Army Chief, Mirza Aslam Beg on three different trips to China. One point which surprised me during these trips was one could often find in libraries of Chinese think tanks and universities a study titled '*The Eurasian Landbridge – A new silk road as motor for economic development*'. This 230-page study was published in English and German in 1996 by a small German political activist group based in Wiesbaden near Frankfurt/Main. The head of this group was Lyndon LaRouche, a US citizen and political activist who was married to the German political activist, Helga Zepp-La Rouche. According to monthly magazines of this group, the couple had visited China often and were received by high-ranking Chinese officials.

This now 17-years-old 'New Silk Road' study from Wiesbaden came to my mind again when China's development plans became unveiled in autumn 2013, subdivided in Silk Road Economy Belt and 21st Century Maritime Silk Road, both today known as 'One Belt One Road' strategy. It proved that China's geo-strategists had worked for years over a strategy which China's paramount leader Xi Jinping and Premier Li Keqiang were promoting during their recent state visits in Asia and Europe.

During his visit to Pakistan in April 2015, President Xi Jinping signed agreements with Pakistan, development projects worth USD 46 billion, a spending which is focusing on building a 3000-km (1800 miles) China Pakistan Economic Corridor (CPEC). This corridor will connect Pakistan's deep sea port, Gwadar, located at the Arabian Sea, to China's western Xinjiang region. International analysts see this CPEC as President Xi Jinping's biggest gambit in the 'One Belt One Road' strategy. Since signing these agreements in April 2015, the vast majority of Pakistan's politicians, economists and strategists believe that CPEC, and in particular, the development of Gwadar will bring Pakistan wealth, prosperity, regional importance and recognition.

But it speaks for good political reporting that also from 2015 onwards, some writers in Pakistan pointed towards soft points within the corridor project. For example, on 19 September 2015, the paper '*The Express Tribune*' published an opinion from a Pakistani analyst under the headline '*Gwadar's string of perils*'. In it, Alvi Sattar says: "What we should be considering though, is that while China has built some roads in Pakistan, it still needs to lay thousands of kilometres of gas and oil pipelines and railway tracks in order to put Gwadar into use. That will cost money, and China may be reluctant to invest if the region continues to be volatile. Furthermore, Pakistan faces a low-scale insurgency in Balochistan, where Gwadar is located and through which the proposed pipelines will pass."

It speaks for the quality of this writing when the guilt for the situation in the Province of Balochistan is not seen coming only from outside Pakistan. Alvi Sattar also writes: "Several tribal chiefs are opposed to large-scale foreign investment, fearing it will bring an influx of outsiders. They demand greater autonomy and royalties for the extraction of natural resources. Although China has developed local infrastructure, it is considered as an exploiter by some segments of the local population."

Pakistan's security strategists see the situation, of course, in a different way. In a paper, given to me in August 2015 by the ISI, they say: "Due to economic potentials, Balochistan has become a venue of geopolitics and battlefield of economic interests between global and regional power players. Balochistan was becoming prone to terrorism and sectarian violence; however these tendencies have been sufficiently contained. An analysis of a summary of terrorism incidents that occurred in Balochistan shows that such incidents resulted in the killing of 2407 civilian/security forces and 5229 injured. However, owing to effective counter-measures by law enforcement agencies

(LEAs), and by restricting the role of dubious INGO's, the situation is improving."

Of course, the ISI in this paper points especially to India's intelligence agency, the Research and Analysis Wing (RAW). For example: "RAW in collusion with other agencies, especially Afghan National Directorate of Security (NDS) is fomenting instability in Pakistan by providing financial support, training, weapons and explosives and sanctuaries on foreign soil...Indian embassies and consulates in Afghanistan are directly involved in funding, coordinating and supporting Balochistan Sub Nationalists (BSN) miscreants and Tehrik-e-Taliban Pakistan (TTP)".

I have no difficulties to quote from this ISI paper because it is widely known that the ISI works in a similar manner in Kashmir – it is simply the name of the game. And in my book about the ISI, published in 2016, I have used clear words about what had happened in Mumbai in 2008: "An operation such as the Mumbai attacks, which needed expert technical assessment, money and time to prepare, could not have been carried out or kept hidden without the knowledge of the service's leadership. Considering the political explosiveness of the event, the COAS as well must have been informed". To say it clearly, the Lashkar-e-Taiba's use of maritime approach on its way to Mumbai in 2008 was already a terrorist act of the same quality like the attacks on USS *Cole* in 2000 and the French tanker, *Limburg* in 2002.

A precondition for a way out of this situation will only be in sight when Islamabad and Rawalpindi put their present Kashmir policy at least for a longer time on ice. China's leadership had recommended this way to Pakistan more than 20 years ago and might do it again now. If Pakistan will follow such advice, terrorism in South Asia, and parts of the Indian Ocean, might drop significantly.

Back to Gwadar and the question of whether CPEC and port Gwadar will become a success story, as I said before, most Pakistanis are very optimistic about it. One could, however, find pessimism in only some writings; for example, in Ghulam Ali's 2013 article in the *Express Tribune* titled *China's strategic interests in Pakistan's port at Gwadar;* or in Ali Sattar 2015 article in the same paper titled, *Gwadar's string of perils*. Recently, in February 2017, James Dorsey wrote the article *Asian Ports: Pitfalls of China's One Belt One Road Initiative*, in which he claimed that the CPEC might not be successful in the end.

I think the opposite way. China's paramount leader Xi Jinping will not end his 10-year term around 2023 with the failure of the CPEC project. Far too much money and prestige have already been invested. Moreover, Beijing's development policy in Western China, even if China's economic growth rate might be lower in future, demands access to the Indian Ocean. China is investing around USD 51 billion in Pakistan's infrastructure and energy, including port Gwadar. Beijing has deployed soldiers to protect Chinese workers and Pakistan has built up a 17,000-man special force to protect its own interest in CPEC. It is therefore all set to keep the so-called low-scale insurgency in Balochistan under control and, if that is the case, thinking about the shortest link from Gwadar to Central Asia via Afghanistan might also be realistic again. Pakistan's political and military leadership have started a new initiative to come to an understanding with Kabul and with major groups of the Afghan Taliban. Whether all this will be successful remains to be seen, as the ISIS, as latest incidents have proven, has also now gained a foothold in Afghanistan.

The Pakistani side will give her utmost to fulfil all financial burdens the CPEC project has loaded on it. The total committed amount under CPEC of USD 50 billion is divided into two broad categories: USD 35 billion is allocated for energy projects while USD 15 billion is for infrastructure, Gwadar development, industrial zones and mass transit schemes. The entire portfolio is to be completed by 2030. With the help of other countries and international finance institutions, they will most likely succeed.

Back to OBOR and other possible pitfalls, there is at present a fragile political situation in Sri Lanka, where China has developed port Hambantota. This is seen by analysts as another question mark within China's string of pearls. They point towards Sri Lanka's former President Mahindra Rajapaksa, who had warned China in December 2016 that public protests would erupt if plans proceeded to build in Hambantota a 6000-hectare economic zone that would buffet a USD 1.5 billion-deep sea port, a USD 209 million international airport, a world-class cricket stadium, a convention centre and new roads.

If political turmoil keeps Chinese investors more careful in spending in Sri Lanka in the future, Beijing has still more options in its string of pearls scenario. There are the container port facilities built by China in Chittagong, Bangladesh, and roads, dams and pipelines built by Beijing in Myanmar. There are the ports of Kyaukpyu and Sittwe in western Myanmar. A Chinese group corporation, CITIC, has won two contracts related to a special economic zone in western Myanmar including building a deep sea port at the Bay of Bengal. The consortia (China Harbour Engineering Company Ltd., China Merchants Holdings, TEDA Investment Holding and Yunnan Construction Engineering Group) will lead projects to build a port as well as an industrial area at Kyaukpyu Special Economic Zone in western Myanmar's Rakhine State. Ports like Kyaukpyu in Rakhine State are of particular interest for China because overland links from there to southern China will help to avoid the Straits of Malacca and will save up to 5,000 kilometres in sailing distance. Two parallel 700-km long gas and oil pipelines are completed on Myanmar's territory and Chinese tankers, coming from Africa or the Middle East, can cross the Bay of Bengal and unload their freight there, from where it can be piped to Yunnan.

But each story has two sides. Over the last three years, there were also disputes between both Beijing and Rangoon for different reasons, most about royalties, prices and compensation. These problems have not yet been solved and contracts might have to be renegotiated. International political observers see, again, Myanmar as a failure in China's string of pearls. To my mind, this is unlikely; both sides will come to an understanding. Beijing needs the short links to Southern China via Myanmar and the Myanmar government the investment and money from the great neighbour.

There is at the end the question of whether China also plans to use Gwadar for naval purposes. The Pakistani, Ali Sattar, wrote in September 2015: "Despite over a decade having passed since China started constructing the first phase of Gwadar, no military-related activity has ever been observed there...its current interest appears to be commercial, aiming at securing an alternative route for its energy supply." Indeed, as far as its naval interests are concerned, China has concentrated so far on the South China Sea. But that might change. Analysts are predicting that after a decade, China might have more war ships than the USA.

And there could still be other problems of OBOR in the Indian Ocean. The Maldives are trying to prove their 'Islamic credentials' by planning to carry out executions again. A 15-year-old girl who had been raped was found guilty of fornication and sentenced to 100 lashes. Saudi Salafism is dominating life in Maldives today. A couple of hundred jihadists from the Maldives are fighting for ISIS in Syria and Iraq. In terms of tourist inflows, one million tourists came to the Maldives in 2014, the majority of them Chinese on package tours. The second largest group was Australians. But the more than 100 luxury resorts dotted on remote islands are unprotected and might be easy targets for jihadists.

Another outlook: Chinese ships en-route to or from Africa might face pirates near the coast of East Africa. Under the pretext of fighting such piracy, China might bring its navy to Gwadar. As Pakistan–China defence ties are already of a cordial nature, Pakistan's leaders in Islamabad and in GHQ in Rawalpindi will agree to such further development.

In November 2016, Pakistani media was full with reports about an Indian submarine trying to enter Pakistani territorial waters aiming to reach port Gwadar for spying. According to a spokesperson of Pakistan's Navy, the submarine was detected through aerial surveillance, was continuously tracked by Navy fleet units and pushed out of Pakistani waters. A spokesman of the Indian Navy of course denied that it had ever occurred – but interestingly, the whole story came up just a couple of days before Pakistan and China started a naval exercise in the Arabian Sea. As a reaction to the whole incident, China handed over two navy ships to Pakistan in January 2017 for joint security along the sea route of the China-Pakistan Economic Corridor. China also promised to deliver two more state-of-the-art ships to Pakistan in the near future.

Iran, for example, seems to have taken all this already into account. In February 2013, it was announced that a new naval base would be built in Pasabandar (Makran) near Iran's border with Pakistan. Iran's navy has also begun to intensify its efforts to develop the Makran coast stretching from Bandar Abbas to Pasabandar.

15

Africa's Arc of Instability

Simon Allison

It is important to discuss the terror issue in Africa along with those in the rest of the world. Unfortunately, when terrorism is discussed, many people in India tend to view the problem as Asia-centric, being limited to the neighbourhood and the neighbourhood being restricted to South Asia! But as President Nelson Mandela of South Africa had pointed out years ago, when he came to India on a state visit, the Indian Ocean connects India with Africa and if you look at the larger strategic neighbourhood, Africa is definitely part of it.

Terrorism is as much a menace in Africa as it is in other parts of the world. From the east coast of Africa to the west coast, an arc of instability exists which covers Somalia where we have the presence of al-Shabaab, Mali, where the AQIM (Al-Qaeda in the Islamic Maghreb) is active and moving further, the Boko Haram in Nigeria. This paper will focus on the emerging trends in these parts of Africa.

Somalia

Somalia is in the headlines even today. Here, the al-Qaeda affiliated group, al-Shabaab, has been on the offensive for the last few month, despite the fact that it has steadily lost ground over the last five years. This fact needs to be noted. First, al-Shabaab lost control of the capital, Mogadishu, in 2011 and was then pushed out of the major cities and towns. This was largely due to the efforts of the African Union force of 21000 soldiers from Ethiopia, Kenya,

Uganda, Burundi and Djibouti which is supported by the UN and also by the Somali National Army. The al-Shabaab leader, Ahmed Godane, was killed in a US airstrike in September 2014 and the new leader, Sheikh Ahmed Abu Ubaida, has been leading the group ever since. But we need to analyse why there is now a surge in attacks by al-Shabaab, when it was literally down and out. Over the last few months, the group has managed to reassert itself and, in repeated offensives, has taken over some of the towns from the African Union troops in Somalia. The group has increased its attacks on African Union bases, Somali government facilities and on targets in Kenya. Why has there been a surge in al-Shabaab activities and its attacks in Somalia when this organisation has been engaged by African Union forces which are supported by the United States? Two reasons can broadly be attributed to this development.

The first is the withdrawal of Ethiopian forces from Somalia. This was a force of over 2000 troops that Ethiopia provided to the AMISOM (African Union Mission in Somalia). Ethiopia also deployed 4000 soldiers who operated outside the African Union (AU) framework, but they operated in tandem with the AMISOM. The Ethiopian government pulled out its forces that were not part of the AMISOM subsequent to the declaration of a six-month Emergency by the Ethiopian government in 2016. The Ethiopian communication affairs minister stated that the country was unable to continue with the heavy financial burden and that the international community should take a greater role in dealing with the Somali problem.

The second reason for the surge in violence by the al-Shabaab is that AU has commenced plans to withdraw from the AMISOM beginning from 2018, a process which is to be completed by 2020. This has been triggered by the fact that the AU, by itself, is not in a position to fund the counter-terrorism measures required against al-Shabaab. It depends on financial support from external powers like the European Union for funding their budget and the European Union has announced a budget cut for AMISOM by 20 percent. This in turn led to an announcement by the AU that it is planning to withdraw its mission from Somalia. Uganda, one of the providers of troops to AMISOM, has also said that it will pull out its contingent by the end of 2017. Kenya has also threatened to withdraw its contingent if the European Union did not rethink its budget cut.

A combination of these two factors has led to a surge in al-Shabaab activity in Somalia. Just recently, on 14 March 2017, an oil tanker was hijacked off the coast of Somalia. Reports of this hijacking suggest that among the people who carried out the hijacking, about a dozen were affiliated to al-Shabaab. So, the connection between al-Shabaab and revival of piracy is something which we really need to take note of. This is the first incident of piracy since 2012 in the Indian Ocean Region (IOR). The relative stability achieved led to talks of pulling out of the combined force which has been taking care of the counter-piracy missions in the IOR. The recent piracy attack would necessitate a review of such a decision.

Mali

The security scenario in Mali is alarming. Here, a motley lot of extremist groups which have for long tormented the civilian population have joined hands and come under some kind of unified leadership which has brought the AQIM, al-Shabaab and some local terrorist groups under a common umbrella. The avowed aim of this grouping is to 'avenge the injustices against them'. The group has aligned with the al-Qaeda leadership as is seen in videos released by them. In the videos, the group has stated its allegiance to al-Qaeda, putting to question talk being heard of the al-Qaeda being down and out. On the contrary, it would appear that there has been a resurgence of the al-Qaeda in Mali and even in Somalia. I need to point out here that the rise of al-Shabaab in Mali and its close links with al-Qaeda in the Arabian Peninsula is a dangerous trend. If allowed to continue, it spells dangerous portents for the region as it could potentially lead to exchange of terror groups between Yemen and Somalia which would have negative ramifications not only for Africa, but also for the Asian region. So that's one of the reasons why we have to look at what's happening in Africa very closely.

Nigeria

In Nigeria, Boko Haram has been the ruling terror group. It began a military campaign to impose Islamic rule in northern Nigeria in 2009. The conflict has since spread to neighbouring states. In counter-terrorism operations carried out by the Nigerian Army codenamed 'Operation Lafiya Dole', the commander of the force, Man Gen. Lucky Irabor, claimed victory over Boko Haram, stating in December 2016 that the Army had won a great victory. The Nigerian President, Muhammadu Buhari, too claimed victory over Boko Haram saying that the terrorist group had been routed in its key north-eastern stronghold. However, such claims need to be taken with a certain measure of caution.

While the group may be on the back foot in Nigeria, it is by no means out. In 2014, the group had acquired the infamous title of 'world's deadliest organisation' and in the last seven years, under the leadership of Abubakar Shekau, Boko Haram has continued to target civilians with impunity which has led to the death of over 20,000 people, creating 75,000 orphans, displacing 2.6 million persons and causing a loss of over USD 9 billion in property. In March 2015, in an audio tape released by Boko Haram, its leader, Abubakar Shekau, swore allegiance to the Islamic State in Iraq and Syria (ISIS) or Daesh. Abu Bakr al Baghdadi, the head of Daesh, promptly endorsed the alliance calling Boko Haram "our jihadi brothers". Boko Haram was quickly rebranded as the 'Wilayat al-Islamiyya Gharb Afriqiyah', or the Islamic State in West Africa Province (ISWAP). The group however splintered in 2016 when Daesh named Abu Musab al-Barnawi as the new leader of Boko Haram. The long-time leader of the group, Abubakar Shekau, denied he had been replaced and vowed to continue the insurgency. Evidently, Shekau was not keen to follow the diktats of Daesh, and so he struck out on his own.

Since then, Boko Haram has continued to launch attacks in the region and while there has been a reduction in violence levels in some parts of Nigeria, in the northeast, violence has by no means been eliminated. An important trend that has emerged is that Boko Haram activities have spread to other parts of the region, specially in Cameroon, Niger and, to a lesser extent, to Chad. Similarly, in Mali, the AQIM and the other groups have also spread out in the neighbouring regions and to some of the other countries in West Africa. We are now witnessing two kinds of trends that are emerging in the case of terror attacks in Africa. First, there is a rise of al-Qaeda-led groups in Africa and secondly, these groups are not limiting their attacks to the host country but are moving out and spreading their tentacles in other countries in the neighbourhood.

What then is the solution to this problem? Obviously, military force cannot be the sole option and multiple options need to be tried out, the mechanisms of which are already available. The AU has a history of various kinds of frameworks available wherein the African countries have looked for an African solution to their problems. They have to look for frameworks that will deal with countering terrorism. In 2004, the AU came with a protocol on countering terrorism but it took them almost a decade to ratify this protocol. This shows that while there has been a lot of talk by the African countries in terms of finding African solutions to their problems, they have been very slow on the implementation front. There appears to be a lack of political will among the leadership in Africa and until and unless this is rectified, forward movement will be slow.

The concerned governments are also looking at other measures to prevent the youth from joining terrorist organisations. Here, a quote from the governor of Nigeria's north-eastern Bono state is significant. He said, "Once we create jobs, once we engage with youth, this madness will evaporate. This is the year of youth in Africa as declared by the African Union and I hope that there would be some movement in this direction." Summits are organised every year by the African Union Commission, in an attempt to find solutions, but it remains to be seen whether they come up with something that will yield the desired results. While there are no easy solutions to the problem of terrorism, they need to realise that terrorists are people who are a part of their own society. So, looking at the root causes of terrorism is as important as military solutions. While military solutions may give short-term benefits, long-term resolution will have to look into eliminating the root cause of the problem.

India has been, in recent years, engaging with the African continent in a big way and in the last India-Africa Forum Summit, the declaration also brought in the fact that India and Africa should cooperate in the field of counter-terrorism. There has been some engagement in this regard, mainly in terms of training and exchanging information, but there is scope for greater cooperation. Indian civil society is by and large not aware of the situation in Africa and only when public opinion within India thinks of terrorism in Africa as being relevant to India too, will we see some kind of forward movement in this regard. Government-level contacts and cooperation are one way of resolving this issue but ultimately it is the people of India and Africa who will have to look at cooperating with each other in future.

16

Islamised Radicalism or Radicalised Islamism?

Takeshi Kohno

An analysis of the global terrorism database, compiled by the University of Maryland and which is based mainly on news reports, is revealing. From 2000 to 2015, the 15-year span witnessed 87,009 terrorism related incidents. South East Asia accounted for about 7000 of the above incidents of which Philippines accounted for 3558 and Thailand for 1115, Indonesia about 500 and Malaysia for 39. The dominant numbers, thus, come from Philippines and Thailand. When we look at the type of incidents in the Philippines and Thailand, the so-called jihad-related incidents are only about ten percent of the total.

In the Philippines, of the many incidents reported, some of which led to casualties and others which did not, most related to separatist sentiments in Mindanao. That is not to say that there are no serious issues of kidnappings and Islamic State (IS)-influenced issues in Mindanao area and Sulu Island. Apparently, there is this node of the Islamic State, the Abu Sayaf group, in Sulu Island. And in the case of Thailand, about 3112 cases are related to separatist issues against the central government. While there are a few incidents of terrorism incidents, most cases pertain to how the regions in the southern part of Thailand are expressing their opposition and resentment against the central government.

This does not mean that there is an influence from international elements which transcends from outside Southeast Asia to Southern Thailand. In the case of Indonesia, the most famous case was in 2002 of the Bali bombings in which 202 people were killed; there were also a series of bombings in Indonesia. I was present in the Japanese embassy at that time and the perpetrator was the Jemaah Islamiyah, which originally was created by Indonesian clerics who fled to Malaysia and then they started this organisation with a hope of establishing an Islamic State in Southeast Asia. So, the idea of establishing an Islamic State in the Southeast Asia region was already there. We can thus see a general trend of seeing the one extreme interpretation of Islam, using the rhetoric of or rather the selective rhetoric of holy texts to justify the idea of terrorist acts.

This has had an influence not only in Indonesia, but in Malaysia, Singapore, southern Thailand and the southern part of Philippines. It is also interesting to note that a group consisting of people from Southeast Asia are getting together to fight in the name of Islam in the Islamic State in Iraq and Syria (ISIS). If you trace this grouping of South-east Asians, it's not just what we see in Syria and Iraq; it can be seen in the Afghanistan conflict too where a group of Malaysians, Singaporeans, people from Philippines and Thailand tend to congregate together. So they do not really mix with other Arab fighters but tend to congregate among themselves. It is, therefore, important to see their grouping tendencies as Southeast Asians.

Eventually, all these fighters will return to their respective countries and it could be sooner than we think. Some have already left. What is to be done with these people when they come back will be a challenge for their respective countries. There is one serious debate going on in Europe on whether we should understand this issue of terrorism as Islamised radicalism or radicalised Islamism. Radicalised Islamism is easy to understand because there was al-Qaeda; there was, though very secretive, a foundation of understanding of Islamic teaching which got radicalised. But we have seen quite a large number of people who are not very familiar with the teaching itself, but they have been radicalised and use Islam on top of their radicalism to act and to kill. That is the Islamised radicalism trend. There is a tendency towards radicalised Islamism and also towards Islamised radicalism. Both have to be dealt with at the same time and this poses its own challenges to the counter-terrorism effort.

17

Need for a Long-Term Strategy

Bilveer Singh

There is no gainsaying the fact that Southeast Asia too is impacted by terrorism. I would like to look at the granular dimensions with regard to the region, the linkages between South Asia and Southeast Asia and what we need to do to resolve an issue as complex as terrorism.

First of all, we need to walk the talk. In this context, the experience of South Asia, especially of India, goes back to the Forties of the last century. We can learn a great deal from the manner in which terrorism has been handled by India and mutual experiences need to be shared.

Second, the phenomenon is highly complex. It cannot be looked at as a linear concern. The process is complex and conflict resolution will take a long time, perhaps over a few generations. We thus need to put a time frame over what we propose to do. If we think that the problem can be resolved in one term of any particular government in the region, then we are not being realistic. That is not going to happen. So how do we condition strategies which are long term and with which politicians are not really familiar with?

Third, the causes are not simple. It is as difficult as defining an elephant in a dark room. Causative factors for the growth and spread of terrorism are many, each having local and national, and at times regional and international ramifications. Multiple cross-currents exist, which too need to be understood, instead of simply understanding the dimensions of the conflict. This would be critical for conflict resolution. To determine the medicine to be given to a patient, we need to understand both the medicine as well as the disease and this is not easy. Indeed, it is a very difficult proposition. So, while we are discussing the problem, we should comprehend and appreciate the difficulties of the situation. It is not simply a guy carrying a bomb and blowing himself up. No mother will give birth to a terrorist; he or she becomes one. We need to understand the underlying motives that prompt an individual to take up such a path. Even after such an individual's surrender, or then apprehended, their minds need to be de-radicalised; merely sending such individuals to jail will not solve the problem. A radicalised individual can motivate others to take to the path of violence and this must be prevented if terrorism is to be rooted out.

Fourth, we also need to take a close look at the nexus between terrorism, narcotics smuggling and human trafficking, be it in any part of the world. The linkages between transnational crimes and terrorism are complex and need to be understood.

Fifth, we must look at the growth and spread of technology. Technology is terror neutral and can be used for good as well as for evil. The virtual world is increasingly being used to spread radical thought and this recognises no man-made borders or boundaries. It is thus increasingly being used to promote and spread radical ideologies, imbued with hate. The virtual world is as real as before; hence the need to understand this dimension in its totality. This is a relatively new phenomenon. Terrorists have an advantage over the security forces in this regard, because they have the initiative, while the security forces can only react to their actions. For the terrorist groups, this is a very cheap and inexpensive way to propagate their cause and to carry out terror attacks. They are able to turn around people at a rate faster than the ability of the security forces to prevent such actions. Most times, by the time the security forces react, the terrorists have moved on and the game is over. So, this is the dimension that we need to assimilate and understand at the same time.

While counter-terrorism is critical, both hard and soft measures are very important. We need to collate information, we need to cooperate with each other. If the terrorists can network together, if they can come together and collaborate, then nations across the world need to do the same, faster and on a bigger scale. While nations may have concerns of sovereignty and borders, appropriate mechanisms need to be set up to allay fears on this score.

Much has been spoken of over the years for the need to create a united front to combat terrorism. This is a necessity because no country is in a position to tackle the problem by itself. As terrorism has transnational linkages, measures to fight terrorism must also transcend national boundaries. One of the prime reasons for nations not being able to tackle terrorism effectively is their inability to cooperate with each other. We will, thus, always be behind the terrorists, playing a catch-up game. The time for talk is long over and what is required now is hard action. It is for the counter-terrorism practitioners to think and do, otherwise we will continue to read of more and more bomb blasts across the world.

It is a well stated truism that shared prosperity and peace can only be achieved if we share our threats too. Terrorism is a shared threat and shared measures are necessary to fight it. Only then will we be fighting for shared peace and security. Unless we cooperate, even if a thousand angels descend from the heavens to tell us about the threat of death, it would make little difference because at the end of the day we will still go back into our little cocoon, while the terrorists will be planning to blow us up. We need to do everything together to contain this scourge, and stop making distinctions between 'good terrorists' and 'bad terrorists'. Such distinctions are an insult to humanity, and we must condemn in one voice, all forms of terrorism.

Some states use terrorism as a tool of statecraft and, unfortunately, are also getting away with it. They must be confronted and told to stop such support in unequivocal terms. In any case, such states will in the long term pay the price for such support, because snakes grown in one's backyard, will sooner or later bite the hand that feeds them. Therefore, we must demolish the myth of 'one man's terrorist being another man's freedom fighter'. Terrorism is an evil to mankind and if you don't accept that, we will be back to mourn the loss.

As of now, especially in the Middle East, we have the Islamic State, al-Qaeda and al-Nusra (Jabhat al Nusra) being very active in spreading terror. While they are being pushed back, that by itself is not the solution to the problem but could perhaps be the beginning of another. An apt example could be that of the Mujahideen in Afghanistan, which after being pushed back, started a new problem with which we are still grappling with, even 30 years later, as they came back, armed and well trained.

The next front could perhaps be a result of the returnees who have been fighting for a long time for Daesh and al-Qaeda, to their respective countries. In South East Asia, many don't even know about the returnees. The returnees are not very clear on why they went to fight in a distant land for a cause which was at best nebulous. But many of these young men and women remain inspired by what has happened in the organisations, in which they fought and they want to become like them, in their own countries. We can see the impact already in Indonesia, where there is a clamour by such groups for Islamic rule. They have morphed from the Mujahideen, from al-Qaeda, from Daesh and are extremely adaptable. We need to be prepared for the next fight which will take place in our backyards.

But, are we prepared for the next fight? We need to put our brains together and determine the contours and the shape of the conflict which is likely to engulf us. In the Philippines, a predominantly Catholic country, the Islamic State gained traction in the Muslim parts of the island of Mindanao. Isnilon Totoni Hapilon, also known by the nom de guerre Abu Abdullah al-Filipini (Abu Abdullah the Filipino), was designated as the 'Emir of all Islamic State forces in the Philippines' in April 2016. His death was rumoured in 2015, but that did not turn out to be the case. He was formerly leader of the Abu Sayyaf group before its battalions pledged their allegiance to Abu Bakr al-Baghdadi.[1]

Within South East Asia, suicide attacks have taken place, so the problem in this part of the world too, is real. We have multiple nationalities fighting for an Islamist cause which creates unrest in the region. The key threats remain from the Islamic State and from al-Qaeda. ISIS has appointed two emirs for the region. Jemaah Islamiyah (JI), meaning 'Islamic Congregation', remains active in the region. It is a Southeast Asian militant extremist Islamist rebel group dedicated to the establishment of an Islamic State in Southeast Asia and has cells in Indonesia, Singapore, Malaysia and the Philippines. It is linked with the al-Qaeda and is also thought to have links to the Moro Islamic Liberation Front and Jamaah Ansharut Tauhid, a splinter cell of the JI which was formed by Abu Bakar Baasyir on July 27, 2008. Terrorism has led to more than a thousand deaths in Indonesia and even in a developed country like Singapore, people have been joining JI. Sixty-seven such persons have been detained which simply means that the problem is not just related to poverty but has many other causes which need to be comprehended to effectively tackle the situation.

NOTES

1. Hapilon was killed later by the Philippines Army in the battle of Marawi on 16 October 2017.

18

Zero Tolerance to Terrorism

Dam Phu Cuong

My country, Vietnam, operates a policy of zero tolerance to terrorism. If an individual joins a terrorist organisation or in any way engages in terrorist acts, then the Vietnamese security forces will get that individual and we have no qualms about it. Even Vietnamese civil society fully supports such action.

Vietnam has gone through many years of war and strife and the country will not tolerate any threat to its peace and stability. We will not support terrorists of any hue, regardless of which country such terrorists operate against or to which country they belong. So, no terrorist, regardless of his nationality or cause, will be given succour or support in Vietnam, whether he be a Chinese, Khalistani, Mujahideen or any other designation.

The government of Vietnam will use all legal instruments including political and economic tools, use of military force and international cooperation to weed out such elements from its soil. In this, our stand has been principled and taken in full consciousness. We have both hard and soft laws and we can put people in prison for 20 years if we need to. If a terrorist is prepared to blow up Vietnamese citizens, then, I think, it is in order that such a person forfeits his or her life. This appears brutal but is essential to preserve peace in our society. We are not prepared to start a cycle of violence through which we have suffered for many years.

We need strict laws to track the perpetrators of terrorism. We also need to understand the ideological construct of terrorist organisations and, as a long-term measure, prevent the spread of such ideology. There can be no tolerance to such an activity, even in the name of democracy, for all it takes is just one bomber to rip society apart. Imagine the impact, if one Muslim jihadi sits in a crowded MRT (mass rapid transport) train in Singapore and blows himself up and kills 100 people!

We are not prepared to accept even a single bomb blast and so will use our laws to get to such persons before they can carry out such acts. This is in conformity with Vietnam's zero tolerance policy towards terrorism. Only then can we succeed in our counter-terrorism effort. While the government is doing what it can to prevent terror activity in the country, it would require the support of the entire civil society too to prevent such acts. No one should operate outside the radar of the security forces and for a successful counter-terrorism effort, a joint approach by all the organs of the state along with civil society is required.

19

Indonesia's Fight Against Terrorism

Hamidin

I am a practitioner. From 2005 to 2009, I was the Chief of the Striking Force Unit of the Critical Response Team of Special Detachment 88 of the Indonesian National Police. Indonesia has suffered greatly from terrorism ever since Indonesia achieved independence in 1945.

Since 1949, Indonesia's first President, Sukarno was attacked no less than 23 times, seven of which were direct attacks on him. He is perhaps the only leader to have been attacked with a MiG17 fighter aircraft, on 9 November 1960. We have also been subjected to hijacking of an Indonesian aircraft. This took place four years after the hijacking of a Japan Airlines flight by the Japanese Red Army in 1977 in Dhaka. On 28 March 1981, Garuda Indonesia Flight 206, registered as PK-GNJ, was hijacked on a domestic flight from Kemayoran Airport, Jakarta, to Polonia International Airport, Medan, by a member of the Islamic extremist group called Jihad Command. And it was in Indonesia that the Japanese Red Army attacked four embassies in one day, on 14 May 1986.

The group of terrorists, namely al Jemaah al Islamiyah (JI), a transnational organisation with cells in Indonesia, before NII (Negara Islam Indonesia), was active in Indonesia and perpetrated the Bali bombings on 25 October 2002. It is no longer active in Indonesia but its former JI cadre have now joined the Islamic State which remains a problem for Indonesia.

Today, terrorism represents the greatest threat to global peace and human development, causing huge loss of life, property, livelihood and sustainable development. Terrorists always take advantage of any situation and any place to accomplish their mission. Terrorists kill to obtain public exposure. To combat terrorism, the international community has to work together in order to achieve the development needs for a better world. Such a partnership will reduce the risk of political challenge and lead to global security and stability. The nature of threat that the world is confronted with, requires from all parties of the international community, dynamic responses and policies that promote growth and when are more equitable for poor countries.

Indonesia's anti-terrorism effort consists of both hard and soft measures. Today, we are more committed to soft measures. For us in Indonesia, terrorism is not a new phenomenon. In 2006, statistics showed that Indonesia ranked 38 in the Global Terrorism Index of a group of 50 states. As recently as 14 January 2016, Jakarta was subjected to a serious attack by terrorists. Multiple explosions took place and gunfire was heard near the busy Sarinah shopping mall in Thamrin Street, the very heart of Jakarta. The police quickly swung into action and killed the perpetrators and thereafter went after the network, which was connected to radical groups in Indonesia, and arrested more than a dozen persons throughout the country. On interrogation, some of them said that they had studied under Aman Abdurrahman, leader of al Jamaah Ansar Ud Daula, currently detained at a high security prison in Nusakambangan, an Indonesian island near the south coast of Java.

President Joko Widodo, in a televised statement, called these attacks 'acts of terror' and said, "Our nation and our people should not be afraid. We will not be defeated by these acts of terror." With that spirit, the residents of Indonesia, took the statement 'We are not afraid', to social media with the hashtag, '#KamiTidakTakut' and that was widely used on Twitter as a counter narrative statement to eradicate the impact of the terrorist attack. Meanwhile, the following United Nations Security Council press statement was issued by Council President Elbio Rosselei of Uruguay:

> *"The members of the Security Council condemned in the strongest terms, the 14 January terrorist attacks in Jakarta, which resulted in the death of at least two civilians, as well as many more injured, for which the ISIL (Islamic State in Iraq and the Levant/Daesh) has claimed responsibility. The members of the Security Council expressed their deep sympathy and condolences to the families of the victims and to the people and Government of Indonesia. They wished the injured a speedy recovery. The members of the Security Council paid tribute to the swift response and courage of the Indonesian security forces in responding to this attack."*

As I stated earlier, Indonesia has both a hard and a soft approach to combat terrorism. The hard approach focuses on law enforcement and the use of force, which includes among other things, tactical raids, arrests, infiltration and killings. The underlying principle here is inter-sectoral coordination, preserving the rule of law and respect for human rights. The soft approach, on the other hand, is seen as the function, role and activities of the non-security apparatus, such as the Ministry of Education as also non-state actors such as Islamic organisations, Ulemas, community and society. Here, force is not resorted to. The focus is on countering radicalisation and on deradicalisation. The former is done through enhancing awareness, enhancing ability and through counter propaganda. For the latter, focus is on rehabilitation of terrorist prisoners and of ex terrorists, their families and their networks.

In recognition of the fact that cooperation with other countries is a vital element in combating terrorism, Indonesia has established cooperation at both the bilateral as well as the multi-lateral level. Internationally, Indonesia, as part of the regional and global community, has signed and ratified ten International Conventions related to terrorism as under:

- 1963 Convention on Offences and Certain Other Acts Committed on Board Aircraft;
- 1970 Convention for the Suppression of Unlawful Seizure of Aircraft;
- 1971 Convention for the Suppression of Unlawful Acts Against the Safety of Civil Aviation;
- 1980 Convention on the Physical Protection of Nuclear Material;
- 1997 International Convention for the Suppression of Terrorist Bombings;
- 1999 International Convention for the Suppression of the Financing of Terrorism;
- 2005 International Convention for the Suppression of Acts of Nuclear Terrorism;
- 2005 Amendments to the Convention for the Physical Protection of Nuclear Material;
- The ASEAN Convention on Counter Terrorism 2007 (ACCT); and
- The ASEAN Treaty on Mutual Legal Assistance in Criminal Matters.

Indonesia is fully aware that international cooperation is essential for any effective criminal justice response to terrorism. By making use of international cooperation, we can cross-pollinate thinking on new ways to combat terrorism. The evolving terrorism risks call for new ideas and new collaborative approaches to help sustain global and regional cooperation in combating terrorism. We must reaffirm our commitment to strengthen legal, regulatory and operational frameworks, to detect, disrupt and prosecute terrorist and foreign terrorist fighters, and to promote stronger future collaboration and innovation in regional and multi-lateral areas. In addition, we still have the challenge of implementing regional cooperation such as coordination and harmonisation of policies and best practice legal approaches by involving stakeholders in the private sector and civil society in the region and associate them with the cooperative efforts and the integration process.

The threat which Indonesia faces from returning foreign terrorist fighters is very real. As of date, there are more than 30,000 fighters from about 100 countries who are joining terrorist groups, particularly ISIS and Jabal al Nusra in Syria and Iraq. As per intelligence estimates, there are about 200 Indonesians waiting to join these terrorist organisations, which already have about 800 Indonesian fighters. They have travelled mostly through Third World countries such as Malaysia, Turkey and the Middle East. Many of them are now becoming agents of the Islamic State. Propaganda of the Islamic State in their home countries has motivated these people to join. Since the beginning of the rise of ISIS in 2012, many youth have been influenced by such propaganda to pay allegiance to ISIS. However, the presence of a large number of foreign terrorist fighters from many different countries in Iraq and Syria and their support base in Indonesia may change the situation as we have witnessed recently in terrorist attacks in Jakarta. We cannot ignore the fact that the availability of easy Information technology such as the internet has facilitated terrorist networks making it easy for them not only to communicate with each other but also allowing them easy access to the technical aspects of military operations such as bomb making and terrorist financing.

To guard against the growing threat of foreign terrorist fighters, Indonesia has taken certain comprehensive measures. The first of these measures relate to raising community awareness to sensitise civil society against the danger of ISIS and to make society more resilient so that the youth do not fall prey to ISIS propaganda. The second, is the intervention programme in our prisons, which aims at rehabilitation, re-education and reintegration of terrorist prisoners and in lessening their support to ISIS. The third is the Indonesian Government's monitoring system through immigration and the intelligence apparatus to prevent Indonesians from travelling to Syria and Iraq to join ISIS. The fourth, is the strengthening of law enforcement measures to prosecute those who return or are attempting to join ISIS. And the fifth is strengthening regional and global cooperation to combat terrorism through the exchange of information in real time, capacity building for law enforcement and other stakeholders, harmonising legal aspects through national, and creating an international, framework model for legal assistance.

By strengthening and bettering cooperation between countries and partnership with the private sector, we can effectively fight terrorism. Indonesia is always ready to strengthen international cooperation at all levels to combat terrorism. It is up to us, as the global community, to transform commitment in fighting against terrorists to one unified policy.

Proactivity is important. The Government has the duty and responsibility to create an environment which is infertile for terrorism and radicalism otherwise you are going to peak all the snakes in your area. Our job is to eliminate terrorists and ensure that new ones do not take their place. Finally, the thing that I want to leave you with is a question: We talk a lot about radicalisation, de-radicalisation, counter-radicalisation, re-habilitation and the like but we also need to ask two questions. One, why do people in society take to the evil deed of terrorism? Two, why do some of us in a society that has not been radicalised become terrorists? An answer to these questions could point to the way for an effective approach to counter-terrorism.

20

The Challenge of New Armed Groups

Min Zaw Oo

This paper will focus on the emerging security challenges in Myanmar pertaining to the emergence of new armed groups during Myanmar's transition to democracy. I will discuss the reasons why these groups emerged during the period when Myanmar was transiting to democracy and its security implications for both Myanmar and the region.

Terrorism in Myanmar is not yet a paramount threat to the state. Some of the armed groups in Myanmar occasionally use terrorist methods to stir instability and discredit the government. But despite occasional bombings, since 1989, none of the groups have taken responsibility publicly for their actions. In this respect, these armed groups differ from terrorist groups in other parts of the world where groups carrying out terror attacks acknowledge their action.

While terrorism is not a paramount threat in Myanmar, the country still has the largest number of armed groups in the region. There are about 30-plus armed groups that are active and their strength is estimated between 60,000 and 100,000 personnel. This number, however, does not include the para-military and militia groups which are now affiliated with the government. A bit of historical background is necessary to understand the status of armed groups in Myanmar.

The Communist Party of Burma (CPB) has been the largest internal security threat to the country since independence in 1948. It remains a banned organisation. The CPB has been effective, both in its military campaigns as well as in inciting internal unrest and protests against the government. However, this calculus changed in 1989, after the military took over power and set up a military regime, after it cracked down on the pro-democracy uprising.

The military government, after assuming power, reached out to the armed groups and offered them a ceasefire deal. The deal was not signed on paper but 40 armed groups took up the government's offer as a gentleman's agreement and decided to abide by the same. Some of these groups were affiliated with the CPB and some were ethnic groups. These groups got sucked into the operations of the rank-and-file of the Communist Party. The ethnic groups worked against the communist leadership and they drove it out, maintaining at the same time their ethnic identity as armed groups.

In 2009, the military government made an outreach to the 25 armed groups that were still armed and fighting the state. With the coming into force of the new constitution in 2008, the military regime put pressure on them to transform into either the border guards or into militia groups under the command of the armed forces. Under this pressure, five large groups were transformed into border guard forces and 15 groups were transformed into militia. Five of the large groups refused to merge with any side.

In the elections of 2016, the National League for Democracy (NLD) won a landslide victory. However, the 2008 constitution, written by the military junta, includes four provisions that limit the NLD's power. First, it assigns the Tatmadaw[1] 25 percent of all seats in both houses of the legislature. Second, it requires a majority of more than 75 percent to approve any constitutional amendment. Third, it prohibits anyone with a foreign spouse or child from becoming president, and four, the 2008 constitution continues to give the Tatmadaw control of three key ministries: border affairs, defence and home affairs.

When it came to power in 2016, the NLD tried to pursue a new course in the peace process and made attempts to reach out to the remaining armed groups. It was during the period when the nation was transiting to democracy and civil rule from 2011 to 2015 during which five new armed groups emerged. In 2010, elections were held for the first time in 20 years in Myanmar and the main military-backed party, the Union of Solidarity and Development Party (USDP), came out victorious though opposition groups alleged widespread fraud and many Western countries condemned the vote as a sham.

When the military was ruling, it reduced the number of armed groups through coercion, military pressure and persuasion. However, when the transition to democracy took place, what was witnessed was the emergence of more armed groups. During the transition period from 2011 to 2015, five new armed groups emerged. Thereafter, under the present government, led by the NLD, one new armed group has emerged. Myanmar has thus witnessed the phenomenon of new armed groups emerging under the transition to democracy.

Why did new armed groups emerge during this period when the nation was transiting to democracy and not when it was under military rule? There are certain underlying factors for this. The first is traditional historical grievances. Many armed groups were tied to distinct ethnic identities. They had a history of suppression and human rights abuses and they disliked the idea of assimilation into the majority. Under-development and the legitimacy crisis of successive military regimes was also a contributory factor. But underlying grievances alone do not create new insurgencies. If that were so, they would have appeared during the military regimes also. This leads us to the consideration of another dimension and that is that when a major armed group anticipates a breakdown of a ceasefire and in outbreak of conflict, they tend to provide weapons to smaller ethnic groups to create new armies – new proxy armies. This was a factor in the emergence of new groups like the Arakan Army and other groups.

Another factor pertains to strategic depth, as these groups had safe havens in countries bordering Myanmar from where they could smuggle arms and equipment and also carry out military operations against the Myanmar government. There is also the issue of higher expectations in the peace process itself. Generally, during any peace process, violence levels should decline. However, sometimes, when the peace process creates higher expectations, some smaller groups want to have a seat at the table. They thus resort to violence to get attention and a place in the negotiations. An interesting incident in regard to such a phenomenon was that a person from the Rohingya group approached me when I was abroad and sought my help to enable them to ask the government to engage them in the peace process. I was not aware of the implications at that time, but later, it was the Rohingya who took up arms and it is possible that they started armed violence for this purpose. The peace process thus can be said to create higher expectations and becomes an incentive for new groups to emerge.

Myanmar has 135 ethnic groups and the community is very fractionalised. When one group is armed, then the other groups, which have had a historical conflict with that group, feel insecure and they too take up weapons to protect themselves. This cycle also leads to the phenomenon of the emergence of new armed groups.

Another dimension is the emergence of international terrorist groups. Some groups within Myanmar see these international groups as espousing causes that they consider dear to themselves, and so they extend their support to them. This phenomenon is seen in the emergence of Rohingya groups on Myanmar's western border. The linkages are evolving, and while we do not know much of such linkages, we have seen technology and fund transfers from international groups to the Rohingya.

What then are the implications of the emergence of new armed groups in Myanmar? First, it has led to an increase in the drug trade. New groups have to finance themselves and while the older groups have natural resources in addition to drugs to finance themselves, the new groups have to rely mainly on illicit drug trafficking. In the period 2011-2015, we have seen drug seizures increase by three times. The Arakan coastline appears to have become a new route for drug trafficking, perhaps because of the animosity existing between Rohingya and Buddhist groups in the Rakhine state.

The next implication is weapon smuggling. A lot of weapons from the northeast of Myanmar on the Chinese border are now being transported to the western border. This means that some of these weapons will end up in Bangladesh and some in Northeast India. Reports indicate that about 10,000 rifles and other heavy weapons have come in from across Myanmar's borders in the east and these are slowly being sent to the western side of Myanmar. This has security implications for both India and Bangladesh.

Lastly, the network and technology transfer among these groups may no longer be confined within Islamic groups but are taking place between Islamic and non-Islamic groups as well. In a 2013 bombing incident conducted by one of the rogue elements in one of the ceasefire groups, the organiser was a Christian and the operative a Buddhist who was asked to blow up a Buddhist pagoda to create a wedge between Muslims and Buddhists. But the triggering device in the bomb was the same as used in Pakistan and Afghanistan. The fact that such a device was used in this bombing points to the fact that the triggering device was procured through Muslim groups in Myanmar. This convergence between armed groups of all shades is a matter of concern. The emergence of new armed groups in Myanmar is, therefore, not just a matter of concern to Myanmar but to the region as well.

NOTES

1. Tatmadaw is the official name of the Armed Forces of Myanmar.

21

Influence of West Asia on Terrorism Worldwide

Daniel Pipes

West Asia is very important when it comes to terrorism in South Asia. It has been the centre for terrorism in its own right and it has been an exporter of terrorism to other regions, notably to South Asia. It pretty much began with the Palestinians who, starting in the 1960s, saw that they could not take on the Israelis in conventional warfare as they lacked planes, tanks and ships, and so, instead, started targeting civilians. The aim of targeting civilians was partly to achieve specific policy goals, for example, to get some prisoners released, or some other specific purpose, and it was also to demoralise the Israelis and hit and harm their economy.

In the early 1980s, the Islamists picked up on this tactic and shifted from the earlier forms of terrorism to suicide bombings. Now, there were no more policies – they were not asking for anything – they just simply attacked. The most important example of transfer from West Asia to South Asia was Abdullah Azam, the Palestinian, who was the key in the founding of both the al-Qaida and also the Lashkar-e-Taiba.

In early March 2017, we witnessed an attacker in Lucknow who was an ISIS follower and was thus someone influenced by West Asia. So, whether the year is 1980 or the present day, we see the imprint of West Asian impact on violence in South Asia. The question that I therefore put forward is: will this influence continue or is it something that will become part of the past?

To understand the influence, we need to look at the sources. For me, the primary issue today is Islamism. By Islamism I mean a certain kind of understanding of Islam, namely, the application of Islamic law in its severity and in its entirety. The underlying idea here is that the Muslim world would be strong if Muslims return to full application of the Sharia. An example of such dedication to the application of Islamic law would be ISIS or Daesh in Syria and Iraq, Boko Haram in Nigeria, al-Shabaab in Somalia, Taliban in Afghanistan and other groups around the world. This, historically, has been a West Asian phenomenon and it might be noted that throughout the centuries, it has been West Asia that has exported ideas to other parts of the Muslim world. Islam itself comes from West Asia; Sufism comes from West Asia and so does Islamism.

The origins of the Islamism surge have a lot to do with the belief that the Muslim world has not kept up with modernity. In the last two centuries, as modernity has come and impacted the entire world, we see three era responses to it. In the first era, from about 1800 to 1920, the majority Muslim response was to emulate Britain and France, the liberal Western states. In the second era of 1920-1980, the majority Muslim response was to emulate the illiberal Western states, namely, Germany and Russia. Finally, since the 1980s, the majority of responses has not been to emulate the West but to go back into Islamic tradition and emulate the Muslims of a millennium ago.

For this reason, I would dispute those who hold the view that good governance shrinks the space for terrorism. I do not think so. If you look at North Korea, Zimbabwe or Haiti, you see three examples of terrible governance, atrocious governance, each in its own way. Yet, one does not find terrorism coming out of these three countries. Contrarily, if you look at France, Australia and Canada you see three countries which despite having good governance are indeed suffering from terrorism. I don't see a co-relation either between governance or personal standing and jihadi violence. Rather, what I see is an attraction to an idea. This is a powerful idea.

I would go further and argue that just as communism was a radical utopian ideology that had great attraction to many people, particularly the educated, as did fascism, now it is the turn of Islamism. And Islamism has great attraction for those that have dynamism and creativity to think about the world and particularly to think about the Ummah – the Muslim community. Such people are saying that the way to strengthen the Ummah is by going back and applying

Islamic law. So, it is not about governance; it is not about personal status – being rich or poor, employed or unemployed, educated or not. It is about attraction to this idea.

Jihadi violence results from this deep sense that the Muslim community, the Ummah, has not done well in the modern era. But it results also from other factors in West Asia. West Asia was renowned in decades past for its dictators – figures like the Shah of Iran, Saddam Hussein of Iraq, Bashar al-Assad of Syria and Muammar Gaddafi of Libya. Murderous regimes certainly still exist in the region, but far more notable is the fact that anarchy has spread, going from west to east. The north of Mali is essentially without rule. Libya itself has two main forces and they fight across the country. In Somalia, since 1991, there has been no effective government. In the Sinai Peninsula, the Egyptian government has lost control. In Yemen, there is a major civil war and there is no central power. In Lebanon, there has been no central power, arguably, since the late 1960s and the Palestinian Authority itself does not rule.

In Syria, there is a tremendous civil war between four main factions – the government, ISIS, other Sunni groups and the Kurds. In Iraq, substantial parts of the country are anarchic. Afghanistan has never, since the 1973 overthrow of the regime, had a government that is in control of the country. Pakistan sees tribal zones, particularly in the Northern areas, not under full government control. As a result of this pattern of anarchy that goes across West Asia and down to South Asia, the national arsenals previously guarded by the state institutions are now open to being plundered. We can see how arms have spread. For example, the Libyan weapons have spread to West Africa and to Syria. In Syria, the ISIS has arms from America via the Iraqi army and from Russia via the Syrian army.

Further, this anarchy means that there are no border controls. For example, if one is standing in front of a border agent, that person is vulnerable. However, no such vulnerability exists when borders like the Syrian-Iraqi border do not exist anymore. In many other cases too, the border controls have essentially decayed providing free movement for jihadis and their weapons. The enormous movement of refugees, especially from Syria, means that jihadis can intersperse themselves amongst the larger populations. As a result, West Asia is the core of Islamist violence. There is no reason to think that it will diminish any time soon; if anything, it is increasing. There are now four countries in which the

Iranian regime is fighting others – in Yemen, Syria, Lebanon and in Iraq. There are troubles in Turkey with the regime fighting the Kurds – wherever we look, the government control is not quite what it used to be in the Muslim Middle East. We, on the outside, cannot fix this – it is up to the Middle East countries themselves.

The attempts to do so, for example, in Afghanistan and Iraq by American-led coalitions failed. Despite trillions of dollars being spent and thousands of lives lost, the goals were not achieved. Change must hence come from within and it appears that there are some positive signs to this effect. There are many in the Muslim Middle East who have concluded that the situation is not satisfactory and needs to be rethought. There are some countries where things are going well, for example, in the United Emirates and Oman where there is not a single jihadi so far. So, from places where things are going right, there are lessons to be learnt from the countries that are successful. But, this is not going to be something that occurs quickly and it is not going to occur seamlessly. West Asia is going to suffer from this wave of jihadi violence of terrorism for some time to come and those of us who live outside the region must take measures to protect ourselves from this violence and the bad ideas that inspire it coming out of West Asia. Whether we be in North America or in South Asia, it is important to insulate ourselves from the dangers, whether it be the weapons, the individuals or most importantly, the ideas.

22

Need for Cooperative Mechanisms in Central Asia

Vladimir Evseev

Central Asia includes five countries – Kazakhstan, Kyrgyzstan, Tajikistan, Turkmenistan and Uzbekistan. For Russia, it is a very important region because we have huge mutual borders with the region. As an example, the Russian border with Kazakhstan is bigger than Russia's border with China. But it is not due to borders alone that the region is important to Russia. It is also due to the very strong economic, cultural and other linkages that Russia has with the Central Asian Republics (CAR); around 2 to 5 million people from CAR work in Russian territory as migrant labour forces. About 10 percent of Russia's labour population comes from Central Asia, the majority being from Tajikistan, Kyrgyzstan and Uzbekistan.

India and Russia have great scope and potential to cooperate in the field of counter-terrorism in Central Asia and strong grounds exist for it. In the near future, India will become a full member of the Shanghai Cooperation Organisation (SCO)[1] and this will enable us to cooperate more closely with the counter-terrorism effort in Central Asia. People in the CAR are now increasingly talking about the need for counter-terrorism action. The reasons are complicated, and many of the reasons are internal. But there are also external factors that are exerting influence. As a result, we have about 10,000 people from the CAR and from some areas of Russia who have left the region and gone to fight for the Islamist cause in Iraq and Syria. This indeed is a very large number and we assess that about 8,000 of these fighters will eventually return to their respective countries.

The challenge before us is to prevent the return of these people to CAR or to Russia. Both Russia and CAR are trying to collectively work together on security matters to deter and create obstacles in the path of the returning fighters. This is necessary. We also find that due to the proximity of the Afghanistan border to the Central Asian countries, a large number, estimated to be in the range of about 4,000 fighters from CAR, have taken part in the activities on the side of radicals in Afghanistan. This too is a serious problem for us and for the Central Asian countries.

However, foreign influence is not the only factor that is causing a rise in the spread of people in the CAR taking to terrorism to fight for the Islamists. A large part of the problem has much to do with conditions inside the country which lead to such action. Here, I am referring to the socio-economic problems and high levels of corruption in these countries.

In the near future, it is necessary for us to assert our strength to fight terrorism, especially in Kazakhstan and Tajikistan. We find that during times of leadership changes, especially during the transitional periods, radical groups resort to terrorism to change the status quo in the country. Kazakhstan is a very important country for Russia because it is a more open country than others in Central Asia. Its very openness enables terrorist groups to influence more people there. For a long time people in Kazakhstan thought that their country was immune to terrorist attacks. However, since 2011, the country has seen some terrorist attacks. For example, on 5 June 2016 in Aktobe, which is located on the western part of Kazakhstan, two attacks occurred at gun stores while a third attack was aimed at a military unit. Multiple shootouts between terrorists and police occurred over the next few days which left seven people dead and 37 injured. Eighteen attackers were killed and nine arrested. Then, in July 2016, in another terrorist incident, this time in Almaty in the southern part of Kazakhstan, a gunman killed three policemen and a member of the public.

Such incidents are likely to continue as the attacks are not accidents but part of a process, which we must comprehend and understand. The number of people engaged in terrorism in the Kazakh republic is estimated to be about 1,000 or so. This is by no means a small number. For example, a sleeper cell may have only 50 people but that number is enough to create huge problems in small cities. So, a city like Aktobe can be held hostage by terrorists if they find an opportunity to do so.

It is of course possible that the people of the Kazakhstan Republic solve their own problem. But let us understand that the real basis for terrorism in the Kazakh Republic is the spread of Salafism – an ultra-conservative movement within Sunni Islam that developed in Arabia in the first half of the 18th century. As per estimates, there are about 15,000 people who follow the Salafi movement in Kazakhstan. In Kyrgyzstan, the number of radicals is estimated to be about 2,000. However, there are also estimates that more and more people are ready to join the radicals and this number is estimated to be about 10,000. This however is my estimate. Many people in Kyrgyzstan believe the number is far higher, probably in the range of 40,000 to 50,000. This is a large number and it is necessary to reduce it if we are to control the spread of radical ideology.

Now, let us take a look at the Tajik Republic. Tajikistan has a 1,344-km-long porous border with Afghanistan. This is a very different situation from that prevailing with Uzbekistan which has only a 100-km-long border with Afghanistan. Uzbekistan is doing well in the economic sphere and is in a position to keep control over its border with Afghanistan. However, while it may prevent the movement of radicalised individuals from Afghanistan, it may find it more difficult to stop a similar movement of radicals from Tajikistan to Uzbekistan.

Tajikistan has a weak economy and the country has limited earnings. There are temporary Russian military bases in Tajikistan and the Russian military patrols the border with Afghanistan. Corruption is rampant and foreign remittances constitute an important source of external financing. While Russia is prepared to help the Tajik republic, most of the problems there are internal and a result of faulty policies. There is little effort to halt the growth of radicalised Muslims. It is important for Russia that a check be kept on radical Muslim groups on the border with Afghanistan.

The Collective Security Treaty Organisation (CSTO) has been formed with six countries – Russia, Armenia, Kazakhstan, Kyrgyzstan, Tajikistan and Belarus – as a military alliance. Unfortunately, two countries, Uzbekistan and Turkmenistan cannot be members of the CSTO. However, Russia does have a bilateral security agreement with Uzbekistan and is helping that country.

The situation in Turkmenistan is however worrisome. About 80 percent of its army is deployed on the border with Afghanistan, but it is ill-equipped and ill-trained to deal with the threat of terrorists on the border as also with controlling the spread of radical Islam which will produce future radicals. The situation is hence difficult but with cooperation and help from security organisations of other countries, we may create additional opportunities to fight terror. This is important not only for Russia and for Central Asia but also to ensure regional security.

In Russian estimates, radicals may organise attacks on the border with 1,000 or 2,000 radicals. So it is necessary to be ready and to deter them from Central Asia and it is hoped that this deterrence would be effective. In Afghanistan, we are aware that the Islamic State has a very visible presence. In Russian estimates, there are about 7,000 to 8,000 rebels in Afghanistan owing allegiance to the Islamic State. The problem in addressing terrorism here is that Turkmenistan has an agreement with Taliban that they will not fight against each other. But what will Turkmenistan do against the Islamic State fighters who want to enter Turkmenistan. The border area in Afghanistan on the Afghanistan-Turkmenistan border is a zone that is practically not in the control of any one. A lot of radicals owing allegiance to the Islamic State have their presence here making it a very difficult situation to handle now and in the future.

It is necessary to organise mutual defence to cooperate not only in security, but in defence as well. It is hoped that India would be in a position to help in creating a regional security architecture for the mutual benefit of all. Russia too has good experience in countering terrorism and is ready to cooperate with other countries. With the combined effort of India, China and other countries in the region it is hoped that we may be able to deter terrorism. I hope we may do that because terrorism is not only a problem for the Russian federation, or for the Central Asian Republics. It is as much a problem for India and other countries too. It is necessary to fight this together as our mutual war against terror.

NOTES

1. India became a full member of the Shanghai Cooperation Organisation (SCO) at the Astana Summit on June 8-9, 2017.

23

Terrorism in West Asia: Possible Trends

Ilan Berman

This paper focuses on the future – what we can expect from the West Asia region and how we can respond. Over the last two years, since early 2014, the rapid takeover of parts of Iraq and, subsequently, parts of Syria by the group popularly known as the Islamic State (IS or ISIS or Daesh) has captivated and captured global attention and its brutality has held global attention. The media today is filled with images and narratives of the brutality and hostility of life under the Caliphate. As a result, very logically, the Islamic State has become the near single focus of international counter-terrorism policy and certainly of the Western response to contemporary terrorism. I would however posit that the struggle against ISIS is only one part of a much larger contest and something that is going to require sustained interest and sustained coordination for several years. What will that field look like? In my view, there are five trends that we need to focus on in the next several years.

The first trend pertains to the Islamic State and its potential of a decline. By way of reference, at the height of its power in late 2014 and early 2015, the territory of the Islamic State covered 81,000 square miles which is roughly equivalent to the size of the United Kingdom. It held sway over a population of 8 million civilians, roughly analogous to the population of Switzerland. During that time, ISIS was estimated by US intelligence sources and private intelligence institutions to be generating a revenue of USD 1 billion annually making it the richest, most well-funded and well resourced threat group in modern history. Today, the fortunes of the Islamic State have declined considerably, as a result of coalition pressure with the application of hard and soft power on Islamic State resources. As a result, the reach of the groups has significantly eroded. As of the summer of 2016, the British intelligence consultancy, IHS Jane's estimated that ISIS had lost a quarter of its total territory, roughly the size of Ireland, and its finances had declined by roughly half as well. This is attributable certainly to bright spots in Western counter-terrorism policy, particularly to what the US government officials call the 'Line 5 Effort,' which is the effort to counter ISIS financing by targeting its various income streams.

The setbacks on the part of the Islamic State have forced changes to the modus operandi of the groups and forced them to implement cost-cutting measures such as slashing the salaries of its foreign fighters. But is the Islamic State truly on the ropes? The conventional wisdom in Washington is that ISIS is now in terminal decline like it was said of al-Qaida several years ago. I would, however, offer the argument, that the answer is 'no'. Despite all these setbacks, the Islamic State is a resilient actor and is still a capable one, which has a diverse funding stream that includes everything from black market energy trade to, most importantly, taxation of the citizens under its control. These elements continue to challenge the ability of the United States and its allies to neutralise them. In addition, the Islamic State still has global reach. The group has succeeded in fielding at least six (what it calls) armies in Libya, Egypt, Nigeria, Saudi Arabia, Yemen and Afghanistan. In addition, it has multiple independent cells that are inspired by its ideologies. What this means is that it is still possible to envision, maybe, a geographically smaller Caliphate but one that is territorially and economically sustainable no matter how successful the coalition is in the near future. In other words, we can envision a future in which the Islamic State is degraded but not totally depleted and we need to contend with that future.

The second trend we need to focus on is the groups that have tethered themselves to the Islamic State itself. Today, no fewer than 34 separate radical groups from virtually every region in the world have made common cause with ISIS or have pledged allegiance to its Emir, Abu Bakr al-Baghdadi and these patterns are inevitably going to be affected by the current path of decline that is being seen on the part of the Islamic State. But these groups are not going to go away as a result and it is facile to think so. In virtually all the cases, except for the groups that have sprung up in Syria themselves, these organisations pre date the creation of the Islamic State and have autonomous personnel, infrastructure and capabilities. A great example in this regard is Boko Haram in Nigeria, which has split over the question of allegiance to the Islamic State. However, both halves of the larger Boko Haram whole maintain autonomous capability and will continue to be a threat, both nationally in Nigeria and also regionally in Central Africa. As a result, the decline of the Islamic State could usher in an era of diffused localised jihad where the former partners of the Islamic State, in the absence of a coherent central guidance, begin to seek to promote their own radical vision for their respective regions. This is something that we all need to be prepared for.

The third trend that we need to account for is the future of al-Qaida. We all know that the Islamic State is a spawn of the al-Qaida – a product of it and an evolution of its ideology. We also know that over the past three years, the two groups have become bitter rivals and have competed for what we call 'hearts and minds' throughout the Islamic world with regard to affiliation and allegiance. In that context, the Islamic State has won, at least so far. But what is not understood well is what has happened to al-Qaida as a result because we have seen a pretty significant evolution of its own ideology and modus operandi in response to the innovations that the Islamic State has made. As a result, al-Qaida today holds more territory than at any time in its history. From Yemen to Syria to Afghanistan, al-Qaida has become entrenched in large parcels of territory, exploiting empty political space in conflict zones and exploiting the local reaction and local aversion to the excesses of the Islamic State, to promote itself as a relatively moderate alternative – and it is succeeding. This long-term strategy, moreover, has benefitted tremendously from lack of attention on the part of the United States. The USA has been preoccupied with the Islamic State, or which some of us call the 'shiny object', the object that is capturing all the media attention and sucking up all the oxygen in the room. Consequently, the USA has allowed al-Qaida to continue to flourish in the shadows in these peripheral regions where it is now making its base. By doing so, the bin Laden network has laid the groundwork for long-term strategic presence as a global actor.

The fourth trend we need to focus on is a new generation of jihadists. Over the last half decade, the struggle between the regime of Bashar al-Assad in Syria and its political opponents has steadily transformed from a local conflict into a global jihad. Thanks to the influx of tens of thousands of foreign extremists, we can say that Syria has become the new Afghanistan. It has become a crucible for today's terrorist and an indoctrination and breeding ground for tomorrow's terrorist.

The analogy to Afghanistan is very instructive. The Soviet invasion of Afghanistan in 1979 touched off what we know as the first jihad. It resulted in the mass mobilisation of radicals throughout the Muslim world and over the years that followed thousands of people made their way to South West Asia to wage jihad against the Soviet Union. All told, scholars estimate that as many as 20,000 foreign fighters joined the ranks of the Afghan Mujahideen, in the decade between 1979 and the end of the war in 1989. Over time, this alumni network became battle hardened, field tested and became closely coordinating. Once the Afghan jihad ended, some of these alumni sought out other conflicts. As an example, they moved to the conflict zones in Chechnya and the Balkans. The rest returned to their own home countries to carry out subversion at a local level. But today, the foreign fighter problem that is being incubated in Syria has the potential to be much worse than what was seen in the 1990s. This is because, since its rise to prominence in Iraq and Syria in the period 2014-2015, the Islamic State is estimated to have attracted nearly 31,000 foreign fighters. Put in another way, the Islamic State in two-and-a-half to three years has marshalled more than one and a half times the number of foreign fighters than what the Afghan jihad marshalled in a decade of fighting. As the Syrian civil war winds down and ends, if and when it does as all wars must inevitably end, we can expect to see a massive outflow of Syrian alumni in ways that are going to destabilise the regions where they come from including places like Central Asia, Russia, South East Asia and South Asia as well.

The fifth trend is one that is talked about far less but it bears noting and that is the threat that is posed by a reinvigorated Iranian threat network. The contemporary focus on ISIS, at least in the USA, has diverted attention from the growing potential of Shiite religious radicalism – a phenomenon which is causally linked to the expanding capabilities and strategic ambitions of the Islamic Republic of Iran. As a result of the nuclear deal signed between Iran and the P5 plus one powers in 2016, the Iranian regime has received what amounts to an enormous economic windfall; one that encompasses upwards of USD 100 billion in direct economic relief as well as billions upon billions of dollars of defence and energy related post sanctions trade. This has set the Iranian economy, which was previously rickety, on a path of modest growth.

As Iran's economy stabilises, its strategic ambitions have expanded. The last year and a half, amongst many other initiatives, the Iranian regime has deepened its military footprint in Syria in support of the Assad regime; it has redoubled its investments in Shiite militias operating in Iraq and it has provided extensive military assistance to Yemen's Houthi rebels and empowered their political lives. Today, the cumulative effect of this is that one can say that Iran is in control of four separate Arab capitals – Beirut, Damascus, Baghdad and Sanaa. This has two important implications for the USA and its coalition allies. First, is the possibility of a surge in capabilities of radical groups that are supported and funded by Iran. Even before the lifting of multi-lateral sanctions as a result of the nuclear deal, Iran was estimated by the US government to be spending between USD 3.5 billion and USD 16 billion a year on the support of groups like Hezbollah and Hamas. Given the importance of these proxies in Iran's strategic foreign policy as force multipliers and asymmetric allies we can expect these contributions to grow as Iran's economy becomes more and more solvent.

The second trend line, which appears to be very ominous, is Iran's complicity in a secondary and less known foreign fighter flow. A lot has been said and written about foreign fighter flows going to the Iraq-Syria battle space in support of the Islamic State. Not much has been said, however, about the idea that Iran is supporting and directing a secondary Shiite fighter flow, state directed, very narrowly tailored but implicating radicals from Afghanistan, Pakistan and Iraq and flowing into Syria, in support of the Assad regime to fight against the Islamic State as well as other forces there. This trend line is significant precisely because it is state directed. If the worry about foreign fighters flowing out of Syria and Iraq after the war is that it will be an undirected stream and that these fighters will go wherever they choose, there is worry that Iran, which has weaponised foreign fighters in its fight in Syria, could weaponise them again in the future against other countries.

So where does that leave us. For the USA and its allies, the contemporary focus on ISIS is logical because of political promises, because of a new administration in Washington which has hung its strategic hat on the idea that the USA will erode and degrade the Islamic State. But the US counter-terrorism policy over the long term has to be broader and more strategic and must anticipate the future complexion of the battlefield. There is a difference between political rhetoric and reality and the allocation of resources. In this process, we are going to see over the next year a very significant evolution in the official thinking in Washington. But I hope we also see far greater investment in international cooperation in combating the future complexion of the battlefield and also in beginning a serious process in the discussion of the centrality of ideology in the spread and proliferation of these trends.

24

Economic Impact of Terror and Terror Financing

Lt Col Vivek Chadha

Terrorism aims at achieving its political objectives using force and intimidation. Often, innocent bystanders end up as its most frequent casualties. The cost of terrorism and its finance, as seen from the prism of human suffering, tends to remain a manifestation of this harsh reality. It is therefore not surprising to find the statistical representation of terrorism in terms of a mix of figures that indicate fatal and non-fatal casualties of civilians, security forces and terrorists. Further, success, as relative as it may be, also becomes a reflection of these ratios, with graphs in different coloured lines indicating the meandering course of its journey.

There can be little dispute over the human element's importance while assessing the impact of terrorism. In fact, it should remain the foremost factor for any analysis. However, in doing so, its economic dimensions are often lost sight of. Its relevance is also obscured by the very nature of the challenge that assessing the economic impact involves. As an illustration, the sustained instability caused due to terrorism is most likely to impact investments flowing into a country or region. Conversely, it can also be a result of poor economic policies or changing global economic climate. It is therefore a challenge to assign a percentage of economic downturn to each of these elements.[1]

The attempt to analyse the economic costs of terrorism must, therefore, segregate the known and the relative unknown, to arrive at a better understanding of its overall impact. This in some ways relates to the costs in tangible and intangible terms. The psychological and emotional sentiment that impacts economics is often the most difficult to analyse, given the absence of parameters to accurately include each contributing factor. Conversely, the specific losses suffered because of terrorism and the expenditure incurred to fight it are relatively easier to comprehend, even as each of these may not be available in the public domain. This paper attempts to calculate the tangible costs of terrorism and the finance of terrorism. It will also give an indicative impact on the economy through various case studies both in the Indian context and regions beyond that have been affected by terrorism. An endeavour will also be made to understand the reasons and nature of the impact that terrorism can have on an economy with reference to India as the case study.

The Direct Costs of Terrorism and Terrorist Finance

The direct cost of terrorism and terrorist finance should be relatively easier to calculate when compared with the indirect costs. This should be even more relevant for countries that have a clear structural system in place for the same like the Department of Homeland Security (DHS) in the USA. An assessment of its annual budget should be a clear indicator of the costs involved. However, this is complicated by several factors. The DHS looks at other issues besides counter-terrorism to include disaster management and access control measures. Further, organisations have budgets that may be utilised for counter-terrorism; however, these are not in the public domain. And finally, expenditure on certain aspects straddles both counter-terrorism and developmental initiatives. Scott Stewart reinforces this and indicates that the US efforts are "spread across nearly every agency in the government."[2] Gordon Adams, a national security budget expert, commenting on the scale of expenditure, says, "The answer is a lot and very hard to break out".[3] However, he goes on to provide an estimated USD 100 billion as an approximate annual expenditure.[4] Yet another estimate places the figure of counter-terrorism related intelligence spending in 2013, based on the leaked Snowden papers, at USD 16.6 billion.[5]

The direct cost of terrorism can be related to many elements that are impacted by it. This includes the following:

- Cost of losses in terms of people and property;
- Ex-gratia payment because of death and destruction of property;
- Monetary allocation for raising, maintaining and modernising a force specifically for counter-terrorism; and

- Creation and maintenance of organisations and infrastructure specifically for counter-terrorism.

One of the most stunning terrorist strike remains the 9/11 attack in the USA. There have been several studies that have attempted to analyse the economic cost of this incident. The Comptroller of the City of New York concluded that the physical capital loss was estimated at USD 21.8 billion.[6] This included the cost of replacing the towers, repairing or replacing the office space surrounding the twin towers, repairing or replacing of utility infrastructure and underground trains, contents, fixtures and computing technology within the buildings, clean-up costs and compensation. Beyond the immediate site of the terror strike, insurance claims because of the strike are estimated at USD 40 billion.[7] It also had a cascading effect on the cost of providing insurance for terrorism related cover, a phenomenon, which was also noticed in India after 26/11, as will be discussed later in the paper.[8] Because of 26/11, it was also estimated that the Gross City Product of New York came down for the last three months of 2001 and 2002 by approximately USD 27.3 billion.[9]

In contrast, a small province, the Basque Country in Spain, when affected by prolonged terrorism saw its per capita GDP decline by 10 percentage points.[10] It reinforced the fact that political instability has a negative impact on investments and savings and that it is bad for economic growth. However, for the same to kick in, the impact of either political instability or terrorism as a tool for creating political instability must adversely affect the nerve centre of an economy. This includes a few variables to include, productivity, expenditure, foreign investments, domestic infrastructure, savings, consumption, etc.

In the Indian context, 26/11 provides an indicator of the direct costs of a large-scale terrorist strike. While specific details for each of the targeted installations is not available, a rough estimate is provided by the settled insurance claims. This is especially so in the case of major targets like hotels. According to the Insurance Regulatory and Development Authority (IRDA), a pool of Rs. 400 crore was created over a period of two years to settle claims arising from the attacks. The insurance companies paid a substantial premium because of the damages due to the attack. The Annual Report of the IRDA for the year 2009-10 indicates that of the Rs. 306-crore terrorism pool created, Rs. 214 crore was paid during the year of which Rs. 212 crore was specific to the 26/11 attack.[11] During the year 2010-11, the claims paid were 76.18 crore.[12]

Besides the specific impact of 26/11, the annual cost of insurance claims for the last three years has remained within a range of Rs. 2-2.60 crore. The relatively low payout could relate to the low number of individual household properties insured against terrorism and the limited number of major commercial establishments targeted by terrorist attacks. Claims made due to terrorism and paid during the last decade are listed below:

Year	*Account Paid (Rupees in Crores)*
2006-07	1.61
2007-08	1.05
2008-09	50.67
2009-10	214.00
2010-11	76.18
2011-12	41.50
2012-13	6.73
2013-14	2.22
2014-15	2.58
2015-16	2.04

Other than the data of claims available, data available from some of the individual commercial establishments further provides details of the costs incurred due to 26/11. The Oberoi Hotel at Mumbai was one of the major terrorist targets. Its renovation cost the management USD 45 million. "The earnings of East India Hotels, the publicly-listed company that operates the hotels, fell nearly 70 percent in the nine months ended in December, compared with the same period a year earlier" though this was also due to the 2008 economic downturn that had a worldwide impact on the hospitality industry.[13]

A major economic cost of terrorism emerges from raising and maintaining a force specifically for fighting the same. The recent past has witnessed several such counter-terrorism related forces being raised in India. The Rashtriya Rifles, which presently has 63 battalions, five Force headquarters and 21 Sector headquarters, was raised to fight terrorism in Jammu and Kashmir. The annual expenditure for maintaining the Force can be gauged from the Defence Services Estimates for the year 2016-17. It indicates that the total amount spent under both Capital and Revenue heads totals Rs. 6336.37 crore.[14]

The Assam Rifles is the oldest paramilitary force of the country. Its role is primarily related to counter insurgency (CI) operations in Northeast India. The budget allocation for the organisation for the year 2017-18 was Rs. 4801.84 crore.[15]

The National Security Guard (NSG) is a counter-terrorism (CT) force which has witnessed an increase in its ranks after 26/11. Its budgetary allocation for 2017-18 was Rs. 816.10 crore.[16]

The newly-raised India Reserve Battalions, of which 48 of the allocated 51 have already been raised for supporting CI operations in Northeast India, were allocated Rs. 68.90 crore. Of the 51 battalions, nine each have been allocated to Assam, Tripura and Manipur, seven to Nagaland, five to Arunachal Pradesh and Mizoram, four to Meghalaya and three to Sikkim.[17] In addition, 10 Specialised India Reserve Battalions have also been sanctioned.[18]

The states of Northeast India are allocated funds for supplementing their security-related expenditure. This is utilised primarily for CI-related expenses. The state-wise allocation of the same is listed below:[19]

Table 1: Details of Security Related Expenditure (Rupees in Crores)

Funds Released	*Assam*	*Nagaland*	*Manipur*	*Tripura*	*Meghalaya*	*Arunachal Pradesh*	*Total*
2004-05	75.40	26.49	9.44	36.17	1.56	1.35	150.41
2005-06	63.91	24.83	33.65	27.00	13.17	1.35	163.91
2006-07	90.86	25.55	13.60	18.24	3.91	1.28	153.44
2007-08	75.61	21.97	14.45	16.47	5.88	3.02	137.40
2008-09	108.60	33.13	21.58	45.04	6.24	5.45	220.04
2009-10	60.56	41.23	27.26	11.85	1.93	7.17	150.00
2010-11	92.04	79.81	27.28	21.12	3.16	16.57	239.98
2011-12	153.04	83.11	28.88	39.25	27.82	17.90	350.00
2012-13	108.96	69.36	20.62	11.32	-	50.74	261.00
2013-14	134.83	30.12	25.01	26.42	16.60	4.53	237.51

Note: Budget provision for Financial Year 2013-14 is Rs. 290.00 crore.

The LWE states also incur expenditure for security-related issues which is reimbursed by the Central Government.[20] An overview of the same provides an indicator of the additional financial burden that it brings to bear on the economy.

A broader perspective of the estimate for all states affected by terrorist violence can be based on the gross amount for SRE for the financial year 2017-18 as allocated in the Union Budget is Rs. 1222 crore, which is an increase of over Rs. 380 crore from the previous year.[21]

A substantial expenditure is also done for modernisation of state police forces. However, the entire amount is not linked to CT activities of the forces. As an indicator, it amounted to Rs 1551.06 crore including J&K, states affected by militancy in Northeast India and the Naxal impacted states (excluding

Table 2: State-wise Details of Funds Released Under the Security-Related Expenditure (SRE) Scheme for Left Wing Extremism (LWE) States During the Last Three Years and till 31.7.2014 (Rupees in lakhs)

	2011-12	*2012-13*	*2013-14*	*2014-15 (as on 31.7.14)*
Andhra Pradesh	1072.77	1512.82	1798.02	509.56
Bihar	1364.91	786.83	1710.89	1344.67
Chhattisgarh	4237.08	5074.01	4214.41	1480.50
Jharkhand	7535.95	6754.94	4778.74	2471.30
Madhya Pradesh	27.50	65.05	55.75	70.00
Maharashtra	762.91	460.44	738.51	632.50
Odisha	2156.62	1531.34	4813.30	1823.31
Telangana	-	-	-	509.56
Uttar Pradesh	200.01	550.11	533.28	133.12
West Bengal	1390.68	1330.70	2065.10	713.19
Total	18748.42	18066.24	20708.00	9687.71

Note: Under the SRE scheme for LWE affected states, expenditure incurred by the state governments on counter-LWE operations, inter-alia, including expenditure incurred on training of state police forces personnel are reimbursed as per the existing guidelines.

Maharashtra) for the year 2014-15.[22] This was followed by an additional allotment of approximately an equal amount in September of the same year, taking the amount spent to a little over Rs. 3000 crore.[23]

The government has also been spending a substantial amount for civic action programmes, which are undertaken by the army and central police organisations. The amount spent on the same in Northeast India over the years has been aimed at supporting the people and alleviating their hardships due to insurgency related challenges. Details of the same are as given below:[24]

Table 3: Statement of Funds Released Under Civic Action Programme

Name of Organisation	*2010-11*	*2011-12*	*2012-13*	*2013-14*	*2014-15*	*2015-16 (Up to 31 Dec. 15)*
BSF	345.80	200	230	262.50	50	150
CRPF	216	51	150	0	27	150
ITBP	0	85	100	68	75	100
SSB	218.16	165	150	17.76	69	70
Assam Rifles	405.45	300	200	350	200	350
Army	105	100	120	150	179	180
Total	1290.41	901	950	848.26	600	1000

Auth: Ministry of Home Affairs Annual Report 2015-16 (Amount in lakhs).

The total amount granted under the head includes Rs. 19.30 crore to the CAPFs by the MHA and Rs. 54.40 crore by the MoD to the Indian Army.[25] While the RR undertakes major CI responsibilities in J&K, the CRPF is the primary counter-terrorism force in the country. It has a total of 230 battalions, of which 60 were deployed in J&K, 35 in Northeast India and 116 in Left Wing Extremism affected zones. The CRPF also has 10 COBRA battalions, which have a specialised CT role.[26] Some of the battalions deployed in these areas may not necessarily be tasked for the same; however, in 2011, the CRPF raised 70 battalions which were specifically tasked for a CT role and were to be trained and equipped for it.[27] While two thirds of the CRPF remains deployed in CI areas, however, for the purpose of this paper, a figure of one-third will be considered, since this is the allocated number for the same. In terms of budgeting, the total budget allocation for the CRPF for the year 2017-18 was Rs. 17,868.53 crore. A rough estimate of a third of the same amounts to Rs. 5956 crore.[28]

Indirect Costs of Terrorism and the Finance of Terrorism

A co-relation of the direct and indirect costs of the 9/11 attack provides interesting indicators. It suggests that as the direct cost could be USD 22.7 billion against the total cost estimates which varied from USD 50 to 80 billion.[29] The substantial indirect costs of terrorism include the economic confidence of both domestic and foreign investors. Therefore, a measure of foreign direct investment (FDI) into a country and its spread across both normal and terrorism-affected periods becomes a useful indicator. This is despite the reality of other macro-economic factors that might have an impact on inflow of investments. Before analysing the impact of the same on India, it would be useful to analyse the same on other countries which have dealt with terrorism.

Pakistan provides an interesting example, given the scale of deaths due to terrorism in that country and yet it being a sponsor of the same in its neighbourhood, both in India and Afghanistan. The cost of creating, nurturing and financing the terrorist factory in the region led to a blowback affect and a rise in terrorism-related violence in Pakistan. A study indicates that FDI into Pakistan were impacted in a "significant manner" on the basis of terrorism-related violence from 2003 till 2013.[30] It adds, "Private capital flows, particularly FDI, demonstrate a sizeable drop due to terrorist activity…Region-wise and country-wise flows indicate no specificities signalling that investors and remitters from all major source areas react in a similar fashion to bouts of terrorism."[31]

Yet another significant study by Blomberg and Hess in 2005 suggested that the "presence of terrorism, as well as internal and external conflict is equivalent to as much as 30 percent tariff on trade."[32] Interestingly, they also suggest the "need for development, democracy and openness in encouraging peace in terrorist nations."[33]

The indirect cost of the 26/11 attacks in Mumbai also provides estimates which are indicative of the losses that were suffered due to the attacks. Despite these indicators, the stock markets bucked the trend. After 26/11, the markets were closed the next day and on 28 November 2008, the Sensex rose by 66 points. It ended the month at 9093 points and in December 2008, it rose further to 9647 points, crossing 10,000 soon thereafter.[34] Similarly, foreign institutional investors (FIIs) bought USD 159 million net of Indian stocks and bonds (with bonds exceeding equities) on 28 November, followed by purchase of USD 433.5 million in equities and USD 155.4 million in bonds during December 2008.[35]

Even as the Sensex did not show any signs of adverse effect due to the 26/11 attack, there were significant indirect costs that impacted the industry. This was in the form of the cost of insurance, which went up by an estimated 30 per cent from the next year. This adversely affected the cost of doing business and the overheads that the corporate world had to bear as a result of the attack. The specific rise in costs as indicated by the IRDA in their Annual Report for 2009-10 as follows:[36]

Premium Rates for Terrorism Risk Insurance
(w.e.f. 01 April 2010)

	Total Sum Insured per location (MD+LOP)	*Risk Category*	*Rate (per Mille)*
1.	Up to Rs 750 crore	Industrial Risk	0.30
		Non-Industrial Risk	0.20
		Residential Risk	0.10
2.	Over Rs 750 crore and up to Rs 2000 crore	First Rs 750 crore as per (1) above PLUS on Balance Sum insured as under:	
		Industrial Risk	0.25
		Non-Industrial Risk	0.15
3.	Over Rs 2000 crore	First Rs 2000 crore as per (2) above PLUS on Balance Sum insured as under:	
		Industrial Risk	0.20
		Non-Industrial Risk	0.12

Note: MD – Maximum Damage; LOP – Loss of Profit.
Source: IRDA Annual Report 2009-10, p. 38.

The hospitality and tourism industries were amongst the worst affected industries as a result of the strikes. Unfortunately for the industry, the strikes coincided with the slowdown of the economy, which further had a negative impact on hotel occupancy and tourist footfalls in Mumbai as well as India.

Economic Impact of Casualties on GDP and FDI: Pakistan

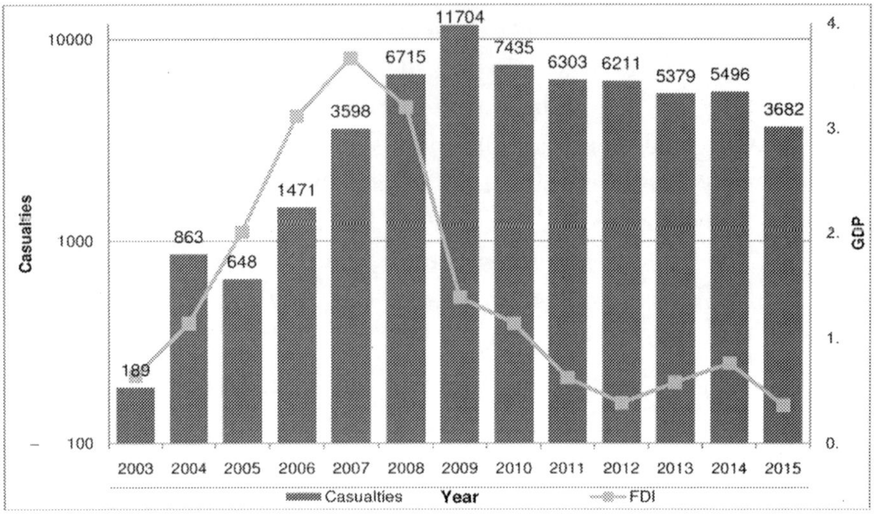

Source: World Bank.[37]

Economic Impact of Casualties on GDP and FDI: India

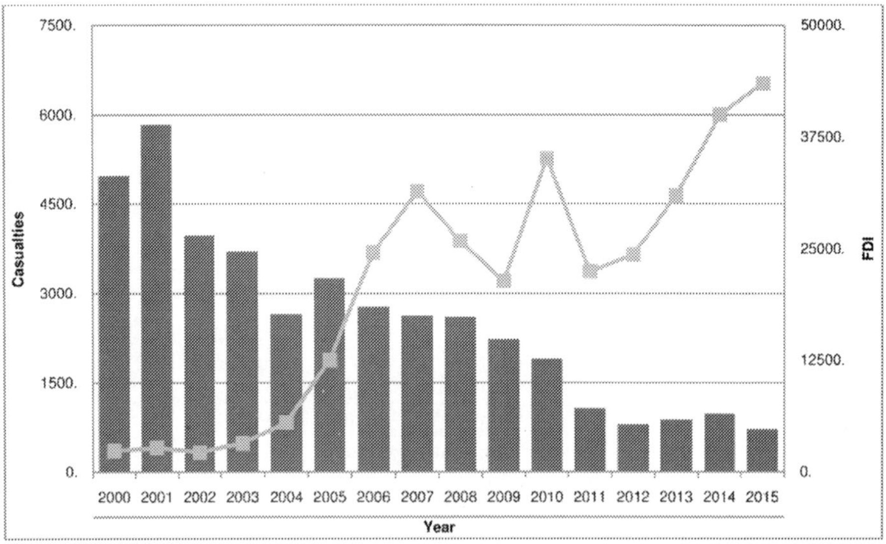

Source: Government of India.[38]

Concluding Observations

The data of terrorist incidents analysed provides interesting insights. It clearly suggests that terrorism has a considerable economic impact. While this is more significant for the immediate region of its influence, it could also affect the country at large. This is evident from the two FDI charts above. In the case of Pakistan, even as violence influenced FDI over a period, the sentiment associated with it kept inflows down despite stable casualty figures. On the contrary, a country like India, which is much larger, displayed greater resilience to terrorist violence. In fact, the rise of the Sensex after 26/11 is in stark contrast to the violence. Similarly, FDI inflows have displayed a steady rise despite violence in specific geographical regions. This contrast is ironical, as Pakistan's employment of terrorism seems to have hurt its economy and people more than it has affected India.

These figures indicate the tangible economic costs. However, it is not difficult to conclude that the real impact of the same is felt by individuals who suffer human losses and, as a result, linked sources of income over a long period of time. Similarly, small businesses, which are directly impacted by bandhs and protests and tourism are more likely to be affected adversely. The impact of such incidents can also have a cascading effect on neighbouring regions that draw their income from the same source. As an illustration, a drop in arrival of tourists to Kashmir also brings down numbers in Jammu and Ladakh. The economic linkages between areas therefore become critical to assess the negative fallout of terrorism.

Besides the direct and indirect costs, for policy makers the cost involved with uncertainty in decision making leads to postponement of developmental and welfare initiatives. The challenge of decision making in an informational vacuum further affects economic measures. This in turn has an impact on every individual who is a direct or indirect beneficiary of the system in place.

NOTES

1. See Adam Z. Rose and S. Brock Blomberg, "Total Economic Consequences of terrorist Attacks: Insights from 9/11", Peace Economics, Peace Science and Public Policy, Volume 16, Issue 1, Article 2, 2010, http://create.usc.edu/sites/default/files/publications/total economicconsequencesofterroristattacks-insightsfrom9_0.pdf, accessed on February 20, 2017, p. 4.
2. Jeanne Sahadi, "The cost of fighting terrorism", *CNN Money*, November 16, 2016, http://money.cnn.com/2015/11/16/news/economy/cost-of-fighting-terrorism/, accessed on March 01, 2017.

3. Ibid.
4. Besides Gordan Adams, an independent estimation by John Mueller and Mark G. Stewart in "Evaluating Counterterrorism Spending", http://pubs.aeaweb.org/doi/pdfplus/10.1257/jep.28.3.237, accessed on March 01, 2017, also points to a similar figure of US $100 billion.
5. Drew Desilver, "U.S. spends over $16 billion annually on counter-terrorism", Pew Research Centre, September 11, 2013, http://www.pewresearch.org/fact-tank/2013/09/11/u-s-spends-over-16-billion-annually-on-counter-terrorism/, accessed on March 01, 2017.
6. Patricia Grossi, "Property Damage and Insured Losses from the 2001 World Trade Centre Attacks," Peace Economics, Peace Science and Public Policy: The Economic Impacts of the September 11, 2001, Terrorist Attacks, Volume 15, Issue 2, Article 3, 2009, http://forms2.rms.com/rs/729-DJX-565/images/terr_911_grossi_2009.pdf, accessed on February 20, 2017, p. 2.
7. Gail Makinen, "The Economic Effects of 9/11: A Retrospective Assessment' Report for Congress, Congressional Research Service, September 27, 2002, https://fas.org/irp/crs/RL31617.pdf, accessed on March 03, 2017, p. 4.
8. Gail Makinen, quoting the Insurance Information Institute, New York, NY, October 21, 2002 and Jackie Spinner, "Terrorism Insurance Bill Moves Forward", Washington Post, October 18, 2002, in "The Economic Effects of 9/11: A Retrospective Assessment' Report for Congress, Congressional Research Service, September 27, 2002, https://fas.org/irp/crs/RL31617.pdf, accessed on March 03, 2017, p. 4.
9. Gail Makinen, "The Economic Effects of 9/11: A Retrospective Assessment," 2017, p. 5.
10. Alberto Abadie and Javier Gardeazabal, "The Economic Costs of Conflict: A Case Study of the Basque Country", *The American Economic Review*, Volume 93, Number. 1. (March, 2003), http://links.jstor.org/sici?sici=0002-8282%28200303%2993%3A1%3C113%3ATECOCA%3E2.0.CO%3B2-C, accessed on March 03, 2017, p. 114.
11. Annual Report 2009-10, Insurance Regulatory and Development Authority India, November 24, 2010, Hyderabad, India, p. 38.
12. Annual Report 2010-11, Insurance Regulatory and Development Authority India, November 24, 2010, Hyderabad, India, p. 42.
13. Vikas Bajaj, "Mumbai Hotel, a Killing Zone, Is Grand Again", *The New York Times*, April 20, 2010, http://www.nytimes.com/2010/04/21/business/21hotel.html, accessed on March 01, 2017.
14. Defence Services Estimates, 2016-17.
15. "Union Budget 2017: 17 announcements by Arun Jaitley for MHA, internal security", indiatoday.in, February 02, 2017, http://indiatoday.intoday.in/story/union-budget-2017-arun-jaitley-mha-internal-security/1/872724.html, accessed on March 01, 2017.
16. "Major boost for police modernisation and infrastructure in Union Budget-2017", *The New Indian Express*, February 01, 2017, http://www.newindianexpress.com/nation/2017/feb/01/major-boost-for-police-modernisation-and-infrastructure-in-union-budget-2017-1565920.html, accessed on February 22, 2017.
17. Annual Report 2015-16, Ministry of Home Affairs, New Delhi, 2016, http://mha.nic.in/sites/upload_files/mha/files/AR(E)1516.pdf, accessed on February 22, p. 16.
18. Ibid., p. 25.
19. "Details of Security Related Expenditure", Ministry of Home Affairs, http://mha.nic.in/sites/upload_files/mha/files/Annex1-300913.pdf, accessed on March 01, 2017.
20. See Unstarred Question Number 3741, Lok Sabha, August 5, 2014, http://mha1.nic.in/par2013/par2014-pdfs/ls-050814/LS%203741.pdf, accessed on March 02, 2017.

21. Pushpita Das, "An Analysis of the Internal Security Budget 2017-18", IDSA, February 21, 2017, http://www.idsa.in/idsacomments/analysis-internal-security-budget-2017-18_pdas_210217, accessed on March 02, 2017.
22. "State-wise tentative allocation under MPF Scheme 2014-15 (Plan and Non-Plan)", Ministry of Home Affairs, Government of India (Police Modernisation Division), March 11, 2014, http://mha.nic.in/sites/upload_files/mha/files/SAP-140314.PDF, accessed on March 01, 2017.
23. Ibid.
24. Civic Action Programme, Ministry of Home Affairs, http://mha.nic.in/sites/upload_files/mha/files/Annex3-300913.pdf, accessed on October 10, 2017.
25. Annual Report 2015-16, Ministry of Home Affairs, New Delhi, 2016, http://mha.nic.in/sites/upload_files/mha/files/AR(E)1516.pdf, accessed on February 22, p. 28 and Annual Report 2015-16, Ministry of Defence, New Delhi, http://www.mod.nic.in/writereaddata/Annual2016.pdf, accessed on March 03, 2017, p. 150.
26. Pankaj Kumar Singh, "Police Force: Staunch Sentinels", Defence and Security Alert, http://www.dsalert.org/assertive-china-and-crpf-for-internal-security/638-central-reserve-police-force-staunch-sentinels, accessed on February 22, 2017.
27. "CRPF creates 70 battalions for exclusive CI operations," *The Hindu*, September 11, 2011, http://www.thehindu.com/news/national/crpf-creates-70-battalions-for-exclusive-ci-operations/article2444746.ece, accessed on February 22, 2017.
28. "Major boost for police modernisation and infrastructure in Union Budget-2017," *The New Indian Express*, February 01, 2017, http://www.newindianexpress.com/nation/2017/feb/01/major-boost-for-police-modernisation-and-infrastructure-in-union-budget-2017-1565920.html, accessed on February 22, 2017.
29. See Adam Z. Rose and S. Brock Blomberg, "Total Economic Consequences of Terrorist Attacks: Insights from 9/11", *Peace Economics, Peace Science and Public Policy*, Volume 16, Issue 1, Article 2, 2010, http://create.usc.edu/sites/default/files/publications/total economicconsequencesofterroristattacks-insightsfrom9_0.pdf, accessed on February 20, 2017, pp. 6-8.
30. Amar Iqbal Anwar and Mazha Yasin Mughal, "Foreign Economic Flows and Terrorism in Developing Countries," CATT WP No. 1, Centre d'Analyse Théorique et de Traitement des données économiques, September 2013, p. 12.
31. Ibid., p. 15.
32. S. Brock Blomberg, and Gregory D. Hess, Terrorism or Tariffs: Which Has a Bigger Tax on Trade?", 2005a, mimeo, as quoted by S. Brock Blomberg, and Gregory D. Hess, "From (No) Butter to Guns? Understanding the Economic Role in Transnational Terrorism", http://citeseerx.ist.psu.edu/viewdoc/download?doi=10.1.1.590.8184&rep=rep1&type=pdf, accessed on October 10, 2017.
33. S. Brock Blomberg, and Gregory D. Hess, The Lexus and the Olive Branch: Globalization, Democratization and Terrorism" November 2005, Part of a World Bank Workshop on Society and Development, Washington D.C., May 26-27, 2005. p. 24.
34. Swami S. Anklesaria Aiyar, "26/11: Buying opportunity, not economic disaster", *Times of India*, January 4, 2009, http://timesofindia.indiatimes.com/sa-aiyar/swaminomics/26/11-Buying-opportunity-not-economic-disaster/articleshow/3932144.cms, accessed on February 20, 2017.
35. Ibid.

36. Annual Report 2010-11, Insurance Regulatory and Development Authority India, November 24, 2010, Hyderabad, India, p. 42.
37. "FDI Net Inflows" World Bank, https://data.worldbank.org/indicator/BX.KLT.DINV.CD.WD?end=2014&locations=PK&start=2000&year_low_desc=true, accessed on October 10, 2017.
38. "Financial Year Wise FDI Equity Inflows", Government of India, https://data.gov.in/catalog/foreign-direct-investment-fdi-equity-inflows, accessed on October 10, 2017.

25

Technology and National Security

Ajey Lele and Natallia Khaniejo

The twenty-first century has witnessed a dramatic shift in the way technology and society interact today. The constant march of progress has led to an increased coalescence between technological advancement and social development. The emergence of technologies like the Internet of Things (IOT), Artificial Intelligence (AI) and Cloud Computing have led to an increased interdependence between Information and Communication Tools (ICTs) and Critical Infrastructure (CI). National security strategies are increasingly dependent on technological advancement for the sake of safeguarding sovereign interests. This intermingling of technological progress with State power has led to the emergence of techno-strategic national security. In the last few decades, the world has witnessed several significant events that have changed the global security landscape and, as a result, developing a well-rounded security architecture has become the need of the hour for nation states.

Some of the most noticeable incidents that demonstrate the need for such a techno-strategic shift are the end of the Cold War and the 11 September 2001 World Trade Centre (WTC) terrorist attacks (9/11). The end of the Cold War could be seen as the phase responsible for projecting global unilateralism with the USA being in 'command' of world affairs while the 9/11 attacks have challenged that hegemony and paved the way for the advent of a multi-polar world.[1] Both these events have had significant fallouts on the way technology is now approached and co-opted by the various actors across the globe. The emergence of cyber networks and ventures linked to cyberspace has led to a further shift in the dynamics of conventional military warfare and these developments have culminated in the emergence of asymmetric and hybrid modes of warfare. Furthermore, the dual use nature of technologies and the relative ease of their proliferation has made it more difficult to control the effects of malicious intent. The need to regulate and control cyberspace has been a major agenda for several countries across the globe and there have been several discussions regarding the potential application of International Law onto cyberspace. While the fifth iteration of the United Nations Group of Governmental Experts (UNGGE) was unable to reach a consensus regarding the means of applying International Law to Cyberspace, the emerging desire to militarise it, arises from the growing belief in containing the threat to sovereign ICTs and CIs. This paper attempts to examine the relation between technology and national security and the subsequent paradigm shift that has occurred over the years.

The Need for Increased Integration between Technology and National Security

In a report titled *Science, Technology, and US National Security Strategy*, Raymond Dubois argues that, "A dominant theme of the twenty-first century is the democratisation of science and technology (S&T). It is a driving force throughout global society and pervasive throughout all aspects of human endeavour to include national security."[2] In order to deal with emergent challenges in a complex threat scenario, countries across the globe have increased their investment in the realm of technology. Given the increased interdependence of technology and society, such investments hold the potential to offer solutions to many social and geopolitical challenges, if not all. While the levels of investment in scientific research and development (R&D) vary from country to country, there is nevertheless an almost universal shift to an engagement with the field at the very least. Some states have gone on to incorporate this research into their national security strategies as well, thereby attempting to create a well-rounded approach to responding to the world's problems today. In an increasingly interconnected globalised world order, the balance of power relies on more than mere military might. States understand that in the modern age, sovereign security can only be maintained through three major pillars. These are the readiness and capabilities of military forces, their engagement with other states in order to prevent conflicts from occurring and the strength of their respective economies.[3] Military strength, economic growth and commitment to institutional cooperative measures, therefore, have now become the three key means of global power projection in the current day and age. The incorporation of technology into national strategies, therefore, represents the belief across the world that scientific and technological advancement provides a direct link to progress. This has led to the emergence of several key technologies that have reshaped socio-political hierarchies as we understand them. This is particularly evidenced by the central nature of technology in modern conflicts such as the Gulf War, the Kosovo conflict, the US invasion of Afghanistan and Iraq, the various cyber-attacks such as Petya and Wannacry, and the nuclear/technological escalation being undertaken by rogue states and non-state actors as well. As DuBois states, "High-technology weapons are no longer the exclusive domain of only a few nations...The democratisation of technology has also given some non-state actors (from small groups to individuals) access to capabilities that in the past have only been reserved for nation states." He further goes on to state that "indeed, the technologies of destruction and the attendant increased capabilities of communication and surveillance, create a threat landscape unlike any we have faced."[4]

Shifting Paradigms of Security and Technological Innovation

The global security architecture has undergone a tremendous shift in the last couple of decades. The shifting power balance that exists today is dependent on the precarious geo-strategic environment and security climate. Twenty-first century defence preparedness necessitates the demonstration of technological strength, a display of technologies via various military exercises.[5] These exercises and the 'testing' of new weapons/delivery platforms all serve to increase a country's soft power radius by projecting the image of a sovereign state capable of securing its borders at every level. Concepts like credible deterrence and asymmetric/hybrid warfare have emerged as a result of these shifting geopolitical paradigms and the nature of threats faced by nation states today has also mutated as a consequence. The current security architecture, for example, is rather nebulous given the amorphous nature of cyberspace and the limitations involved in controlling and negotiating the boundaries of such a transnational phenomenon. As Joseph Nye states, "Understanding deterrence and dissuasion in cyberspace is often difficult because our minds are captured by Cold War images of massive retaliation to a nuclear attack by nuclear means. The analogy to nuclear deterrence is misleading, however, because many aspects of cyber behaviour are more like other behaviours, such as crime, that states try (imperfectly) to deter."[6]

The intersection between technology and the military is not a new concept. This can be traced all the way back to the ancient Greeks. History is replete with examples of technological innovation in the realm of defence. The transition from stones and spears to guns is evidence of how technological progress has affected military engagement. More specifically though, recent generations have witnessed a change in how technological tools are used vis-à-vis military modernisation efforts. The relation between technological development in the civilian field and the military field has been reversed. While a lot of technologies that are currently used in the civilian sphere computers, and more importantly the Internet, have their origins in military settings, this trend has now been reversed. The increased privatisation of scientific R&D in the civilian sector has led to a tremendous amount of innovation. Some examples of technologies that have dual purpose development histories are artificial intelligence, cloud computing, drone technology, 3D printing, etc. While there are nevertheless several technologies that are strictly experimented on within the military paradigm such as hypersonic technologies and automative militarisation, the changing nature of modern threats and the increased emergence of dual-use technologies has certainly reduced the proportionate primary investment in these fields.

Revolutions in Civil and Military Technology

If one were to trace a rough timeline of the way technology has evolved through history, it could be broken down into five phases. These phases have been responsible for most of the technological comforts and innovations that we enjoy today, but they have also changed the perception of nation states and redefined the methods used to ensure national sovereignty. The innovation of the steam engine can be seen as the beginning of the first industrial revolution (1780-1840). The second industrial revolution (1840-1900) began with the emergence of the railways and the steel industry which revolutionised the concept of travel, created faster avenues of troop/weapon mobilisation and also provided materials for further innovation in the fields of technology. The third revolution (1900-1950) produced the electric engine, heavy chemicals, automobiles and consumer durables. The fourth revolution in technology can be attributed to the developments that occurred post the 1950s with increased predominance of the oil industry and information technology.[7] The fifth revolution in technology can be attributed to the emergence of low-cost microprocessors in the 1970s.[8] This is the phase that we are currently in. None of these phases are concrete and are constantly in flux with innovations from one phase impacting subsequent phases with a certain degree of flexibility. Nevertheless, the increasing technocratisation of society that has occurred in the aftermath of the fifth phase has paved the way for a tremendous amount of research in novel technologies like quantum computing, AI, cloud computing, etc.

Sciences like Materials Science, have also received a big boost with the invention of innovative methodologies and the discovery of new techniques. The interest in fields like bio-technologies and nano-technologies can be attributed to the multidimensional applicability of these fields which is what makes them such rich areas of research. Nano-technologies have wider applicability than bio-technologies as they can be used both for electronic as well as material progress. Recent advances in materials science involve the nano-structural reconfiguration of pre-existing materials with the aim of developing super materials. Some of the most well-known of these are graphene, silicene, black phosphorene, aerogels, etc. These advances are not limited merely to military realms but have actually arisen out of civilian research projects aimed at examining the ways in which the fundamental properties of materials can be manipulated and improved. Bio-technologies, on the other hand could bring in a revolution in the logistics supply chain. They would help in carrying lighter foods which have more shelf life and nutrition (this would help in having a leaner "tooth-to-tail ratio").[9] The human ability to heal has also inspired scientists to attempt to create self-healing materials that might be able to repair themselves in the event of a threat/attack. Such materials could go a long way in reducing the threats to life faced by soldiers in situations of war. Recent history has also demonstrated how non-state actors have turned to chemical and biological warfare with the aim of destabilising global security. The need to create a holistic national security strategy keeping all these developments in mind has become the foremost priority of most nation states. All these changes have had and continue to have a direct impact on the way in which wars were conceptualised, strategised and fought.

Digitising the Military

Progress in the civilian sector has permeated to the military sector as the latter have begun adopting technologies that were hitherto being researched purely in civilian terms. Technologies such as cloud computing, AI, quantum technologies and material sciences have impacted the direction military modernisation is taking today. Major technologies that have changed the way in which militaries function today have been the Information Technologies and Space Technologies. The collusive effect of these two have led to a revolution in military affairs. The advent of the GPS and the utilisation of radar systems have emerged as responses to the layered approach required to deal with modern conflict. Satellites have become essential for the purposes of electronic intelligence (ELINT), signals intelligence (SIGINT), communication intelligence (COMINT), and radar intelligence (RADINT).[10] IT and space technologies have been the main departure from the traditional dichotomy of military-civilian technological research.

These fields have necessarily dual purpose and their benefits can be reaped by militaries as well as civil society. It has now become necessary, therefore, for militaries to engage with the research being conducted in civilian spheres as well. The shifting nature of emergent threats necessitates a national security response that is flexible and well rounded. Militaries have begun engaging with technologies such as AI in order to develop a more well-rounded response to emergent threats. Recently, there have been reports regarding the usage of AI in the fight against ISIS. "Project Maven is a crash Defence Department program that was designed to deliver AI technologies – specifically, technologies that involve deep learning neural networks – to an active combat theatre within six months from when the project received funding. Most defence acquisition programs take years or even decades to reach the battlefield, but technologies developed through Project Maven have already been successfully deployed in the fight against ISIS."[11] There are several such instances where civilian and military fields have begun colluding, as developments in the former have motivated innovations in the latter.

This adoption of civilian technologies for military research has led to a more holistic and flexible approach and such collaborations should be further encouraged. Another instance of such a collaboration can be seen in this article that states that "at the beginning of May, a group of Ph.D. students from across Georgia Tech, all part of the Sam Nunn Security Program (SNSP), travelled to Tampa, Florida to brief U.S. Special Operations Command (SOCOM) senior leadership on disruptive and game-changing technologies for national defence."[12]

Current and Future Trends

Currently, AI, quantum computing, cloud computing, materials science and cyber security are now becoming central aspects of military modernisation. National security strategies are increasingly dependent on the progress in these fields due to the rising coalescence of civilian and military infrastructure. While militaries have resisted adopting technologies like cloud computing due to security concerns, digitisation is becoming the need of the hour and states are attempting to negotiate the boundaries between creating un-hackable private military networks and maintaining transnationally connected global communication lines. The UNGGE, the IGF, the SCO and several other global multilateral forums are attempting to negotiate the ways in which these boundaries can be traversed without militarising all of cyberspace. However, maintaining that distinction is becoming increasingly difficult as it is no longer possible to prevent technological proliferation and harder still to limit/control it. The dual use nature of most modern technologies has made it impossible to determine the intent underlying the acquisition of these technologies. Furthermore, attributability is another key issue that prevents states from engaging in direct confrontation regarding breaches and hacks vis-à-vis cyberspace.

Nation-States are engaging in these conundrums in various ways. One such development is the application of quantum computing in the military realm. For example, recently, "China announced the launch of its Jinan Project, a quantum information effort billed as 'the world's first un-hackable computer network'. Building on its launch last year of the world's first quantum-enabled satellite, China has made significant strides in quantum technology, a field with rapidly increasing relevance to national security. Its satellite has been hailed as a major step toward 'unbreakable' encrypted communications".[13] Therefore, there are key developments occurring across the world today that are increasingly conflating the boundaries of development and progress in civilian and military technologies. The increase in asymmetric warfare and hybrid warfare, the emergence of chemical and biological, as well as WMD threats from non-state actors, the rising cases of cyber breaches and network hacks are all leading to an environment of global insecurity and fear. It is necessary for States to keep in mind the shifting paradigms of this global security landscape and incorporate modern means to counter emergent threats. If national security strategies are not modernised, they might fade into obsolescence, thereby leaving open loopholes that could cause severe damage to the functioning of civil society as well as critical infrastructure.

NOTES

1. Lele, 2009.
2. DuBois, Gerstein and Keagle, 2017.
3. Lele, 2009.
4. DuBois, Gerstein and Keagle, 2017.
5. Lele, 2009,
6. Nye, 2016.
7. Lele, 2009.
8. Pundhir, 2017.
9. Lele, 2009.
10. Lele, 2009.
11. Allen, 2017.
12. Georgia Tech Students Brief Military on Disruptive Technology for National Security 2017
13 Fontaine 2017.

REFERENCES

DuBois, Raymond F., Daniel M. Gerstein and James M. Eagle (2017), *Science, Technology and U.S. National Security Strategy*, Center for Strategic and International Studies, Washington: CSIS.

Nye, Joseph S. (2016), "Deterrence and Dissuasion in Cyberspace," *International Security* 41.

Fontaine, Michael J. Biercuk and Richard (2017), *The Leap into Quantum Technology: A Primer for National Security Professionals*, November 17. Accessed Jan 04, 2018. https://warontherocks.com/2017/11/leap-quantum-technology-primer-national-security-professionals/.

____ (2017), *Georgia Tech Students Brief Military on Disruptive Technology for National Security*, May, https://www.iac.gatech.edu/news-events/stories/2017/5/georgia-tech-students-brief-military-disruptive-technology-national-security/591902.

Allen, Gregory C. (2017), *Project Maven brings AI to the fight against ISIS*, December. https://thebulletin.org/project-maven-brings-ai-fight-against-isis11374.

Lele, Ajey (2009), *Technologies and National Security*, http://www.indiandefencereview.com/news/technologies-and-national-security/0/.

Pundhir, Avinash Singh (2017), *Fifth Technological Revolution: Challenges and Opportunities*, https://www.linkedin.com/pulse/fifth-technological-revolution-challenges-avinash-singh-pundhir.

PART III

INTERVENTIONS AND INITIATIVES

26

Role of Governance and Civil Society

E S L Narasimhan

The words 'terrorism', and 'terrorist', are often used as interchangeable words, their sole objective being to frighten, to cause panic and physical destruction and to cause destabilisation of an elected, established government. Governance is perhaps one of the most important instruments to address the issue of terrorism. Many times, people mistake governance for government. The former is, however, a composite term encompassing within its ambit a vast array of institutions – the executive, the legislature, the judiciary, the media, human rights organisations, civil societies, etc. If all these function as they ought to, then we are talking of good governance. Shortcomings in any of these institutions have an impact on governance. Government is basically an executive, but all these organisations and institutions put together, give what we call governance.

A fundamental flaw in our approach to countering terrorism has been the excessive reliance on a militaristic approach. Our actions are mostly reactive, though at times, a proactive stance is adopted, using intelligence as a tool. For some time now, however, we have also begun looking at and addressing causative factors and this, I believe, will be the key to conflict resolution. If we do not understand what drives a person to join terrorist organisations, then we will rarely come up with the right solutions.

Why does a person turn to terror? There is evidently a sense of frustration, disillusionment and disappointment with the established order which constitutes the 'push' factor. Terrorist organisations offer relief and that becomes the 'pull' factor. This then is the motivation – a desire for relief from frustration and disillusionment in the established order which terrorist groups promise to deliver. Good governance then is an effective tool to counter-terrorism as the prime motivation to join terror groups will no longer exist.

There is a great deal of talk of 'minimum government' and 'maximum governance,' and the like but what are the challenges faced in the delivery of good governance. The list is long and includes issues such as demographic transitions, moral and physical corruption, crises in national values, leadership crises, poverty, poor education leading to unemployment and so on. One of the major problems today is of a perceptible loss of faith in our institutions such as the judiciary, the media and the bureaucracy, whose institutional integrity is increasingly coming into question. This is not meant to belittle any of these institutions, but to simply inform of how these institutions are perceived by a large segment of the population.

There is perceptible concern about the judicial process, especially of the delays in justice delivery. The judiciary is the last hope of freedom, but is it executing its role as it is mandated to do? There is a perception that justice is inordinately delayed, and as we well know, 'justice delayed is justice denied'. When a person does not get justice for his grievance, a feeling of frustration and anger sets in. I personally have been impacted when I lost my brother, who was an IAS officer, a divisional commissioner in Jorhat in Assam. He was killed on 6 April 1981, by a bomb planted in his chair. All the accused were influential people and some of them were powerful ministers in the then state government and no action was taken against them. Later, when arrests did take place, the case was transferred to the CBI. Every single one of them was acquitted by the court, which indicated a miscarriage of justice. Such incidents drive people to pick up the gun to seek justice. The perception that justice is only for well-to-do people and not for the ordinary man thus gets ingrained in the public eye. Today, people who are influential, if arrested after committing a crime, immediately develop medical problems and get transferred to a posh hospital instead of spending time in jail. That seems to be reserved for ordinary persons who languish in jails for years.

We also need to question whether the media is playing the role it should play. Today, the media itself is promoting a certain amount of disenchantment. This has much to do with its phenomenal spread in recent years. Earlier, the print media had just a few newspapers. Today, we have a plethora of both the print and electronic media. This has led to the phenomenon of 'breaking news,' with each media house trying to outdo the other. In news debates, at times it appears that the media is the prosecutor, defender, juror and judge, all rolled into one. Trial by media is now a common occurrence which influences public opinion. When ultimately justice is delivered, which is not in consonance with public perceptions, it leads to disappointment and a feeling that justice has not been done.

The executive has a very important role as a policy-maker, but the implementation of policies is where we suffer. This is in the hands of the line institutions such as the bureaucracy. Good policies can come to nought if poorly implemented and if welfare measures do not reach the intended segment. There is also a feeling that civil servants lack empathy and are often arrogant. They do not have the time to meet people and hear their grievances due to work pressure, meetings and other activities. This causes loss of faith by the public and leads to a feeling of being excluded from governance structures. There is thus a need to reaffirm the faith of the people in the bureaucracy and to ensure the implementation of government policies which are all well intended. A perception also exists about the legislature that debate has given way to noise. It may be a good idea to stop live telecasting of legislature debates, as the very fact that the debate is being aired live, leads to the lawmakers posturing for the cameras rather than focusing their energy on reasoned debate. This creates more of discord in society and raises doubts in the minds of the public.

Another key issue is the all-pervasive spread of corruption which is deep-rooted in society. The question arises, are we fighting corruption or are we just making a pretence of doing so? The anti-corruption drive cannot be a show but must deliver and be seen to be delivering. It is a sad fact that the big fish are seldom caught and, if caught, are seldom successfully prosecuted. There is little point in convicting people for petty crimes when the big criminals, who have committed huge frauds, get away scot-free! These are the questions being asked by the public and each time they remain unanswered, a bit of faith in our public institutions gets eroded. Over time, this leads to frustration and some people then turn towards terrorism in an effort to seek justice. Obviously, something needs to be done to make the functioning of civil servants more accountable and for justice delivery to be swifter and sure.

Thought also needs to be given to reform the process of elections.

Unfortunately, the electoral process has been reduced to a slanging match with parties hurling criticisms at their opponents rather than outlining their plans for the development and upliftment of society. Huge expenditure incurred in each election is also a cause of corruption. We need electoral reforms and an idea suggested to stop elected representatives from moving from one party to another and cause the downfall of a government was that in such cases, President's Rule be imposed for the rest of the term rather than have another government elected at all. There are many suggestions, but this is an aspect that needs to be seriously looked into at the earliest.

Another cause of concern is the frequent leaks to media houses of classified information which sets off a frenzied trial by the media. What is not being questioned is how has a top-secret document found its way to a media house? Is there a case for making the media a subject of the RTI Act? There needs to be some level of accountability on the part of media houses too, else, in their search to improve their TRPs (Television Rating Point) they say what they want with scant regard to the truth, sowing in the process, doubt in the minds of people on institutions and on government capabilities to govern, of benefits reaching the people, on the capabilities of the police force, etc. There is a need to go back to the slogan 'Satyameva Jayate,' both in letter and spirit.

Another aspect of governance pertains to core government responsibilities like education and health. These cannot be bartered away to the so-called public-private partnerships. In education today, we boast of opening IIMs and IITs all over the place, but are we providing quality education or are we quantifying education? Many educational institutions lack proper facilities and some are poorly staffed. In Telangana itself, 75 engineering colleges had to be closed down in 2016 as there were no students. In Plato's *Republic*, everything could be done except for converting a man into a woman. Today's education has been commercialised and we have unfortunately converted Saraswati into Laxmi. Issues concerning healthcare and education need to be seriously addressed as they constitute an important part of governance. If the education system is such that a large number of youths remain unemployable, then a ready-made platform is being provided to terrorist organisations to recruit them and swell their numbers.

The field of health care also presents a picture that is not rosy. It is the government's responsibility to provide affordable healthcare to the common man, but that is still a far cry. Failures to address challenges in education and health care drive people away from the mainstream and increase the possibility of their potential recruitment into organisations that are inimical to the state.

What is required in governance structures is accountability, periodic audit of performance and transparency. While the Right to Information (RTI) Act has injected some element of transparency into the system, it is being misused in its application and at times used as a tool of blackmail. While RTI is a useful tool, those seeking answers through RTI should also be held accountable for their actions. As Governor, I once made a trip to the Bastar Division in Chhattisgarh where I visited a temple in Jagdalpur. Promptly, there was an RTI query seeking information on whether 'the temple visit was part of the Governor's itinerary, whom did the Governor meet there and what did he discuss.' I replied that the visit was indeed part of my itinerary, I met Lord Balaji there and prayed to him to please give good sense to people like the applicant!

Such types of RTI queries are meaningless but are increasingly becoming common. Similarly, Public Interest Litigations (PIL) are also becoming tools to block development. Any person who feels aggrieved goes to the court and gets a stay order. Why are the courts giving such stay orders that block development schemes for years? Why cannot the court hear the case on a day-to-day to basis and decide on the matter one way or the other?

The time has come when governance issues need to be addressed with full seriousness and with priority. The issue of corruption in public life needs to be addressed as a core priority to restore faith in the system. Alongside, we need to inject some element of accountability and responsibility into all the institutions of governance and into civil society. This must encompass non-government organisations (NGOs), human rights organisations, the media and the public. In Chhattisgarh, there was a case where an individual was apprehended for his links with the Maoists, tried and convicted by a court. It was surprising that Nobel Laureates came from all over the world to plead for this man and seek his release. But no such voices were heard when Maoists gunned down 38 policemen while they were sleeping in a barrack. Human rights cannot be a one-way street applicable only to terrorists, their sympathisers and to anti-social elements. The security forces too have rights which are often glossed over by such organisations. They need protection for their actions as they are operating in a very difficult environment and if such protection is not afforded they will have little motivation to fight against elements inimical to the state.

Addressing issues of governance is an important tool in the fight against terror. This will reduce the catchment area for terrorists and inject a sense of responsibility, both in institutions of governance as well as in civil society. Good governance alongside an effective justice delivery system will go a long way in eliminating the scourge of terrorism in the country.

27

Building a Constituency of Peace

Mehbooba Mufti

Terrorism, as is well known, is the biggest threat that the whole world is facing at this point of time. Unfortunately, the countries that are fighting terrorism are not fighting together. There is shadow boxing between the various super powers to retain hegemony over world affairs and it began with the then Soviet Union's invasion of Afghanistan. That was the first time that Islam was used as a tool by the USA, along with Pakistan, to serve a political purpose. We are still facing the brunt of that action.

We see similar shadow boxing going on in Syria where the game has been taken to the next level. A shadow war is taking place between the USA and Russia with the actual fighting being done on sectarian lines between Shias and Sunnis. The same story is being repeated in Iraq and in Yemen.

India too has been a victim of terror for many years but here we see shadow boxing between India on one side and China and Pakistan on the other. India has consistently been trying to declare certain groups and people as terrorists, but China has been blocking all such attempts. These terror groups have since long inflicted a great deal of pain on India. It appears that here too, while there is unanimity on the need to fight terrorism, there still appear to be countries who believe in the existence of good and bad terrorists. Apparently, the terrorists who are being used by Pakistan as tools of their foreign policy are being classified as good by China and Pakistan. Fighting terrorism will hence be a long battle so long as states extend support to certain groups of terrorists based on their belief that such groups can further their political interests.

Both good governance and military action are useful instruments in the war against terror. However, governance is unfortunately the first casualty when terrorism rears its ugly head. The focus of the government shifts from governance to maintaining law and order, and protecting the life and property of people becomes its first and foremost duty. That has been my experience, both when my father was the Chief Minister of J&K from November 2000 until 2005, and subsequently too.

Addressing issues of terrorism must, of necessity, comprise a multi-pronged strategy. While addressing governance issues and dealing with terrorists is undoubtedly an important component of governance, there is also a need to revitalise the political process and build a constituency of peace. This is important because any issue, any grievance, any conflict, if left unaddressed, is like a wound. It first gets infected, then gangrene sets in necessitating life-saving surgery, which could involve amputation of a part of the body.

When Atal Bihari Vajpayee became the Prime Minister of India in 2002, he set about building a constituency for peace. He took effort in creating proper harmony between the NDA government in the Centre and the state government in J&K. Vajpayee understood the pain of the people of J&K and tried to address both the internal as well as the external dimensions of the conflict. Towards this end, he took many steps to build bridges with Pakistan. He took a bus ride to Lahore despite the fact that a night earlier, seven young boys were killed, just to sabotage the visit. That did not deter him. Vajpayee did not abandon his quest for peace, despite the Kargil war of 1999 or the attack on India's Parliament in 2002, which led to both countries mobilising their forces on the border. From Srinagar, the capital of the state, he not only sent a very great message to the peoples but delivered it in a language that the Kashmiri people understood. He spoke of Kashmiri saints and poets, quoting from the life of Hazrat Sheikh Noor-ud-din (Rahmatullah Allaih), a 14th-century Kashmiri saint, born in 1377, whom the Kashmiri people lovingly refer to as Nand Rishi. He also quoted from Lalleshwari, a Kashmiri mystic of the Kashmir Shaivism school of philosophy, locally known mostly as Lal Ded and also from Peerzada Ghulam Ahmed Mehjoor, who is credited with introducing modernism in Kashmiri poetry and bringing lyricism and folklore in it. This touched a chord with the 40,000-odd people who had come to hear him, most of whom were youth.

It was during this talk that Vajpayee said, "I'm ready to extend a hand of friendship with Pakistan". It was fortunately reciprocated from the other side and that led to a ceasefire that lasted for many years. We had a dialogue process established for the first time. Journalists from Pakistan visited Srinagar and other places and when they went back, they told Mr. Musharraf that Kashmir is not like what they thought, because unfortunately, the media creates its own picture which is often distorted. The process also led to Musharraf stating that the United Nations resolution is not important any more and that we need to fulfil the aspirations of the people of Kashmir, the rest of India and the people of Pakistan. When Vajpayee visited Lahore, Musharraf said that the soil of Pakistan would not be used against India and consequently infiltration levels came down. We had a window of peace. All these had an impact because Vajpayee was the first Prime Minister who not only said but also ensured a free and fair election. Though my party got only 16 seats in the 2002 elections, it was not the numbers, but the credibility of the process that was important and my father became the Chief Minister. We allied with the Congress to form a government and had a common minimum program with them. We thus came together and that common minimum program became the basis of the foundation to change the whole narrative in the J&K state, not just internally, but also in Pakistan.

We assured the people that if we come together we are going to revoke POTA (Prevention of Terrorism Act, 2002). POTA was a draconian law that led to great angst among the people and so we revoked it. We made it a point in our common minimum program that there has to be a dialogue with all the stakeholders, both internal and external. This was important, as Vajpayee had rightly observed that we can change our friends but not our neighbours. It was thus essential to have a working relationship with Pakistan, which hopefully would be cordial and which would benefit both the countries. It was at this time that my father, while speaking at Baramulla, asked for opening of routes to other parts of Pakistan-occupied-Kashmir (POK). "Why do we need the guns and grenades from the other side," he asked? "Why can't apples go from this side and money come from that side?" And that is when Vajpayee started doing the spadework for the Muzaffarabad Road, which later became a reality when there was a UPA government in power at the Centre.

Unfortunately, the process did not last for long. When we talk about good governance, it is an important thing. We got an opportunity because a feel-good factor was created with the revocation of POTA; then Mr. Vajpayee's visit and then a host of factors such as the financial package for the pony owners who had suffered a lot because of the militancy. We stopped crackdowns where people were asked to come out of their houses in temperatures of well below zero degrees and wait outside while their houses were searched. Such measures gave us a window of peace to show our good governance. At that time, my father also started an anti-encroachment drive against all illegal construction and the result was so positive that many people voluntarily came forward to demolish illegal structures they had built on public land. We were committed as seen by the fact that even though we had to fight elections in Pampore, the anti-encroachment drive was not stopped. A lot of shops had been demolished in Pampore when I went to campaign there. I spoke to my father and told him that we were unlikely to win this seat because "Pampore looks like Tora Bora." He said that he was not going to do anything about it and the demolition of illegal structures would continue. It was here that one of our opponents came and told a young girl, "Look what Mufti has done to your village. He has demolished all the houses and everything. Are you going to vote for his candidate?" The girl's reply was heart warming. "He is not going to take this road to his home," she said. "This is for us."

This simply underlines the point that while good governance and military action are very important, they by themselves cannot resolve conflict or end terrorism. For that, we also need to build a constituency of peace, which in turn would require addressing issues and grievances, confidence-building measures and the political process. It was at that point of time, during my father's tenure as Chief Minister, that the Kashmiri Pundits got more confidence in visiting Tul Mul in huge numbers. It was he who started building transit accommodation in Sheikhpura in Budgam district, Mattan in Anantnag district and Tul Mul in Ganderbal district. There were no protests against this move; it was a very normal part of the whole governance process. When elections were again held in 2008, they too were conducted freely and fairly, which was important from the point of view of credibility of the electoral process, as was the case in the 2002 elections which were conducted when Vajpayee was the prime minister.

In the 2014 elections, the BJP got 25 seats in Jammu and my party, the PDP, got 28 seats in the Valley. So we came together with the hope that the work started by our former Prime Minister, Shri Atal Bihari Vajpayee, would be taken forward. It is unfortunate that the political process, which was taken forward till about 2005, came to a standstill thereafter. Nothing happened on the roads that led to POK, except for barter trade and meetings between family members on either side. My father's vision was that it should go beyond the barter system into proper trade relations.

In an interesting anecdote, my father told me that when he went to receive the people from the other side of Kashmir in April 2005, the first thing they asked him was "Mufti Saab, *kya hum yahan namaz padh sakte hain*?" (Mufti Saab, can we read the namaz here?) He told them that they could offer *namaz* anywhere. Such misconceptions can be removed with greater interaction between people of both sides. We need to open new routes, new roads and take confidence-building measures to the next level so that anybody, anytime, can go and see what is happening in POK and they in turn can come and see what is happening here.

The misconceptions, unfortunately, are still there. I went for Umrah (a pilgrimage to Mecca, which can be undertaken at any time of the year) sometime back and we met many Pakistanis there. My sister, Ruby, who lives in Chennai was with me and she was asked, "Can you offer *namaz* in J&K?" "Off course, we can," she replied, "not just in J&K only, but throughout the country. I live in Chennai and when I get up in the morning, I hear *azaan* from all five sides."

So, this kind of misinformation still exists in Pakistan, which even the media does not try to dispel. We see too many debates in the media with generals on either side breathing fire at each other. The need of the hour, however, is to reach out to each other and build goodwill amongst the people of the two countries. That is why we formed a government with the support of the BJP and had an agenda of alliance that led to the making of a common minimum program.

It was my father's vision and faith in Indian democracy that in our earlier government too, we had a common minimum program with the Congress and now we have a common minimum program with the BJP. In the former case, we were able to implement a lot of measures and the results are there for all to see. Now, we have this agenda of alliance with the BJP and we should not shy away from talking about revocation of AFSPA. When the situation deteriorates, we are not shy of asking for more troops and asking the Army to be more proactive. Similarly, when the situation improves, we should not shy away from moving the security forces back to the barracks to bring in a semblance of normalcy in our daily lives. We would rather see our children chasing birds and bees and butterflies rather than carry stones in their hands to throw at security forces.

As part of the normalisation process, we could look into issues such as transfer of power projects to the state which are with NHPC, opening of new routes such as between Kargil and Skardu, and even participation in the China Pakistan Economic Corridor (CPEC). Building a peace constituency is important to create a conducive environment for progress. That is why, I appeal to the people of India to give me that window of peace that I can build on and consolidate the gains from earlier years. From 1989, we have been fighting militancy. We need to fight it together, not just by military means or police force or by talking about good governance. We need to build bridges between us and people of the state, we need to have a dialogue with everybody as was done by Vajpayee. I do hope Prime Minister Modi takes this up with all seriousness. Kashmir is a jewel in the crown of India so all of us together have to regain that jewel. I am hopeful that Prime Minister Modi, who has the moral authority and vision to think ahead, will take forward the process begun by former Prime Minister Vajpayee.

It is my view that we need to have a political process in place as well as confidence-building measures, so that we in Kashmir get a window of opportunity to give good governance, which would then reduce the space for terrorists to operate in. I need help from the country, I need help from the Central Government and I need help from the media. We are a great country and we need to give peace a chance.

28

Uphold the Constitution

N N Vohra

A lot has been said about the means to tackle terrorism through a combination of means such as good governance, use of force, building a peace constituency et al. We must, however, understand the terrorism that has been imported into our country by our adversaries in the form of a proxy war as in J&K. That species of terrorism is of another kind and ipso facto and ab initio, may not relate to governance. It, however, impacts governance as the very raison d'être of such terrorism is to cause paralysis of the government by shifting its entire attention, energy and time towards fighting terrorism. While not delving further into the categories of the various kinds of terrorism, we need to distinguish and separate foreign-sponsored terrorism from home-grown militancy and insurgencies that have now blossomed into terrorism. While governance is an important and vital component in conflict resolution, in the case of foreign-sponsored terrorism, the argument of governance becomes somewhat irrelevant. It remains important, but it is not the answer to the resolution of the imported species of terrorism.

With respect to governance, there are various institutions that come into play such as the judiciary, the executive, the media, civil society at large, RTIs and PILs, each of which have an impact on the problems that we face and what needs to be done to bring things under control. As far as governance is concerned, where have we gone wrong? I think we need to answer that question. While a host of activities are now taking place to improve governance, why were they not done for the last 60 to 70 years? Who is accountable? Who is to be held responsible for these failures?

India's Constitution is based on cooperative federalism. We have the three organs of the Constitution – the Legislature, the Executive and the Judiciary and, of course, the media which has become the fourth arm. We have the Union, we have the States and we have a division of responsibilities between state subjects, central subjects and subjects on the concurrent list. We also have a sharing of resources, a finance commission and various other institutions, where taxes and resources are reasonably well allocated and distributed.

If good governance is the tool to counter-terrorism, then the question that first arises and which needs answers is, where has the governance gone wrong? I would submit that governance becomes inefficient or mal-administration emerges when there is inefficiency, lack of accountability and dishonesty. When elected elements play politics all the time, it impacts directly and immediately on the appointed executive, that is the public services, bureaucracy, civil police and judiciary. And when you run a government through nepotism, through caucuses and through groups, accountability begins to erode and public institutions get diluted, losing effect and impact. Consequently, public delivery systems become inefficient and corrupt and the public at large, especially the poorer segments and those who live in remote and difficult areas, suffer the most. When there is neglect, discrimination, lack of equity and accountability and where there is open corruption from top to bottom, the poorer elements, the neglected elements, they get angry, frustrated and cynical and over a period of time they get alienated.

Today, we have alienation in various parts of the country that can be traced to various sets of circumstances, each different in its own way. The situation in the Northeast is not comparable to Bastar in Chhattisgarh, which in turn is not comparable to what happens in J&K. Hence, when we seek to tackle terrorism through governance, we are trying to restore governance to what it should be. And what it should be is simply governance by the Constitution and governance by the rule of law. Because, if governance is not delivered within the parameters of the law, then what we have said in the preamble to the Constitution, a promise… "to secure to all its citizens: JUSTICE, social, economic and political; LIBERTY of thought, expression, belief, faith and worship; EQUALITY of status and of opportunity; and to promote among them all FRATERNITY assuring the dignity of the individual and the unity and integrity of the Nation," will be hard if not impossible to achieve. Justice, Liberty, Equality and Fraternity are not mere words. They have to be delivered.

Towards efforts in good governance, the example of the Government of Chhattisgarh stands out. Years of neglect and discrimination are being addressed by action on the ground, such as building roads and bridges, providing schools and providing facilities for higher education, skill development and opportunity for employment. The Chief Minister of the State has been able to accomplish this by posting the best officers he has, both IAS and IPS, to the areas affected by violence. This also highlights the point that the instruments of governance – the officialdom, the public services and the like, all have a great role to play but they cannot play it on their own unless the elected representatives, the political masters, also become answerable and focus on their responsibilities to the electorate that brought them into power.

As part of governance, it is important to restore efficiency, accountability and transparency and, simultaneously, do away with corruption. Eliminating corruption is in itself a huge task. We have been talking of a Lok Pal for half a century now, but the political will to constitute this institution is still to come about.

With respect to the role of the uniformed forces, I dare say for the sake of clarity that if we are talking of terrorism that is not home grown, such as the proxy war we see in J&K, sure enough, then, without debate, it is the security forces of the country who are called upon to deal with the intrusions, infiltration, subversion and sabotage that takes place from morning to night. When it is a home-grown situation, then I daresay that there will be a nuanced difference in the role of the uniformed forces. The forces are certainly required in the initial stages when there is a total breakdown of law and order and the government declares the area as 'disturbed'. The Army then takes over, but after having restored order or is in the process of restoring order, then it is the bounden duty of the political executive and the appointed executive, the services, to play their role to bring things in order. It is here that responsibility and accountability must be clearly defined. Whether it is education, health, communications, sanitation or basic law and order on a day-to-day basis or providing the people at large with the basic minimum essential services that they require, remains a prime responsibility. Failure to do so will sooner, rather than later, sow the seeds of unhappiness, discontent and dissatisfaction, which will progressively graduate into alienation. And alienation lends itself very readily to picking up the gun to settle scores.

29

The Power of Democracy

Kiren Rijiju

The policy of the Government of India with respect to terrorism has always been consistent and very clear. India believes in conflict resolution through peaceful dialogue, as a result of which, the government has, over the years, entered into a dialogue with many groups. In India's Northeastern region, the government entered into a Suspension of Operations (SOO) with some of the groups. With others, it has entered into certain memorandum of settlements. And with yet others, the government has negotiated a ceasefire agreement and is in talks with them. Some of the militant groups were hardcore groups that believed in violence till some time ago, but good sense prevailed and they have also come to the negotiating table. This indeed is an encouraging sign.

In J&K too, some individuals have abjured the path of violence and now have faith in democracy and the power of the ballot. As is the wont in any democracy, some of these people have been successful and some are yet to achieve victory through the ballot. That is the power of democracy. Eventually, it is the people who will choose their representatives, and belief in the ballot is the only way that we need to choose. This is a symbol of the success of India's democracy.

The story of Mr. Hagrama Mohilary illustrates the success of the democratic path. He was, till a few years ago, the leader of a violent movement for the creation of a Bodoland state. Through the ballot, he is today, ruling the Bodoland Territorial Council and is a very successful politician in Assam. He has also successfully brought along his people with him. Mizoram is another great example of conflict resolution. The armed revolt by the Mizos in the early nineteen eighties was one of the toughest challenges that India had faced. And there was some very defining movement those days in how the security forces were used and how Indian agencies worked, which finally, led to the Mizo National Front aligning with the mainstream and taking part in the electoral process. Today, Mizoram has transformed into one of the most peaceful states having the highest literacy rate in the country, next only to Kerala. This simply goes to show how things can change. It was unimaginable to think that such a change could take place when insurgency was at its peak in the state.

Assam had a very violent decade in the late nineteen seventies and early eighties. Here too, conflict resolution mechanisms have been largely successful. In Central India, even those people who believe in extremism, especially those who are part of the Communist Marxist and Leninist groups, have entered into the electoral process. Of course, a few of them have not been successful, but that depends on their political agenda which has to be accepted by the people. Electoral success lies in the hands of the people and is not with the government, but to get into the mode of elections is by itself a great success story.

Questions have been raised as to why should the state talk to hard-core militants who have indulged in so many violent acts. That may be so with respect to those groups who wish to overthrow the state with the power of the gun. The state will not talk to such elements. In any case, a country the size of India cannot be broken up, no matter how powerful a militant organisation may be or how many resources it commands or how much support it can generate among the people. Secession from India or the break–up of any part of India is not possible, simply because the strength of India is democracy. In India, everybody has the absolute right for his or her hopes and aspirations. There is no blockade, there is no restriction, so each individual is entitled to his/her own free flow of ideas. In such a situation, to say that one feel's suffocation in the Indian state and wants to break away, simply will not succeed, be it in any part of this country.

As Minister of State for Home affairs, I have met many groups; some are representatives of active militant organisations, some are those who had surrendered, some who are in negotiation with the Government of India. I have clearly told them that the government is ready to talk with only one condition and that is to abjure violence. Talks could be at the official level or at the political level, and we will understand the issue. But if they do not talk, then they will be doing the greatest disservice to the people they claim to represent.

In India, we have the rule of law, and these rules have been made by the people. Rule by bullet can never be a permanent solution to a problem. It will never be legitimate and it will never be accepted. We have seen dictatorial regimes around the world crumble and fall. Permanence is established only through the democratic process and the rule of law. This is what we must aim for at all times.

30

Transformation in Nepalese Politics

Baburam Bhattarai

I would like to primarily focus on the transitional nature of Maoist politics in Nepal during the last two decades. As things themselves suggest, why did the Maoists fighting a protracted people's war come to a peaceful democratic process? How did it become possible? What has been the implication and, most importantly, what does the Nepalese experience offer to others involved in a similar democratisation process?

Firstly, I need to point out that the transitional nature of Nepalese politics is ongoing where some of the long-standing problems continue to unsettle national politics. Today, these challenges have manifested themselves in new ways posing serious questions regarding the tenability of implementing the new Constitution of 2015. After being at the forefront of the Maoist armed struggle and thereafter playing a leading role in the promulgation of a new Constitution, I have chosen a new political course to establish an alternative political force, the Naya Shakti Party, which would genuinely and rightfully address the new challenges of this new era. The task of democratising our society and polity is still in progress with the transition from the bullet to the ballot.

The expression, 'bullet to ballot,' in the plain and literal sense suggests the use of political tools as a means of conducting politics. The 'bullet' theoretically implies a violent method and the 'ballot' suggests the embracing of a non-violent mode of politics. Theoretically and philosophically, it is a tremendously challenging task to arrive at a conclusive understanding about violence and non-violence. Once we enter into this debate, it doesn't end merely with the desirability or undesirability of using violent or non-violent methods or in deciding whether in any given circumstance, violence can be treated as a legitimate act or an act of last resort. Most debates on this issue, very often, assume a moralistic or ethical overtone, leading many theorists to argue over calculation of human cost or the economic and ecological cost of wars. In this paper, I will desist from that debate, as these are extremely contested concepts and any attempt to make an absolute moral judgement can become a rather tricky task. Instead, I will dwell on the grey areas or the avenues where politics assumes a rather complex character. This is because everyday politics is very often about these shades of grey where not everything presents itself as black and white and it is this obscure area that opens up a new possibility for us to think and act differently about how we can restructure the democratic space to accommodate those that remain outside it. This leads me to discuss the specific context of Nepal and the Nepalese Maoists.

The shift in Maoist politics from an armed struggle towards the constitutional side became possible because of a couple of reasons. The first thing that needs to be highlighted is that the Maoist movement in Nepal was a political movement motivated by the idea of social justice and socio-economic programmes that attracted widespread support among the people. What also needs to be recognised is that this movement in many ways resonated with the aspirations of past struggles and revolts in Nepalese history against the autocratic rulers by making a call for democracy. Politically, the struggle between the monarchy and democracy has been the main contradiction in Nepal's modern history. All the major political parties in Nepal since their formative days have led popular struggles against autocratic regimes in one form or the other. With the end of the Rana oligarchy in 1950, space for parliamentary democracy was opened up for the first time in Nepal's history. Let me point out here one major difference between the Nepalese and Indian situations. While democratic institutions functioning in India remained uninterrupted post-independence, in Nepal, a major breach took place within a decade of interaction of parliamentary democracy and this happened precisely because of the existence of the institution of monarchy, more specifically when King Mahendra assumed an autocratic rule under the guise of a party-less panchayat system in 1960. This is the backdrop against which the Nepalese Congress and Communist parties conducted their politics in Nepal. During the mass uprising of 1990, it was primarily a struggle between the monarchy and democracy that shaped the demands of the people and the political parties.

However, this too ended in a constitutional compromise between the parliamentary party and the Shah monarchy. The fallacy of this institutional compromise with the king was exposed when it became possible for an autocratic monarchy to emerge from within the parliamentary system, i.e., when Gyanendra Shah took over complete executive power in 2005. The Maoists who initiated their armed struggle in 1996 identified this union between the monarchy and the traditional parliamentary parties as a major fault-line in Nepalese politics, which has contributed to the poor socio-economic conditions in Nepal. Politicians and scholars alike have not hesitated to acknowledge the competence with which the Nepali Maoists exposed this triangular contestation between the monarchy, the parliamentary parties and the revolutionaries in Nepal. After the royal coup of 2005, the Maoists were the first to call for an effective and coordinated programme among the democratic forces for resistance against the autocratic monarchy and it was this particular initiative that opened up the possibility for the Maoists and the parliamentary parties to arrive at a consensus regarding the abolition of the monarchy and forge a common commitment towards full democracy or 'Poorn Loktantra'.

Clausewitz famously said, both the 'bullet' and the 'ballot' are continuation of politics by other means. The call for making a new constitution through a constituent assembly elected by the people that had remained an unfulfilled aspiration during the earlier uprising was taken up by the Maoists in the new context. Therefore, one has the uniqueness of Maoist politics in Nepal. They had a pivotal role to play in the final battle of monarchy versus democracy through both the bullet and the ballot. In fact, unlike what one would normally expect, it was actually the Maoists who made a call for using the ballot to draft a new constitution. It was not just a circumstantial arrangement of events or a mere reaction to political incidents such as the royal take-over that enabled the Maoists to talk about making democratic innovations. Theoretically too, there had been a rich debate within the Maoist party about the need for the communists to take the democratic process seriously and in a substantive way. Therefore, apart from exposing the problems intrinsic to the system of monarchy and parliamentary democracy, the Maoists were engaged in a project of democratising themselves as well. This is a crucial point. Of course, not all Maoist leaders agreed on this point. There were serious differences among the top leaders regarding the democratising of the party as well as entering into a democratic alliance with a parliamentary party. In fact, I was the first of the few to push for democratic nuances within the party as well as relations with other parties.

Nevertheless, these views were subsequently adopted by the party itself leading to a seminal document titled 'Development of Democracy in the 21st Century'. Here, the Maoists indulged in self-introspection and asked themselves how they could avoid the mistakes of previous socialist communist regimes.

Towards this end, significant resolutions were made to redefine and democratise the relationship between the leaders and the led and between various organs of the party and also amongst the leaders themselves. But the most noteworthy statements were the party views on state power and political freedom. The Nepali Maoists decided that when in power they would allow rival political parties to mobilise and compete with the revolutionary party. Therefore, the Maoist party would also have to acquire a mandate from the people through elections, otherwise they themselves will degenerate into an authoritarian bureaucratic organisation. I consider it important to state these specificities because without an insight into the theoretical and political innovations within the Maoist party, an understanding of the transition in Maoist politics from the bullet to the ballot would be lopsided and misunderstood.

Another important factor for timely transition from the bullet to the ballot in Nepal was the highly sensitive geo-political positioning of the country, sandwiched between two huge states of India and China. A prolonged armed conflict could have had a spill-over effect in the neighbourhood leading to a serious conflagration in the region. In case of a complete win or complete loss of zero-sum conflicts, a new constitution can become a symbol of new political beginnings after the past regime has been brought to an end. Political theorists call this the replacement model. However, political conflicts may often end in a stalemate, without any side emerging as a clear winner or loser. In such cases, constitutional-making can become a part of peace pacts or ceasefire agreements. The constitution can then be an outcome of a negotiable pact or a compromise between the past rulers and the new political force. Nepal's peace process and constitution making stands somewhere in between these two approaches.

By ousting monarchy and establishing a republic, Nepal's new Constitution marks a departure from the past political regime in one way, but at the same time there was also an institutional compromise regarding the parliamentary democracy between the Maoist and the non-Maoist parties. In the process, the parliamentary parties discarded some of their old political beliefs and embraced more radical nuances of socio-economic transformation than traditionally adjustable in liberal democracy. For instance, commitment towards federalism, proportional representation, inclusive and participative democracy, land reforms, etc., were made. On the other hand, the Maoists also had to suspend some of their ideological positions and accept certain ideas conventionally associated with liberal democracy such as protection of private property, rule of law, separation of power, etc. These commitments of understanding or agreement between the Maoists and non-Maoists were instrumental in laying the foundation of a prolonged peace process and constitution-making in Nepal. In other words, these were the basic guidelines in transition from the bullet to the ballot in Nepal.

If we remind ourselves with specific original objectives, then it is not very difficult to understand the complication in Nepal's constitutional process or its democratic transition. This will enable us to understand the reasons behind the uprising in the Terai-Madhesi region and the dissatisfaction among the indigenous population even after the promulgation of the new Constitution. If the structural origin of conflict remains unaddressed and democratic space for articulation of genuine socio-economic and political demands are not made available to the people, then the sustainability of any society's transition towards a stable, peaceful and functional democracy can remain vulnerable. This is one of the most important lessons from Nepal's recent experience. However, we must also refrain from making generalisations because experiences regarding transition from the bullet to the ballot are time- and context-specific. The Nepali case, at best, can be considered a reference from our lessons.

To conclude, the task of democratic transition is a continuous process of progression. Even though the creation of new political institutions and constitutional remedies are crucial aspects, a nation must always make relentless efforts to continuously democratise its relationship with its people. The new mission that I have recently embarked upon is guided by this very understanding. The idea of Naya Shakti, not only as an alternative political party but also as a movement for deepening democracy, is a natural corollary to the transition from the bullet to the ballot. As Christopher Columbus once said, "You can never cross the ocean unless you have the courage to lose sight of the shore." I have mastered the courage to lose the sight of the shore of the bullet and attempted to cross the ocean of progressive transformation of the world through the ballot. Let us all join hands to create objective conditions for peace, prosperity, equality and justice so that nobody will ever have to resort to the bullet.

31

Consensus in Framing the Constitution

R Sampanthan

By looking at the issue of 'bullet to ballot,' even if we look at it superficially, I think choosing the former would not be a difficult choice. But our experience shows otherwise. The choice has been difficult, and one might rightly question, why.

I think it is because human society is so complex and so diverse as to necessitate that governance is structured so as to meet such complexity and diversity. It is the mode and manner of governance that decide the choice between the ballot and the bullet. Governance in a country is based upon the country's Constitution, which plays a vital role in the structure of governance.

Governance encompasses the exercise of the executive and judicial powers. Each one of these fields of authority has a crucial impact on the manner in which a country is governed and on the life of the people in relation to the government and in relation to each other. The Constitution largely depends on the leadership the country provides for framing the Constitution. Wise leadership ensures that the Constitution of a country is largely based upon reasonable consensus. Consensus accommodates diversity and avoids complexity. Societies in most countries are multi-lingual, multi-ethnic, multi-cultural and pluralistic in character.

Constitutional arrangements need to accommodate such diversity and complexity. If there is such accommodation, society is stable. Such stability promotes development and is able to achieve peace and prosperity whereas lack of such accommodation promotes discontent and conflict, instability, lack of development and absence of peace and prosperity.

The ballot provides a democratic way based upon dialogue, a free exchange of views and the making of choices based upon one's judgement. It is a rational process. If this process fails, then it is the bullet, which is not merely a response to discontent and conflict but also an apparent means to seek a remedy to perceived injustice. This has been the experience of several countries, both positive and negative, where the ballot has prevailed and been successful, and also where the bullet has been resorted to, with its painful consequences.

I would like to refer to my own country, Sri Lanka, though small but an important country in the Indian Ocean region, Sri Lanka is a multi-ethnic, multi-lingual and multi-cultural country comprising a majority of Sinhalese and who have their own distinct identity. The Tamils and the Muslims are numerically a minority but have their own distinct identities too. It is accepted in Sri Lanka and it is not a bone of contention. The Tamil-speaking people have historically inhabited the north-eastern part of the country and are in a majority in every district in that part of the country whereas the Sinhala people are in a majority in the rest of the country. This too is accepted and not a bone of contention.

The country got independence from colonial rule in 1948. Before colonial subjugation, there were both Sinhalese and Tamil kingdoms in the country, which were captured by different colonial powers separately and at different times. These different territories were unified together in 1833 under British colonial rule. However, all people – the Sinhalese, the Tamils and the Muslims – joined together in their demand to achieve independence. Sri Lanka's first Constitution was framed in 1948 by our colonial rulers. It provided for majoritarian rule, with certain safeguards which were soon disregarded. Thereafter, we have had two constitutions, one in 1972 and other in 1978, and the latter exists till today.

The 1972 Constitution was framed by one of the two major Sinhalese political parties without the consent of the other major Sinhalese political parties, or the consent of the Tamil political party mainly representing the Tamil people of the Northeast. The 1978 Constitution was framed by the other major Sinhalese political party without the participation of the major Sinhalese political party that framed the 1972 Constitution, nor the consent of the political party mainly representing the Tamil people of the Northeast.

The 1972 Constitution and the existing 1978 Constitution were not framed on the basis of consensus. They were unilateral actions of the political party in power at the relevant time, being empowered by majoritarian rule.

The political culture prevalent in Sri Lanka has unfortunately been that in order to achieve and attain political power, the tendency has been to confer on the majority community, a supremacist position in preference to truth, justice and equality. It must be realised that this approach has resulted in Sri Lanka not being able to maintain or retain its rightful place in the world. The demand for a change in the structure of government has prevailed from shortly after achieving independence. The demand was made by the Tamil people in the Northeast who alleged that they were treated as second-class citizens and injustice was meted out to them in matters relating to their civil, political, economic, social and cultural rights. They were subjected to physical violence whenever they made just political demands and this continued for several decades without any retaliation by the Tamils.

The political demand of the Tamil people for necessary changes in the structure of governance was democratically supported overwhelmingly, by the Tamil people of the Northeast at every general election to parliament from 1956, up to date, and in every other election, whether provincial or local, but the democratic verdict of the Tamil people was not given recognition.

The Tamil people are thus being governed without their consent and against their will in violation of the Universal Declaration of Human Rights adopted by the United Nations. After that, there was an armed revolt by Tamil youth for almost three decades. Such armed revolt commenced more than three decades after the country had attained independence and after all the democratic and political processes had failed. It was a classic instance in which the bullet filled the void created by the failure in the process of the ballot. This highlights the importance of respecting and recognising the verdict of the ballot. Such respect and recognition of the verdict of the ballot is the surest way to dispense with the need for the bullet. The result of all of this has been that up to fifty percent of the Tamil population has left the country and settled in several parts of the world. The Sri Lankan Tamil Diaspora is spread throughout the world, more than 150,000 Tamil people have died or killed during the armed conflict. The old – Sinhalese, Tamils, Muslims – all suffered immensely. Further violence will result in more Tamils fleeing the country. The conflict has received international attention and four resolutions have been adopted by the United Nations Human Rights Council in 2012, 2013,

2014 and 2015. The resolutions deal with violations of international rights laws and international humanitarian laws by parties to the conflict, the Sri Lankan State and the armed rebel outfit.

Intimation of the resolution adopted in October 2015 is being currently reviewed by the International Human Rights Council in Geneva. It deals with transitional justice processes, issues pertaining to land, missing persons, the detainees and the evolution of constitutional arrangements that will bring about a just and acceptable political resolution to this conflict.

In recent times, far-reaching political changes in the democratic process have taken place in Sri Lanka. In 2015, at an election prematurely called after the Constitution of Sri Lanka was amended to enable the then holder of the office of the President to contest even beyond the stipulated two terms, an authoritarian and insensitive regime which failed to be inclusive of all the people who lived in the country was replaced by a new President and a new Prime Minister through the process of the ballot, emphasising once again the utmost importance of the democratic process and the ballot. The new government has committed itself to the making of a new constitution for the country based upon consensus and has commenced the process. The fact that the two main political parties are in alliance with the government offers the country a historic opportunity that was not available for the making of the 1972 and 1978 constitutions.

The main Tamil political alliance in the parliament with the representative of the Tamil people of the north-east is working with the new government to formulate just and acceptable constitutional proposals.

The Tamil people are committed to evolving a just, reasonable, workable and durable political solution within the framework of a single undivided, indivisible Sri Lanka. The parties largely representing the Muslim people are also a part of the process. For the first time in post-independence Sri Lanka, an opportunity is available for the framing of a constitution, based upon a substantial and reasonable consensus amongst all political parties and all the people of the country. This opportunity must be pursued with genuine commitment. That will be the only way to ensure that the bullet no longer has a place in our society.

I quote from a speech delivered by the Indian Prime Minister Shri Narendra Modi to the Sri Lankan parliament on 13 March 2015. He said,

"All of us in this region, indeed every nation of diversity, have dealt with the

issues of identities and inclusion, of rights and claims, of dignity and opportunity for different sections of our societies. We have all seen its diverse expressions. We have faced tragic violence. We have encountered brutal terrorism. We have also seen successful examples of peaceful settlements. Each of us has sought to address these complex issues in our own ways. However we choose to reconcile them, to me something is obvious: Diversity can be a source of strength for nations. When we accommodate the aspirations of all sections of our society, the nation gets the strength of every individual. And, when we empower states, districts and villages, we make our country stronger and stronger. You can call this my bias. I have been a Chief Minister for 13 years; a Prime Minister for less than a year! Today, my top priority is to make the states in India stronger. I am a firm believer in cooperative federalism. So, we are devolving more power and more resources to the states. And, we are making them formal partners in national decision making processes."

In India, all states are powerful, all states have equal power, all people have equal power and so there is no question of India ever being divided. So, when the Prime Minister of India went to attend the Sri Lankan parliament, he urged them to come up with constitutional proposals that would be fair, just and reasonable and that would give Sri Lanka an opportunity. He went on to state:

"Sri Lanka has lived through decades of tragic violence and conflict. You have successfully defeated terrorism and brought the conflict to an end. You now stand at a moment of historic opportunity to win the hearts and heal the wounds across all sections of society. Recent elections in Sri Lanka have reflected the collective voice of the nation – the hope for change, reconciliation and unity. The steps that you have taken in recent times are bold and admirable. They represent a new beginning. I am confident of a future of Sri Lanka, defined by unity and integrity; peace and harmony; and, opportunity and dignity for everyone. I believe in Sri Lanka`s ability to achieve it. It is rooted in our common civilisational heritage. The path ahead is a choice that Sri Lanka has to make. And, it is a collective responsibility of all sections of the society; and, of all political streams in the country. But, I can assure you of this: For India, the unity and integrity of Sri Lanka are paramount. It is rooted in our interest. It stems from our own fundamental beliefs in this principle."

So, while committing himself to Sri Lanka's unity and territorial integrity, the Indian Prime Minister, in the course of his speech, went on to emphasise the importance of all being able to live as equals with dignity and self respect. This is an opportunity to conclusively reject the bullet in my country, Sri Lanka, in favour of the ballot, and we must all join together to ensure that we are able to achieve this.

32

A Personal Account

Sajad Lone

I would like to share certain personal experiences and relate some incidents that became the tipping points of my life. The story which I will now narrate had for me a far greater message than what the reader may feel. It is about the role of three individuals, two of whom became the tipping points in my life, making me realise that this is my country and I have to live here, while the third one delayed it.

When a person like me decides in a multi-party set-up of the separatist spectrum who believe in the bullet and wants to move on to the ballot, there are a lot of problems and impediments. The first is ideological. You have to convince yourself that this is the right path. There is also a perception problem. We speak so much in the media that we become prisoners of our own rhetoric. Trying to break out of that rhetoric is a big problem as you are identified with a certain cause and you are now seen as negating it.

I was doing some research work some years ago and in one of the studies I read the statements of an ex-guerrilla leader who said that he never imagined the impact of their propaganda until he left the guerrilla movement and found what he had to face after he left it. In order to overcome those impediments, a lot of facilitation is needed from governments. I would not say that such facilitation is not forthcoming, but I would say that there is a lot of scope for improvement.

The story I want to tell is a true episode of my life around 1989. I was about 23 years old at that time and I was a typical Kashmiri with very limited exposure. I had just returned from Britain where I had gone to study. Typically, I would not applaud for the Indian team. I had my questions about identity. I was not into politics but my father was a politician; I was not really sure what I had to do. Was I in favour of the bullet at that time? I think not, because I had just come back and there was something at the back of the mind that said, "No! Development is the way out." At the same time there was a very strong sub-identity which actually prevailed over all other identities and it was sort of 'them versus us.'

On a day in 1990, I was at a certain place with another person. It had been two months since my return to India and I had an anglicised accent. That was the time when we were subjected to a raid by the BSF. The next thing I knew was that we were being hauled into a truck. This is where I want to tell you a story of three Indians. A jawan in the BSF, a DIG of the BSF and a very senior officer of the BSF. The tipping point in my transition towards Indianness began in my 45 days of captivity. I am not complaining, but once you are arrested in suspicious circumstances on charges of terrorism, you are not expected to get a five-star treatment and things are very bad over there.

When somebody asked for me and called me by name, I thought they have come to release me because I was in a very bad shape at that time but, unfortunately, that person had come for some other reason. However, on the third day, I met this jawan, my hero of India, my ambassador of India. I don't even know his name but I salute him even today. He was from Haryana and he came into my room on the third day.

"*Arre tu ugravadi na lage, acche ghar ka lagta hai*" (You don't appear to be a terrorist; it looks like you belong to a decent family), he said in a typically Haryanvi accent, and thus started our friendship. He would come and talk to me and ask "*Ki baat hai*" (What happened?) I replied, "*Mein padta tha, vaapas aa gaya, phas gaya.*" (I went abroad to study, came back but got stuck here).

Things were tough. When they took us out, they would blindfold us, but this jawan would come in the evening to talk to me. I still remember his words in chaste Haryanvi, "This is your country. We may pull your ears, but we will not take them out. If your younger brother misbehaves, will you not correct him?"

For me, those days were in that context where everybody around you thought of you as being useless, an enemy deserving to be killed. In that environment, there was this BSF jawan who would sit with me and preach Indianness to me. He has been and will always be my hero.

An important incident occurred on the tenth day of my captivity. We were three in the cell – my brother, another person and I – and the time was 2:00 a.m. The cell door was like a cage with bars and it had a curtain as a cover. I saw a hand wriggling inside which woke me up.

"Who is that," I queried?

It was my friend, the jawan. "It's me," he said. "I have cooked chicken and I thought I would share it with you as you would not have eaten chicken since long."

He handed over three pieces of chicken inside the cell. They were small pieces, and from his pocket he took out four chapattis and passed them over too. "Let nobody see this," he said, implying that he was doing it without the knowledge of his superiors.

My brother and I took a piece each, but the third person objected. "Do not eat it," he said. "It is not *halal*."

"It has been offered with so much love; we will eat it," my brother and I retorted. And eat it, we did. After some time, the third friend could not restrain himself. "Give me a chapatti too," he said, "I will have it with some curry." We were left wondering how the curry had suddenly become *halal*!

Though my friend, the jawan, was a hard taskmaster, we developed a rapport. Everybody was scared of him and if somebody wouldn't break, he would break them. And here he was, showing us so much compassion. When I finally left, he hugged me tightly and said, "You are my friend, and you have far to travel. Stay out of trouble; jail is not the place for you." He had tears in his eyes when we parted.

I gave him my Delhi number, since in those days, we didn't have mobiles. Apparently, he had called me once because I was told that somebody from Haryana had called and I had no friends apart from him but thereafter I lost contact with him for ever. I don't even know his name. But my tipping point from bullet to ballot, from one end of the spectrum to the other, has been that man and it will always be him.

The other person was the DIG Saheb. Now these three people I met, I met concurrently. On the second day, I was blindfolded and taken to DIG Saheb. I remember him sitting there with a map of India on the wall behind him. On the side was a sofa on which two men were seated. There was a table in front of them. I sat on the floor and my blindfold was taken off.

"How do you like it here?" That was the DIG speaking.

I couldn't talk, so my head just drooped.

"Are you ashamed of being here?" he asked.

"Yes sir," I replied.

I looked at the two people sitting on the sofa. I did not know them but they were probably from a department in the Home Ministry.

"How have we been treating you?" was his next question.

I kept quiet. Then he asked me what I was doing there and, while I was replying in English, the men sitting on the sofa interrupted and told me to speak in Hindi. "Are you ashamed of your language," was their caustic comment, but after some time they allowed me to speak in English, a language in which I could connect better with them.

After about an hour's conversation, I looked into the eyes of the DIG and said, "Sir, look into my eyes as you would into that of your younger brother. If you think I am a terrorist, shoot me, but if I am not, then don't treat me like one."

The officer looked at me and I could see that my emotional outburst had won him over. He believed in me. We talked for two to three hours. Then the DIG said, "Sajad, have we not treated you well?"

I kept looking down, so he asked me to speak without fear.

"Sir," I said, "I am sitting on the floor and you are seated on a chair. Why do you want me to answer this question?"

"Get him tea," was his response. So I had a cup of tea. When I was leaving, he said, "I give you my word. We will treat you well, but ask yourself, had you been across the border, how would they have treated you?" He then asked me if anyone had beaten or abused me.

"Yes sir," I said.

He then called everybody and, in his language, told them if anybody touches me, he was going to have it. After that day, nobody dared come near me. That was another Indian hero for me, who said, "You are educated, so I will respect you. I don't know whether you are a terrorist or not, but you are a future Indian and I will invest in you through respect." That is why he is my second hero.

Such was his love that on the 45th day, when the interrogation ended, we were shifted to what was called 'papa 2', which is the current Chief Minister's residence. We were in a storeroom and were happy that the interrogation was over. In the morning, somebody called me saying, "Sajad, some people from the department have come and they are looking for you."

I was afraid that the interrogation would start again. I was blindfolded and taken to another room, but everyone there was very respectful. There are no problems, they said, but added that while they wanted to release me, my statements were not tallying with the 12-odd men they had arrested. This went on for a while and then they said that my release was now problematic.

The Assistant Commandant of the BSF who was there with these men intervened. He told them that as per the orders of the DIG, my interrogation was over and he will not allow any further questioning. Those men then said that they were also from the government, but the Assistant Commandant would not budge. There was a scuffle between the men from the Home Department and the Assistant Commandant over a suspected terrorist and then the latter held me by my arm and took me away, speaking as one would, to his younger brother, "Come on Sajad, let's go. We will not talk to them."

This was the level to which the DIG Saheb went, to keep his promise of not allowing anybody to disrespect me or lift even a finger against me.

I was put through the entire interrogation process. Militancy was still in its infancy and the security agencies were starved of information. Every suspect was thus, a potential mine of information, but even so, the DIG did not allow anyone to use third-degree methods on me nor to abuse me, coerce me or raise their voice against me.

As all stories have to end, mine ends here. But like in the movies, for every hero there has to be a villain, and, in my case, it was a senior police officer. He could not however, undo the tipping point I had reached, but he too was a reality of India.

When one is imprisoned, every person, even a lowly sweeper who comes, is for the jailed person, a superior being and we would seek information from him. I too, would ask anybody who came, "What will happen to me, is there any news about me?" At that time, you believe it's the end of your life. While the jawan and the DIG were pillars of support, the senior police officer was not a good man. At the drop of a hat, he would say, "You are a terrorist and we should have shot you."

Finally, how do I answer the question, why the bullet or why the ballot? I have moved from former to the latter under the most trying circumstances. In cases such as mine, when you are identified with something, you become a villain. The response to a bullet is a sum of many parts; you cannot make it one part. It cannot just be an operational measure, which though important, does not constitute the whole. We require facilitators too, such as the empathy shown to me by the jawan and the DIG. While the state is rightly focusing on operational measures, the other aspect is totally missing, or at least there is a lot of space for improvement.

Love and compassion can achieve a great deal. It is true that every militant and every terrorist will not understand the language of love, but every militant or every terrorist will also not understand the language of operational measures. There are takers for the offensive and there are takers for the language of love. We will have to reach out.

For people who have chosen the path of violence and who now wish to take to the path of the ballot, there is a problem. You are a symbol, you are a hero for one section of the people, and when you try to traverse the distance from the bullet to the ballot, your supporters feel betrayed and consider you a traitor. If somehow, the group which questions the system or is out to overwhelm achieves its aims or objectives, partly or wholly, then they are the heroes. They could survive politically and take part in the political process, winning and losing being part of the game, as that is dependent on the will of the people. I consider myself lucky that I fought the elections, lost once as a parliamentary candidate and then fought again successfully and in fact became a minister. The relationship between the bullet and the ballot will however always be an enigma. My vote however, is for an offensive of love that will prevail and that is far more effective than all the other offensives.

33

My Experience

Hagrama Mohilary

A discussion on the bullet to the ballot is very relevant to my life. I would like to share with you my compulsions, which took me on the path of the bullet. Dissonance of political rights for the Bodos from time immemorial was the motivating factor that compelled me to pick up the bullet, assert our identity and develop ourselves as a distinct community with its own language, culture and tradition in a land of our own. The history of the Bodos is as old as the Mahabharata. We are the descendants of Valandhara, the daughter of the king of Kashi, who was the second wife of Bhim. Of that marriage, a son was born who was named Sarvada.

The holy temple of Kamakhya in Guwahati was built by a Bodo king who is mentioned as Narkas Asur in the Puranas. Among the great Bodo kings, the reign of Kumar Bhaskar Varman is well recorded in history. After independence, the Bodo people expected to have constitutional safeguards in the form of a separate political identity for the survival and sustenance of our distinctive identity.

You are well aware that Assam has for long, remained one of the most volatile and sensitive regions of the country because of the problem of insurgency, ethnic conflict, pressure of migration, under-development, poor infrastructure and connectivity, etc. The Bodos are the largest plains tribes of Assam and they felt neglected, exploited and discriminated against for over four decades. The growth of literacy and education among the plains tribes of Bodo-inhabited districts was amongst the lowest.

We started a movement for self-determination in 1987 in a democratic manner. In order to crush the movement, the government and its agencies unleashed terror on the Bodo people through killing in encounters, gang rapes and destruction of property. Fearing this action from government agencies, the movement took a violent turn. However, violence was undertaken from within the Bodo villages and not from Bangladesh and Myanmar.

In 1993, an accord was signed to end the violent Bodo movement. The Accord provided for the setting up of an elected autonomous council under the state, but it left the question of its territorial jurisdiction open. In 1994, we launched an agitation for non-implementation of the Accord and in 1996, we formed an organisation for the creation of a separate state of Bodoland. Our struggle was against the unjust government and its policies towards Bodo-dominated areas.

While the struggle was going on, the Kargil War erupted in 1999. Responding to the call of the nation, our organisation directed its cadres not to fire on the Army and the security forces. Our organisation also offered, to send its cadres to fight in the battle areas to protect the integrity and sovereignty of the nation. This gesture on the part of the organisation was appreciated by the Central Government, which directed the security forces not to target the Bodos.

In July 1999, The Bodo Liberation Tiger Force (BLTF) declared a unilateral ceasefire in response to the Central Government's appeal for talks. During the protracted negotiations that lasted nearly three years we fearlessly and logically put forward our concerns but at the same time appreciated the limitations of the government. We never asked for a sovereign state but settled for a suitable status of a separate state with special provisions.

In February 2003, the Central Government, the Government of Assam and the Bodo Liberation Tigers (BLT) came to an agreement for the creation of an Autonomous Council under modified provisions of the Sixth Schedule of the Constitution. As a part of the Accord, the Bodo language was included in the Eighth Schedule of the Indian Constitution.

Under this Accord, the Bodoland Territorial Council would have legislative, executive, administrative and financial powers with respect to the subjects as per 2E. This includes ten measures in socio-political areas. The Council would have 40 elected and six nominated members. The Accord also provided for adequate devolution of funds and special Central assistance to create socio-economic infrastructure and development. The jurisdiction of the Council was also determined so as not to repeat the mistake of 1993. The Accord raised the hopes and aspirations of the people. We have been trying to fulfil this since then and have taken many steps with the power given to the Council and the resources made available.

Three times elections have been held for the Provincial Council after the Accord was signed in 2003. In all of them, people from all communities have taken an active interest, and the elections have been, by and large, peaceful.

During the journey of the last 14 years, the Council has taken a number of steps for the benefit of the people living within the jurisdiction of the Council. It believes in the philosophy, '*Sab ka Saath, Sab ka Vikaas*'. The initiatives inter alia include the following:

- Improving connectivity throughout the length and breadth of the Council area;
- Creating institutions and strengthening the infrastructure to raise educational standards, set up a Bodoland University, Central Institute of Technology, skill development, etc;
- Construction of river embankments and bunds to control floods.
- Creation of employment opportunities;
- Putting in place basic facilities in villages through special Central assistance; and
- Upgrading the facilities and availability of doctors and nurses in government hospitals.

We would have achieved much more if some of the provisions of the Accord had not remained unimplemented. Whenever any major initiative projects are taken up in the Bodoland Council area, we consult all the stakeholders and do not impose any decision. The progress and journey from 2003 onwards has benefitted the entire population in the area. There has been overall progress in all spheres with the active involvement and support of all communities. We may not have fulfilled all the hopes and aspirations of the people, but we have come a long way.

The Bodoland people from the regional political party that runs the Council is in alliance with the NDA and it is hoped that the Council area would witness infrastructure and connectivity development at a much faster pace in the coming years. The experience with the ballot has enabled us to preserve our identity, our language and culture and has kept our way of life intact. Our experience of democracy and the federal structure of the Constitution show that conflict can be resolved through dialogue and the ballot and that the bullet is not always the answer.

I am reminded of a quote from a speech delivered on 3 April 1964, at Cory Methodist Church in Cleveland, Ohio, titled 'The Ballot or the Bullet', by human rights activist Malcolm X. In it he advised African Americans to judiciously exercise their right to vote, but he cautioned that if the government continued to prevent African Americans from attaining full equality, it might be necessary for them to take up arms. That is something we all need to remember.

34

Seven Pillars of Wisdom

Muriel Domenach

France has a large number of people who have been radicalised. We are thus very much on the front line of radicalisation and have experiences that are similar to other countries like India, Turkey and others. We have had painful experiences of repeated attacks on our territory and since January 2015, two-hundred-thirty-nine people have been killed in terrorist attacks. Our society remains threatened by such attacks, which is why it is important for us to be prepared to counter the same. Accordingly, we are taking steps to deter and prevent future attacks through administrative measures and through our intelligence system. In this paper, I will address France's response to radicalisation; not the repression part of it. In my current assignment, I am not responsible for repression, but I am responsible for everything that's not repression, including prevention, detection and disengagement.

France is on the frontline in terms of propaganda by Daesh. We believe we have 16,000 people who have been radicalised. This is a very large number, perhaps more than any other West European country, though we don't have the highest number of jihadists per capita. As of now, there are about 700 French people who are currently in the conflict zone, potentially to fight alongside hard-line Islamist groups. In addition, about 200 have been killed and an equal number have returned to France. Our intelligence services also assess that about 290 women have accompanied the fighters. It is also assessed that there are about 400 minors in the theatre, half of whom are under five years of age.

Why is France on the frontline of radicalisation? The reason is partly because of failures, lack of equal opportunities and economic and social crises, but paradoxically also because of our achievements. For instance, France is a country where third-generation migrants have become ministers in the government. This speaks highly of the French system where people of different origins are not discriminated against and it is possible to achieve the highest level of an individual's profession. This is one of those achievements that are being targeted by Daesh. Basically, they are saying the same thing as the Far Right to the children of immigrant parents, "You don't belong here".

It's also because of France's motto that France finds itself targeted by Daesh. We believe in freedom, equality, fraternity, freedom of expression, the right to caricature and even the right for blasphemy. We're very strict on equality between men and women and we are very tough on discrimination. To mark the International Day for the Elimination of Racial Discrimination, the French Government, on 21 March 2016, launched a video campaign to underscore the dangers of prejudices and racism under the banner #TousUnisContreLaHaine (Everyone United Against Hate). This has resulted in a 50 percent decrease in discrimination over the last year. Both fraternity and secularism are integral parts of the French ethos. Here, secularism does not refer to excluding religion in private life, but in prioritising civil law over religious belief and in the prevalence of civil law as an essential condition of the French way of life, to promote unity and fellowship.

How has France tackled radicalisation as a public response in the country? First, as a Jacobin state, with a very strong sense of what the state should be doing, it was for the state to take the initiative in addressing radicalisation. But it was realised that success would not be forthcoming unless the right partnership was struck with civil society, from local government to opinion leaders, artists, community leaders and everything. I would say the public response to radicalisation, or at least the prevention part of it, has seven pillars, like the seven pillars of wisdom.

First, we need to define radicalisation. We need to point out what radicalisation is and what it is not. Radicalisation is violent extremism – anything that connects extreme ideology with a possible turn to violence. If it's not possible to turn to violence, then we're not in a radicalisation process. Also, it's very important to insist that radicalisation is not Islamic by essence. The Quebec attack demonstrated that it can be Far Right ideology, or it can be other ideologies. Sadly, in France, it is Islamic radicalisation that killed 239 people but it's not Muslim by essence, of course.

Detection is the second pillar. It is very important to report both through a national mechanism and also through a local one. Our mechanism is two-fold. We have a hotline that was opened in April 2014 as a response mechanism to stop French citizens from travelling to Syria to join Islamist groups engaged in the country's civil war. People were encouraged to call the number if they suspected a friend or family member was considering travelling to that country or was in danger of becoming radicalised. It has proven to be very successful, with over 45,000 calls being received over the hotline. Of these, less than 15 percent proved to be effective, but that is still a good ratio. And of course, it takes state of law guarantees, like we don't keep data for more than five years, and we would ensure judicial control. The mechanism is also twofold. One part is through the national hotline and the other through local security services that take information from all sorts of local actors like schools, social workers, et al. It is very important to mobilise social workers and all sorts of local actors in the process to enhance effectiveness. Of the 16,000 people whom we believe have been radicalised, information and reports of 12,000 of them came from the national hotline and the remaining 4,000 came from the local security services.

The third pillar is training. We need social workers and public agents to mobilise. We've been conducting the training of 20,000 people and we count very much on them to further train other colleagues. It is important to have social workers develop a sense of ownership in the training process and we are now insisting on the training of social workers to further develop mobilisation.

Counter-narrative is the fourth pillar to prevent radicalisation of minds. This includes counter-narrative from the state as well as counter-narrative from civil society. Counter-narrative from the state, of course, is the key. We developed a government brand called Stop-Djihadisme (Stop Jihadist). Stop Jihadist recently developed a very dynamic campaign in which the experiences of other countries, including the U.K., were collated in terms of the techniques. Eventually, a campaign called #toujourslechoix (alwaysthechoice) was developed. It is like a serious game exemplifying the dangers of radicalisation with men and women. At every step they have a choice, and sadly they end up making dangerous ones. But counter-narrative from the state is limited in a sense, we believe. So, it is for civil society to further elaborate and develop through private initiatives, from artists, humorists, et al. I have a very strong belief that humour is a weapon of mass prevention. Like a Belgian playwright called Ismaël Saïdi is now showing a play called Jihad. It is the story of three young Belgian kids who go to Syria through Turkey and are experiencing all sorts of tragic but also comic events. Of course, counter-narrative takes the mobilisation of all parts of society including those who profess the Muslim faith. I, with my team, meet with Muslim representatives including representatives of those Muslim groups that claim to conduct concrete initiatives in terms of the prevention of radicalisation, be it in the counter-narrative or in training or in the actual monitoring of radicalised youth.

The fifth pillar is the actual monitoring of the radicalised youth. Once a person is assessed as having been radicalised, then this person is referred to a joint family support prevention cell. We have family support and prevention cells in each and every département (department). France is divided into more or less 100 départements. (In the administrative divisions of France the département is one of the three levels of government below the national level, between the administrative regions and the commune. There are 96 département in metropolitan France and five overseas département that are also classified as regions). Each département has a family support and prevention cell that gathers state representatives' security services, social services and social workers. Each person who is monitored has a reference, and our first assessment is that the more the monitoring is disciplinary, social, educational and psychological, the better it is. Currently, about 2400 people are being monitored throughout the French territory along with 1000 families. In many cases, the entire family has to be monitored before social workers can actually monitor the young.

The sixth pillar is disengagement, which is a very difficult process. France is facing a very difficult situation in its jails. We are trying to develop a third way as a complement to jails and what we call the open background, a third way exemplified by a first reintegration centre that was created in Central France this fall. It's very difficult to address the right audience for this third way between an open background and jail, but we are working on it. We will be assessing what has been done so far and, of course, also consider what has to be done with a possible return of those who had gone to fight alongside the Islamists in the war zone, including mothers and children. Again, we believe that many of the French returnees might be minors. So, of course, disengagement will be a difficult process.

The seventh pillar is international cooperation. We have to be creating a coalition of the willing and the ability to defeat Daesh militarily, not only within the EU, but also outside it. To this end, I very much count on exchanges with my Indian colleagues. We have to insist on the internet actors that they should do more in terms of, one, taking down negative contents on their networks and two, promoting positive contents not only through the training of those who are initiating positive contents, but also through the promotion of those positive contents.

These however, the seven pillars of wisdom for dealing with preventive aspects in combating radicalisation. Obviously there is no magic wand but we are developing and promoting good practices. French society is fully mobilised; the French authorities are fully mobilised. The fight against radicalisation will remain a priority with its repression part and its prevention part.

35

The Art of Counter-Terrorism

Boaz Ganor

In this paper, I would like to, first of all, discuss the pillars of counter-terrorism. Before we discuss how we can cooperate in this troubled field, we need to understand what are really the pillars of counter-terrorism. Here I use the term, 'The Art of Counter Terrorism,' for to be a good and effective counter-terrorism expert, is to be an artist.

The first pillar of this art is to identify who is the enemy? Who is the opponent? I would like to suggest the classification of three types of perpetrators of terrorism. The first type is commonly known by the name 'lone wolf.' Perhaps a better word for 'lone wolf' would be 'lone dog,' as so succinctly stated by Avi Dichter.

The lone wolves are people who are being inspired by terrorist organisations. They are being exposed to incitement; they are being radicalised and one day they decide to commit a terrorist act. This is their own decision and they don't have any operational ties with a terrorist organisation at that time. That is the lone wolf.

The second type of perpetrators include those local independent networks that combine a few lone wolves or lone dogs for that purpose. This refers to a bunch of friends or family members as was the case in the 2 December 2015, San Bernardino attack, carried out by a married couple, Syed Rizwan Farook and his wife Tashfeen Malik, in which 14 people were killed. Another example is the 8 June 2016, shooting in the Sarona market in Tel Aviv which was carried out by two Palestinian gunmen who were cousins. These attacks were inspired by a terrorist organisation but did not have any operational ties with a terrorist organisation; this is a different ball game.

The third type of terrorist attacks pertains to organised terrorism. And this is the type that we all have unfortunately experienced in the last few decades. This type of terrorist attack is initiated, planned, prepared and executed by activists of a terrorist organisation. Just to name a few attacks, the Mumbai attack, the attacks in Istanbul, in the Bataclan theatre in Paris, in Zaventem, Belgium and so on and so forth.

When we are talking about the lone wolf attack, most of such attacks do not have many casualties. Here, I do not underestimate any victim of terrorism for that purpose, but a lone wolf attack, by its very nature, will have far fewer casualties than an organised attack by a group. In a lone wolf attack, a few people might be killed or be injured by stabbing, or by running a vehicle over them, and so on. There are a few exceptions, of course, such as the Nice attack, which resulted in dozens of people killed in one lone wolf attack. But generally, in a lone wolf attack, we can expect the number of casualties to be limited.

Organised terrorism is, however, a different ball game. Here, the casualties are large, as we unfortunately witnessed in Mumbai and other places. However, organised terrorism can be sorted out if you have good intelligence, if you have good operational tools and there is good communication between the intelligence agencies and operational units. But, when we talk about lone wolf attacks, it's very difficult to prevent such attacks, mainly because we used to believe that intelligence is helpless and powerless in dealing with these kinds of attacks. I will explain why I use the term in the past tense. The reason is because traditional intelligence, both human sources intelligence (HUMINT) and communication intelligence (COMINT), is based on one common denominator; it is based on the fact that you have at least two people who communicate with each other and share their secret, and this communication can be intercepted. But in a lone wolf attack, everything starts and ends with the sick mind of one person. So, traditional intelligence is useless. But there is a solution for that, which I will elaborate on a bit later.

The other challenge that we all are faced with is what we refer to as the 'hybrid terrorist organisation'. Earlier, we knew about the classical terrorist organisations like the Red Brigades, Baader-Meinhof and the like that used to be some kind of a terrorist underground that conducted attacks. The hybrid terrorist organisation is an organisation that controls both territory and population and is embedded within civilian society. It is engaged also, in addition to terrorist attacks, in pseudo-legitimate activities. Such a terrorist needs to supply water and food, and provide education, law enforcement and other services to the public that he controls. Unfortunately, we, in Israel had to deal with hybrid terrorist organisations for many years. Hamas and Hezbollah are both hybrid terrorist organisations. But until not long ago, many people around the world believed that this was an Israeli problem. This is no longer so, for ISIS is also a hybrid terrorist organisation. ISIS controls territory and population. If I would have been a consultant of Abu Bakr al-Baghdadi, the first thing I would tell him is, "You know what, bring over international spectators and declare free elections in the territory that you control. Bring Jimmy Carter, he will like that, and ask him to even monitor the election." I can almost guarantee that the hybrid organisation will win the elections without guns being pointed at the heads of the voters as some of them would vote for the organisation out of fear and some would vote because they believed in what the organisation had to offer. But an election would put the international community in a tight spot, as they would not know what to do against a politically elected leader of an organisation! A hybrid terrorist organisation is thus more dangerous than a classical terrorist organisation because of the manner in which it is embedded within the civilian society. And when a liberal democracy is trying to contend and fight against the hybrid terrorist organisation that covers itself with human shields, it is very difficult to do so without collateral damage; and we see that in different parts of the world today.

The second pillar of the art of counter-terrorism is what I call the rationale of the terrorists. Many people around the world tend to believe that terrorists are lunatics and irrational actors. I beg to differ. I would like to argue that terrorists, or at least the terrorists I'm familiar with, and I'm generalising here, are rational actors. I can say that because when we discussed what is a rational decision-making process, we understand that the process is a certain way in which you choose between different alternatives. You calculate cost and benefits of each one of those alternatives and you are choosing the alternative which you believe is more beneficial than costly in order to achieve your goal. That's what every counter-terrorism practitioner does every day and that is what the terrorists do as well. Terrorists are therefore rational actors. This, in a sense, is good news, because if terrorists are rational actors, then counter-terrorism experts and counter-terrorism artists can understand the rationale and therefore have some leverage to change their behaviour, or de-radicalise them, or deter them from conducting terrorist attacks. The most important part of this type of activity is understanding their rationale.

Israel has been subjected to quite a few lone wolf attacks wherein the attacker was apprehended after he had stabbed civilians and young children. The photographs of these attackers while being taken to jail are quite revealing. The common denominator in all them was the smile on the face of the attacker. The attacker would probably spend the rest of his life in jail, but he still chooses to smile. This is not an artificial smile as this is not a photo opportunity. This smile is the reflection of the attackers rationale. And until and unless we are able to crack this rationale, we will not be able to communicate with them, to deter them or influence their behaviour altogether. It is my belief that this smile is an outcome of the brainwashing they have received, as a result of which they believe that the activity they have resorted to is an act of honour. To negate such acts and to negate radicalisation, there is then need for a counter-narrative, which should give exactly the opposite message – and that message is that such acts, regardless of the goal, are despicable and dishonourable and have nothing to do with honour.

I had stated earlier, when speaking of lone wolf attacks, that we used to believe that intelligence is not possible to come by in cases of such attacks. However, we in Israel, as also some of our colleagues in Europes have found an answer to overcome this shortcoming in HUMINT and COMINT while dealing with lone wolves. And the answer lies in open source intelligence (OSINT). It appears that a very large number of people who perpetrate lone wolf attacks, perhaps more than 50 percent in the case of recent attacks, both inside and outside Israel, gave some sort of warning on social networks before they carried out their attack. This is a golden piece of intelligence, if you know what to do about it.

The third pillar of the art of counter-terrorism is decoding the formula of terrorism. Now, if you would ask me if I can summarise everything I learned about terrorism for the last 30 years into one sentence, I would reply in the affirmative, as there is a formula of terrorism. It is a mathematical formula that has two factors – motivation multiplied by operational capabilities. It means that when a certain group of people has both motivation and operational capability to conduct terrorist attacks, it would conduct attacks against you. Now, what is counter-terrorism? It is all about lowering the motivation that gives birth to terrorism or lowering the operational capability of the terrorists. It's enough, on the face of it, to deal with one factor because if they have motivation and no capability, they would not launch attacks and vice versa. But the art of counter-terrorism is to be able to lower these two factors together and this is easier said than done. Why, you may ask? This is because we can only lower the operational capability of the terrorists by fighting them, killing them, arresting them or by confiscating their funds and destroying their warehouses and weapons. However, while we do this to degrade their operational capability, it paradoxically raises their motivation level to retaliate against you and that's the boomerang effect in counter-terrorism. How to deal with both factors simultaneously is hence the art of counter-terrorism.

The next pillar is collaboration. Here, we are talking about cooperation at the international and the regional level. Such cooperation is necessary because counter-terrorism is really all about weaving a chain of security. If we talk of the Indian Ocean region, it is a security chain. If one link of that chain is weak, it places the entire chain under risk. Therefore, to tighten this chain of security internationally and regionally is crucial. This cannot be done without a definition of terrorism. This is not merely a theoretical question, but has operational ramifications. It is unfortunate that most scholars, decision makers and legal experts agree that we can never reach one objective definition because this is a subjective term, because we all know the saying, 'One man's terrorist is another man's freedom fighter'. However, I beg to differ.

Terrorism is a strategy, not a goal. Therefore, the definition that I use is, '*Terrorism is the deliberate use of violence aimed against civilians in order to achieve political ends.*' An attack against an army and military targets is not terrorism by the definition that I use; it's guerrilla warfare, it's insurgency. And of course, anyone who deliberately attacks my soldiers or your soldiers is the enemy; you have all the right to fight back. But it's your problem and your problem alone. However, anybody who deliberately attacks my civilians is no more my problem alone; it's the problem of the international community.

As an example, it is understandable that India and Pakistan would never agree on what is a just cause or what is not. Is Kashmir a just cause to conduct violence or not? Is Palestine a just cause to conduct violence or not? Is Kurdistan a just cause or not to conduct violence; we would never agree on that. But we can agree that even if we believe that we have a just cause, the deliberate use of violence aimed against civilians should always be forbidden regardless of whether the cause is just, legitimate or holy. Unfortunately, this basic understanding is not very well accepted in the international community. This is the definition of the Muslim War League which says that terrorism is an outrageous attack carried out by either individual groups or states against human beings, against their religion and against their intellect. So, if you have a just cause, you can do all of the above. I beg to differ. We need to take those causes out of the definition.

To sum up, we have this need to create what I call a 'glocal'. I use the term 'glocal' which is a combination of global and local, for international cooperation. Based on this definition, we should outlaw terrorist organisations without taking into consideration our political concerns and interests. We need to prevent states from sponsoring terrorism and we need to stop incitement for terrorism based on this definition. We also need to create an international alliance, where joint intelligence gathering based on open source intelligence (OSINT) will be the norm. There really is no risk to any intelligence source if OSINT is jointly collected and analysed.

We also need to have a joint counter-motivation campaign. This could be done and should be done together, not alone, not separately by every state, but joint operational capacities need to be built to jointly counter the operational capacities of terrorist organisations. Here, I am talking about joint units. Why should one state, a small state in Europe, have a negotiation team and another neighbouring state, just 15 minutes away, have a separate one? You can use the same skills and shift them from one country to another country; joint training and joint technology are indeed required. So, we need to shift gears, and I would conclude by saying that we need to move on and not merely talk about better international cooperation. We need to talk now about joint counter-terrorism efforts.

36

Countering Maritime Terrorism in the IOR

Vice Admiral G Ashok Kumar

This paper is focused on naval cooperative measures and countering maritime terrorism in the Indian Ocean Region (IOR). Seas that cover about three-fourths of the earth's surface are not only a source of food and resources but also a medium of trade and transportation, and over long distances, the cheapest form of transportation. We are well aware that the IOR is the third largest water body in the world which is accessible through just seven external choke points. This means you can egress into or egress out of the Indian Ocean Region only through these seven choke points. And through these choke points transit over 100,000 ships annually, carrying world trade.

The statistics of the oil that is carried, the trade that is carried and the container shipping that is carried through ships transiting the region make it abundantly clear that any disruption to these International Shipping Lanes (ISLs) or to these choke points would have devastating effects on the global economy. India, in pursuance of its development agenda, is also increasingly turning to the sea as a driver for India's growth story. The 'Sagar Mala' Project and the focus on blue economy are reflective of such efforts. India's foreign policy vision for the IOR is summarised in the acronym 'SAGAR' which stands for 'Security and Growth for All in the Region'. The 'Act East Policy' and 'Project Mausam,' also exemplifies the government's multi-track approach to the IOR.

Let me move on to maritime terrorism. As is well known, there is no internationally accepted definition for maritime terrorism. However, the

Convention for the Suppression of Unlawful Activities (SUA), the principal convention for unlawful activities in the maritime domain, does list some of them. Statistically, you'll also find it interesting to know that incidents of maritime terrorism constitute only a very small fraction of the overall total. This could also be because of the cost-benefit analysis being actually against maritime terrorism.

But yet, maritime terrorism has manifested itself in many forms. These include hijackings, which can actually be used to get some money to fund terrorism, ramming of explosive-laden boats into ships that are trying to prevent unlawful activities at sea, quite like the manner in which a small fibre glass boat carrying C4 explosives and two suicide bombers, rammed into the United States Navy guided-missile destroyer USS Cole on 12 October 2000, while it was being refuelled in Yemen's Aden Harbour. There could also be underwater attacks, as was carried out by the Liberation Tigers of Tamil Eelam (LTTE). India too has not been immune in this regard, as terrorists used the sea routes to infiltrate and launch attacks on land on 26 November 2008. We have also seen that since October 2016, there have been attacks on a number of warships of Yemen and on merchant ships by non-state actors. These attacks have included missile attacks, attacks by surface unmanned vessels and also by mines. In the South China Sea, the Abu Sayyaf group continues to create havoc, killing sailors or kidnapping them for ransom.

In a sense, maritime terrorism has displayed an increasingly hybrid nature with the characteristic of mutating into deadlier forms. In addition to maritime terrorism, other forms of non-traditional threats to maritime security such as piracy, armed robbery and trafficking, whether it is guns or drugs, are also endemic to various sub-regions in the IOR. This has also resulted in a proliferation of a private maritime security business which remains largely unregulated and remains a potential threat to maritime security. The potential nexus between maritime crime and maritime terrorism and, as reports indicate, the increasing conflation of maritime crime with ideology, quite often religious ideologies, exacerbates the challenges to maritime security from non-traditional threats.

With this basic introduction, let me move on to reiterating some existing cooperative mechanisms that India has in the IOR. As enunciated in the Indian Maritime Security Strategy, the Indian Navy is committed to shape a favourable and positive maritime environment for enhancing net security and thereby be a net-security maritime provider in the IOR. The Indian Navy has always been amongst the first responders to any crisis, as was the case in Maldives in 1988 when mercenaries attempted a coup against the then government. Broadly, the concept of net security envisages preserving peace, promoting stability and maintenance of security in the wider areas of interest. India's foreign cooperation endeavours are based on four pillars of capacity building, capability enhancement, constructive engagement and collaborative effort. We believe that the most effective method to counter maritime terrorism is to enable friendly foreign countries to gain and fine tune their capabilities. Towards this end, the Indian Navy is committed towards capacity building and capability development of nations that may require such assistance. Most specifically, Indian naval actions in support of this objective include presence showing and rapid response to emerging threats, maritime engagement with other friendly foreign countries and conduct of specific maritime security operations. For instance, the Indian Navy has remained deployed round the year; one such instance being the Gulf of Aden, where Indian presence has remained since October 2008, fighting pirates in the Horn of Africa and escorting merchant ships safely. Almost 90 percent of the ships that were escorted were actually foreign flag ships. India is also an active participant in international anti-piracy forums such as RECAP (Regional Corporation against Armed Piracy), CGPCS (Contact Group on Piracy off the Coast of Somalia) and SHADE (Shared Awareness and Deconfliction). The Maritime Rescue Coordination Centre, Mumbai, is the RECAP focal point for India's area of responsibility.

Let me move to our ventures with other navies. The Indian Navy along with the navies of Indonesia, Malaysia, Thailand and Myanmar regularly undertake coordinated patrols or what we call CORPAT along respective international maritime boundary lines. This is to prevent arms running and gun smuggling. In addition, the Indian Navy along with the Indian Coast Guard has been providing support to the island nations in the IOR. For instance, in Male, we undertake an EEZ patrol every month with Maldivian coast guard personnel on our ships. Similarly, in the islands of Mauritius and Seychelles, we conduct EEZ patrols once every six months. We also undertake other HADR (Humanitarian Aid and Disaster Relief), NEO (Non-combatant Evacuation Operation) and peacekeeping missions. The interaction, as can be seen, is at a multilayered level which enables us to address sensitive issues without much hassle.

The Indian Navy also conducts institutional exercises with a number of navies. The scope and complexity of these exercises has continuously evolved, and today it includes not only traditional maritime security challenges but also non-traditional ones. In addition, a host of other exercises of varying complexity are being undertaken with a large number of navies. These include passage exercises, which we call PASSEXs, and also occasional exercises such as RIMPAC, the Rim of Pacific exercise which is a multilateral exercise, and also HADR exercises as a part of the ADMM-plus. In the last one year alone, that is 2016, we have visited about 30 countries because we believe presence is actually a deterrence and our presence deters any unlawful activities in the seas around us.

A number of operational interactions to enhance mutual understanding and operational coordination are also undertaken under the aegis of multilateral forums such as Indian Ocean Naval Symposium (IONS) and MILAN (a congregation of littoral navies conducted biennially by the Indian Navy at the Andaman and Nicobar Command in Port Blair), both of which are Indian Navy initiatives. In fact, the IONS includes about 35 countries today and about 17 navies participate in the biennial MILAN exercise which is coordinated by the Indian Navy at Port Blair. Over and above this, we also conduct staff talks with about 20 navies. When it comes to maritime assistance, the Indian Navy provides maritime assistance to friendly foreign nations to address specific requirements such as those pertaining to hydrographic surveys, diving assistance, ordnance disposal, salvage and sealift. For instance, when the Maldives ran out of water because of problems with their water supply, water was shipped by Indian naval tankers to the Maldives.

The other strength of the Indian Navy is the training cooperation that we have with various countries. In the last 30 years alone, we have trained over 11,000 foreign personnel from about 40 countries. We offer about 125 courses, 25 of them for officers and about 100 for sailors of all navies in the IOR. Technical cooperations such as maintenance support, technical advice, repairs and refit, transfer of hardware and construction of ships is also being undertaken for friendly foreign countries. Aircraft and ships have also been provided to friendly countries to augment their capacity and capabilities.

Cooperation is the name of the game and one of the things that India has done is to enter into wide shipping information agreements with various countries. In the last IORA meeting, when India's Vice President represented the country, one of the focus areas was to enter into wide shipping agreements. Now, we are in the process of signing agreements with 30 countries; we already have it operationalised with about nine of them. We have assisted four countries – Sri Lanka, the Maldives, Mauritius and the Seychelles – in enhancing their maritime domain awareness by setting up coastal surveillance radar systems for them. This is in the process of being set up for a few other countries. There would be a mutual exchange of information between India and these countries.

Notably, post 26/11, the Indian Navy has developed a National Command Control Communication and Intelligence Network, the NC3I. This network, not only links the Indian Navy and the Coast Guard, but also fuses information from multiple sensors. For instance, we now have a coastal surveillance network, a series or radars, the national AIS chain which is a Directorate General of Lighthouses and Lightships (DGLL) Project, inputs from the Long Range Identification and Tracking (LRIT) from the DG Shipping, space-based Automatic Identification System (AIS) information which we have contracted for from one of the agencies, and inputs of all our surveillance efforts whether it is ship surveillance or maritime reconnaissance (MR) aircraft which fly in the entire IOR. We also get information from all the technical agreements we have entered into with various countries. So, we do have a consolidated picture of maritime domain awareness (MDA) of the widespread shipping and this helps us is to identify dark ships when we run into them. The Indian Navy is also steering a case to establish a national MDA system which would further integrate databases and sensors of all stakeholders and agencies.

Having covered all this, what are the challenges? The traditional principles of freedom of the seas ensure that almost all vessels, irrespective of type and intent, have almost unfettered access to the seas. Beyond 12 nautical miles, no rule applies to them. So, anybody can be there in waters beyond 12 nautical miles of any nation; they are on the high seas. Surveillance and identification in the vast maritime domain is also another significant challenge. For instance, just out of Mumbai alone, there are about 23,000 fishing boats that sail out on a daily basis. To keep a tab on each one of them is actually a challenge. The tracking of smaller vessels which are outside the purview of international shipping regulations is another big challenge. The success of the counter-piracy effort of Somalia has been on account of the international multi-pronged cooperative and collaborative approach. Challenges to deal with maritime terrorism are likely to be even greater, and so we will certainly require international cooperation and collaboration, not only among security agencies, but also other related stakeholders.

Domestically, despite the significant progress made to strengthen coastal and maritime security, there remain several challenges. These include issues related to a single-point apex body for maritime affairs, consolidation of sensor and data sources, and integration of all agencies into a national level integration system, and review of legislative framework especially with respect to enforcement. Furthermore, strengthening of the Indian Coast Guard and coastal police will be a facilitator for a wider role for the Indian Navy as a net maritime security provider in the IOR.

To address the challenges, some of the key areas require greater focus and these include leveraging existing international cooperative mechanisms such as the IORA and the IONS which have been successful naval initiatives for enhancing maritime security, and continued and focused engagement with other nations in the IOR through a whole-of-government approach. In so far as the maritime forces are concerned, greater traction to foreign cooperation initiatives is imperative. Strengthening of intelligence and information-sharing arrangements at the regional level such as through the proposed Information Fusion Centre (IFC) in the Indian Ocean Region would need to be complemented by the national maritime domain awareness system in India. Establishing an apex level body for maritime affairs, such as the proposed National Maritime Authority, would go a long way in ensuring our fight against maritime terrorism. Review of the international legal framework and maritime security to keep pace with the challenges, and strengthening of domestic law will also go a long way in this regard. Despite the low numbers and localised nature of maritime terrorism, the threat from it in the IOR is real and has now manifested itself in deadlier forms.

The unique nature of the maritime domain compounds the problems associated with monitoring and identification. The international legal framework has also not kept pace with increasing challenges. Furthermore, while operational actions are undertaken by security forces, effectively dealing with international maritime terrorism also needs complementary actions by other nations and stakeholders to comprehensively address the issue. The Indian Navy continues to be committed towards anchoring stability and security, and thereby national development.

37

Need for Win-Win Cooperation

Vladimir Milovidev

What is the art of countering terrorism? What is the art of inventing or designing something? We find that terrorists are permanently inventing new methods and techniques to attack us; unfortunately, we are still unable to combine effectively and synergise our strengths to counter and to prevent terrorist acts. In answer to the hypothetical question I raised at the beginning of this paper, I believe that to counter-terrorism, we need to develop the art of combining as also the art of inventing. We need to invent something new that enables us to combine our interest, helps us in our understanding of ourselves, assists us in identifying terrorists and understanding their rationale and decoding their messages. A combination of methods and technologies would be required if our efforts to identify terrorists and understand their rationale is to bear fruit.

The main problem that I foresee is that while we have a large number of counter-terrorism experts who are all good artists, the difficulty lies in making all of them to work together. This is so because we are individuals, having our own interests and vision. This applies to countries too, as they have their own traditions and view of terrorism. So, the international art of counter-terrorism is simply to find a way for all of us to combine together. And to do this, I think, we need to first see terrorism as a broader phenomenon, which involves a lot of religious, cultural, economic and political factors that we need to take into consideration. We then need to listen to each other and find rational ways to cooperate and combine with each other.

Russia and Russian experts on counter-terrorism have deep concerns about the spread of terrorism, and, thus, have a biding interest in studying and understanding issues related to it. First of all, the terrorist activity of various groups like al-Qaida, the Islamic State and others is spreading to regions located in the close vicinity of Russian borders, and thus presents an immediate danger to Russia and its neighbours. There is not just a security threat from the terrorists, but sometimes, in a broader sense, there is the danger of political destabilisation in Russia's partner countries that would impede the progress of major economic, infrastructural and integration projects in greater Eurasia.

As my initial background is in economics and not in politics, I will stress another factor which makes us very interested in this problem. This region has a great potential to establish a mutually beneficial cooperation, especially in the economic field, along with many other areas of interest in other countries. As of now, unfortunately, we do not have much cooperation in this sphere. In terms of economics, the Indian Ocean Region (IOR) accounts for about five percent of Russia's total exports and 3.5 percent of imports. These are very small figures and Russia would like to increase its presence in this region in a much more active manner. To do this, of course, we need to follow the art of invention and combination, to invent new approaches to cooperation with the IOR countries and also combine our interest. Two of the BRICS countries, India and South Africa, are located in these regions and BRICS, as a group of five major developing nations, have gained importance and influence as a global factor. Likewise, Russian cooperation with CAREC (Central Asia Regional Economic Cooperation) countries is also on the rise, which signifies Russia's growing aspirations for a greater role in the region. In these terms, terrorism and radicalism present the biggest danger impeding the integration processes and cooperation with countries of the regions.

If we look at the map, we see a number of hotspots that are in territories close to the borders of our existing potential partners. This is disruptive as it impacts on trade and transport routes, cultural relations, innovations, techniques and many other ties in various areas. Due to geography, there are no means to bypass such hotspots. In all probability, these hotspots will only grow and increase in the future. We thus have only one choice before us: to have an enhanced, diversified approach, and make joint efforts to bring down and cool the level of violence in these areas. However, it should also be noted that sometimes terrorists are themselves created by outside forces to achieve temporary local results. These terrorists later start acting on their own, often turning against their creators in a big way. Thus, we have the trend of local conflicts and local outbursts of terrorism and violence acquiring a global nature.

Our future benefits lie in cooperation. Any unilateral effort of a country to support radical forces in its territory or its neighbour's, to gain unilateral advantages for itself would be a great mistake. What is drastically needed today is a real reconciliation and consolidation of all anti-terrorism forces in areas where our hotspots match. Win-win cooperation, despite our existing differences, appears to be the only way to guarantee peace and stability in all countries in the region. Economic interest should prevail. While military victory is a desirable solution, it remains a very hard though important step, and is not a full solution.

It is not enough to eliminate the terrorist threat and in no way does it mean eradication of terrorist ideas and practices. In fact, global terrorism has a network structure and can move relatively freely across the globe quite unexpectedly in any region. Military defeat may lead to dispersion of such cells, and it is hard to predict the way in which they will appear after being waved away from any country in the region. We have adequate examples of such cases. Therefore, I think this is a joint effort to create the international art of countering terrorism, and because it is a complex approach, we need to re-cultivate areas previously prone to terrorism together. That involves economic resurgence, education and other political and humanitarian measures in order to prevent new radicalisations anywhere.

38

Role of International Institutions

Martin Kimani

When we look at the role of international institutions to counter-terrorism, the first thing right off the mark that we know to be true is that the global counter-terrorism architecture is made up of a dense and complex web of relationships. These are mostly bilateral and mostly enfolded within the intelligence, military and political systems of states. The entire network made up of these bilateral and sometimes regional relationships respond to quite covert and transnational threats that go across the spectrum of terrorism, drug and human trafficking, illicit weapons, etc., and these particular sets of illegal activities interact with each other in very particular ways.

This architecture is demand driven. It is not permanent; it always shifts with the events it is asked to respond to. And that is what gives it its complexity, because today, Kenya may be dealing with India on a very particular issue, and tomorrow those issues could shift even as each of our countries shift in relation to our other partners.

That architecture, built on member states and their security and political agencies, is where the bulk of financial and human resources reside. A lot of that architecture is hidden from plain sight. It does not share what it knows freely, and it has very strict protocols on how it engages in terms of exchanging meaningful, actionable information.

It is also inside that state architecture, where the data, the knowledge and very often the expertise lives. When you consider that reality, the question then becomes, what can the international organisations add to it. That is the question that needs to be answered. We know that international organisations as a whole are poorly resourced; they never have enough money even when they appear to have a lot of it. We know that international organisations and their officials are largely closed off from their intelligence and security architecture of counter-terrorism. In other words, no one who I know, who works daily on counter-terrorism, calls on an officer of the United Nations every morning.

The UN and other international platforms, sometimes, are captive to virtue signalling, and non-intervention. They are used to show that you are good and they are used to promote notions of the good. I am not denigrating these ideas, but simply stating that a lot of the time they are there for signalling purposes, and, that sometimes runs completely counter to the existence of operational counter-terrorism officers.

Very often, international organisations are catchment areas for academic researchers and their debates. For instance, the very important debate on definitions really makes no sense at all to the terrorists, and certainly, if you are engaging in counter-terrorism, those sorts of issues of definition, as important as they are, do not form a part of your daily life in any meaningful sense.

The question then arises: what are the key competencies of international organisations? If they were branches of General Electric at the time when Jack Welch was the CEO and used to say, "if you are not in the core business, I'll close you down" what would international organisations say is their core competence? They would probably talk about counter-terrorism strategy, the PVE (Prevent Violent Extremism) strategy presented by the UN Secretary-General on 15 January 2016 and a variety of other resolutions, both at the UN and at the regional level. I am sure they can talk a little bit about building of new architectures and I am sure they can talk about bringing certain skills to the table, to countries that need those skills, or to specific sectors within countries that need those skills.

39

The IORA Mandate

KV Bhagirath

The Indian Ocean region is today the centre stage of the global economy is key to the strategic stability of the region, and a veritable lifeline for international trade. In my view, development is a critical prerequisite in addressing the root causes of terrorism. The need for regional and international cooperation amongst states would constitute the second prerequisite.

In early March 2017, an oil tanker was hijacked off the coast of Somalia by Somali pirates. The oil tanker was flying the flag of Comoros Island, an IORA member state, and the hijacking marked the first instance since 2012 of a commercial ship being seized. While the hijacking was unfortunate, the fact that such an incident has occurred after five years is indicative of the anti-piracy measures that have been put in place. The combined navies of various regions working together have addressed the issue of piracy and hijacking quite effectively.

The hijacking has, however, come as a big shock as the eight-member crew, all Sri Lankans, were taken hostage. As Sri Lanka too is an IORA member, the question that arises is, what can the organisation do on the ground to address such issues?

Here I would like to mention the core competence of IORA. It is essentially a developmental organisation for regional economic cooperation in the Indian Ocean. Initially, it was called Indian Ocean Rim Association for Regional Cooperation (IORARC), an extremely difficult acronym to expand. The genesis is based on Nelson Mandela's statement made in New Delhi, when he visited India in 1994. He said:

> *"The natural urge of the facts of history and geography, should broaden itself to include the concept of an Indian Ocean Rim for socio-economic cooperation and other peaceful endeavours and recent changes in the international system demand that countries of the Indian Ocean shall become a single platform."*

It took a few years for officials to come together, especially the five countries in the forefront including India, and IORA was formally launched in March 1997 in Mauritius where its secretariat is presently based. The membership today has grown to encompass 21 member-states, from South Africa in the west to Australia. Two notable exceptions are Pakistan and Myanmar, but the latter is shortly applying for membership of IORA.

Importantly, IORA also has seven dialogue partners which are China, Egypt, France, Germany, Japan, the UK and the USA. The interesting thing is that the IORAs charter very specifically limits its mandate to regional economic cooperation. That was how Nelson Mandela wanted the IORA to function, and that is how the charter has been framed leaving no window for any other activity. It hence does not have a mandate to go into a political or any other role besides regional economic cooperation.

Terrorism is not new to IORA member-states. In fact, the earliest bombings by al-Qaida in 1998 of the American embassies in Dar-es-Salaam, Tanzania and Nairobi, Kenya, both of whom are IORA member states, were perhaps the first ever example of this terrorist group. The Indian Ocean has also witnessed piracy off the coast of Somalia, the Gulf of Aden and the Arabian Sea, resulting from a combination of circumstances including ethnic, language and cultural diversities, arbitrary boundaries, ideological strife and competition for scarce resources, especially water. It was the Somali piracy phenomenon that brought forth proactive steps on the part of IORA. In 2011, India became the chair of IORA and it initiated steps to reprioritise the focus, giving maritime safety and security the top priority in order to counter piracy and terrorism.

Over the years , IORA has also helped numerous conferences to discuss what was important, but as mentioned by Mr. Shanmugam, the Home Minister of Singapore, 'the deliverables that you place on the ground is what is important.' This is important, rather than conferences and discussions.

Indonesia is the present chair of IORA, and last week it commemorated the 20th anniversary by organising and hosting the first IORA Summit in Jakarta on 7 March 2017. Among the documents that were adopted was, interestingly, the IORA declaration on preventing and countering terrorism and violent extremism. It was the first time that IORA had almost, I believe, tried to step out of its mandate. IORA member-states denounced terrorism and violent extremism in all its forms and manifestations and resolved to work and support each other's efforts to counter this threat. In this regard, India announced this proposal in the Summit to reinforce cooperative mechanisms, maritime safety and security, such as wide shipping agreements by setting up an information fusion centre to strengthen maritime domain awareness and proposing to host such a centre in the Indian Ocean Rim for IORA member-states.

The IORA Summit also adopted two other documents – the concord and the action plan – which actually focuses, specifically, on cooperation in maritime safety through coordination and pooling of resources. Quite appropriately, the first Summit had the theme, 'Strengthening Maritime Cooperation for a Peaceful, Stable and Prosperous Indian Ocean.'

What IORA has also been trying to do is to bring into the mainstream some of the countries, Somalia and Yemen, to bring them on board to participate in our capacity-building exercises with the specific idea of bringing them to sit with all the other members of the IORA states, to see how we can get them to work together and learn from other states. It has been useful to us and we have a special Somalia-Yemen programme in IORA, which has been quite successful in organising events for these two states in third countries.

The G7 Foreign Ministers meetings in Germany in April 2015, and in Japan in 2016, took cognisance of what was happening in the Indian Ocean and how to combat terror and have tried to combine their resources with IORA, which had been invited to these meetings. But the fact that the IORA mandate does not permit the organisation to go beyond economic regional cooperation forbids us to get into anything more solid.

On 12 March 2015, the Indian Premier, Shri Narendra Modi, during his visit to Mauritius, remarked:

> *"Indian Ocean Rim Association can be an important instrument for pursuing our vision for a sustainable and prosperous future in the region. The time has come for a strong grouping around the Indian Ocean. We will pursue this with new vigour in the years ahead. We seek a future for the Indian Ocean that lives up to the name 'SAGAR' (Security And Growth for All in the Region".*

I had mentioned earlier about the mandate of IORA being limited to regional economic cooperation. But the fact that the Jakarta IORA Summit had adopted a declaration on counter-terrorism may well be the seed for an expanded mandate. That would depend, of course, on whether the charter can be amended, as most members are reluctant to do so. IORA has a renewed and revitalised architecture that deals with regional economic development which can be an instrument in its own limited way.

40

Role of the United Nations

Elizabeth Joyce

In 1996, the Government of India took the important step of calling for a comprehensive counter-terrorism convention, something which it continues to lead and to work towards in this day in order to secure the global community against the scourge of terrorism. The Comprehensive Convention remains an important goal, and UN member-states are working towards it to reach an agreement. The UN has nevertheless been able to move forward and make great strides in assisting states to tackle global terrorism, even in the absence of the convention.

This has happened primarily due to three reasons. First of all, there is a basket of conventions, 19 international instruments in all, that considered collectively, are considered by some as a comprehensive approach to countering terrorism. They include conventions such as the Convention on Terrorist Bombings, International Convention for the Financing of Terrorism and the Convention on Nuclear Terrorism. The Convention on Terrorist Financing even contains a definition, not of terrorism, but of a terrorist act. As Prof. Gaylord said, terrorism is strategy, not a goal and that has enabled member-states to agree on a definition of an act of terrorism. It is defined as under:

> "*Any act intended to cause death or serious bodily injury to a civilian, or to any other person not taking part in the hostilities, in a situation of armed conflicts, when the purpose of such act, by its nature or context, is to intimidate a population or to compel a government or an international organisation, to do or to abstain from doing any act.*"

That is the legal basis on which the UN has been operating since 1999 when it was opened for signature; the Convention finally becoming operative in 2002. So we do have this Convention as a legal basis.

Secondly, since 2006, the UN has had a global counter-terrorism strategy, adopted by the General Assembly, which is currently under review. Pursuant to that strategy, it also has a counter-terrorism implementation task force which brings together around 39 different agencies that have many and varied roles in tackling terrorism. In a broader sense, pillar one of the strategy instructs member-states to consider the root causes of terrorism, particularly relevant to current considerations of how to prevent violent extremism and this includes UN agencies that would not normally be associated with counter-terrorism (CT), including UNESCO, UNICEF and UNDP.

Currently, this strategy is under review and member-states are considering establishing a high level under-secretary general position to give greater leadership on CT and achieve better coordination and coherence. The Secretary-General has also promised to mainstream CT considerations into the work of the UN more generally. Such a move was unimaginable even a few years ago.

Third, are the measures adopted by the Security Council, many of which have been adopted under Chapter VII of the UN Charter which makes them legally binding on all the member-states. They include the 1267 Regime that was first adopted in 1999 by which the Security Council imposes sanctions on individuals and entities linked to al-Qaeda or Daesh (ISIS). It also includes the 1373 Regime which is a business and counter-terrorism committee and which expects member-states to impose national sanctions against individuals and entities linked to terrorism including, but not confined to, al-Qaeda and Daesh. All this goes to show that a very solid legal base for action exists.

Resolution 1373 was adopted after 9/11. It lays down a very comprehensive set of measures that states are required to implement. The office of Counter-Terrorism Committee Executive Directorate (C-TED) was set up to support the work of that committee. In its bilateral dialogue with each member-state it assessed each of them and their capacity to tackle counter-terrorism. C-TED has grown to become an independent assessment body staffed by members of the UN Secretariat. It has more than 12 years of assessment experience and a vast data base documenting show of force and good practices. It has visited over 120 member-states, many of them several times. It has a deep and ongoing dialogue with each state including, in many cases, at the direct working level with law enforcement officials, judges, prosecutors and police officers. It has a strong focus on the IORA region from East Africa to South East Asia, and, of course, South Asia. It covers a broad range of CT measures, legislative frameworks, effective criminal justice systems, counter-terrorist financing, border control, law enforcement, human rights, etc., and works to ensure that all this is done with respect for due process and rule of law.

Increasingly, C-TED has taken on more cutting-edge topics. Internet communications technologies have led us to discussions with the private sector and the consideration of public and private partnerships. This has been an intense work stream since the last two years, one that was not predicted to be as intense as it has become. In other areas, C-TED has been working on preventing violent extremism and on new ways of addressing threats.

From the very start, the Counter-Terrorism Committee (CTC) was wise enough to recognise that an office of 50 people would not have the capacity to get very much done without international and regional partners and with civil society implementing partners in many cases. So CTC has long-standing relations with organisations like UNODC, Interpol, IKO, IOM, IMO – all the acronyms. When the need for capacity building is seen, the Committee reaches out to its implementing partners and makes a referral. It sometimes even raises funds on behalf of its partners and has them deliver the required technical assistance pursuant to the recommendations. Where the need is felt to facilitate further discussion of norms and standards, the Committee can act as a catalyst to improve the understanding of the states of norms, or even work with the partners to improve standards. A good example of this is the work done by the Committee to prevent terrorist abuse of charities. Our assessments were showing that there needed to be more discussion around the subject, both to raise awareness of the risks and to introduce the concept of proportionate response to the risk. After all, the charitable sector is vulnerable to terrorist financing but it's also worth billions of dollars a year globally and its independent dynamism is an essential global force for good – one of the finest expressions of civil society in action. So, just as we want to prevent its abuse from terrorist finances, the risk is a real one. We do not want it to suffer a chilling effect, either from heavy-handed preventive measures on the part of global financial institutions or from diminished resources from discouraged donors. We discussed these issues with over 80 states and over 100 charities and we achieved not only what we set out to achieve but it also led to greater engagement between the standard-setting financial action task force and the charitable sector itself. In due course there was a revision of good practices and standards.

The recent example of the counter-terrorism regime as framed by the UN is a bit intense, just as the threat has expanded and become more complex. The Security Council CT Regime has worked to address the emerging threats. In the last four years, we have had an unprecedented number of thematic CT resolutions aimed at addressing such trends like the use of kidnapping and hostage-taking by terrorist groups, foreign terrorist fighter phenomenon and, in particular, how to prevent cross-border travel for the purpose of terrorist acts, terrorist trade in religious, scientific and cultural artefacts, issues related to gender and terrorism, internet communication technologies, new threats to civil aviation, links between human trafficking and terrorism and, most recently, in December 2016, the need for enhanced international judicial and law enforcement cooperation.

Speaking now of the role of South Asia in the work of CTC, in terms of those emerging issues, trends and development that the Security Council has had to consider after C-TED had brought them to its attention, possibly no other region has been more effective than South Asia in drawing the attention of C-TED to these issues. The eight countries of SAARC regularly bring their practitioners to the table to bring a real world perspective to the work of the CTC and essentially advising C-TED on what is needed. This is a unique role that member-states have played and we are deeply grateful to the eight governments of the SAARC region for facilitating this and making it happen. Since 2009, judges, prosecutors and police officers of the eight states have been meeting regularly at the practitioner level to discuss the challenges of effectively countering terrorism. These insights have informed and often guided the way in which C-TED designs its assessments and facilitates technical assistance. Recent issues have included urgent concerns about the use of digital evidence and the digital transmission of evidence, interviewing and interrogation techniques, foreign terrorist fighters and, crucially, countries like Afghanistan whose criminal justice officials are under daily and serious threat of direct attack, the need to enhance the physical protection of criminal justice officers as well as the witnesses and victims of terrorism. This dialogue has led to bilateral dialogue with countries outside the region facilitated by C-TED. Sri Lanka, for example has been providing advice and guidance to one of the West African member-states currently dealing with Boko Haram based on its own experience with rehabilitation and reintegration techniques. In June 2017, C-TED will convene the 12th such regional workshop with the additional expertise of UNODC and Interpol. This process has been strongly supported over the long term by all the states of the region but was facilitated, in particular, by the Government of India when Ambassador Hardeep Puri was chair of the CTC in 2011-2012. His dynamic leadership set the stage for prescient initiatives that bear fruit to this day. He convened a special meeting of the CTC, and in partnership with the Council of Europe in 2011, considered for the first time the practical measures that the states were taking and could take to counter incitement to terrorism and violent extremism that could incite and inspire terrorist acts. Some five years later, these themes, and many of the solutions considered in that meeting are still cutting-edge issues and about to be mainstreamed brought in the ministry work of the UN as a whole.

The need to act continuously on urgent basis is warranted by the regional and international nature of the threat today. Horrific attacks in all regions, and no less in the IOR, demonstrate that no state or citizen is insulated against the threat of terrorism. This is true even if the perpetrators are motivated by events that are geographically distant from the locus of their attacks. States in the region have made great strides in their efforts to address the terrorist scourge. We know that no state can successfully address this threat alone and that all tools – diplomatic, military and political – are often necessary to ensure a sustainable victory. We, in the United Nations, stand ever willing and ready to support those efforts.

41

International Cooperation on Counter-Terrorism

Asoke Kumar Mukerji

Terrorism has become the single biggest threat to international peace and stability. However, effective international cooperation based on the United Nations (UN) framework to counter this threat has yet to be felt. Three areas reflect this. These are:

1. Legal cooperation between nations based on international conventions adopted by the United Nations General Assembly (UNGA);
2. Implementation of the United Nations Global Counter Terrorism Strategy (GCTS) of 2006; and
3. Operational cooperation among countries through the United Nations Security Council (UNSC), especially for fettering listed terrorist individuals and entities through the UNSC sanctions lists.

International Legal Cooperation

The idea of using international cooperation to counter-terrorism, based on legal instruments, was initiated by France before the Second World War at the League of Nations. The provocation for the French initiative was the refusal of the Fascist authorities in Italy to hand over individuals identified by French law enforcement agencies as the masterminds of the assassination of French Foreign Minister Louis Barthou along with King Alexander of Yugoslavia at Marseilles in October 1934. The legal principle behind the French initiative was that of "prosecute or extradite". The League of Nations adopted the Convention for the Prevention and Punishment of Terrorism in November 1937. Of the 25 countries that signed the Convention, only India ratified it before the League of Nations was overtaken by the outbreak of the Second World War.

The first sustained post-Second World War initiative to use legal instruments to facilitate international cooperation on countering terrorism took place only in 1972. The terrorist act targeting 11 members of the Israeli contingent to the Munich Olympics of 1972 galvanised the UNGA to adopt its first resolution to seek international cooperation to counter-terrorism. An Ad Hoc Committee on International Terrorism in 1972, consisting of 35 countries including India, was established in the UNGA to flesh out the multilateral legal framework. The Committee, chaired by India in 1979, submitted its report to the UNGA, which included the proposal for the negotiation of an additional international convention or conventions based inter alia "on the principle of extradition or prosecution to combat acts of international terrorism not yet covered by other similar international conventions."

The growth of terrorist activities, especially after the end of the Cold War in 1989, led the UN to adopt conventions setting up a robust international legal architecture to counter-terrorism. These included instruments to suppress specific acts of terrorism like bombings (1997), financing (1999) and nuclear acts (2005). The UN's attempt to adopt a comprehensive convention on international terrorism (CCIT), however, remains gridlocked.

Flowing out of discussions in the UNGA, India had proposed the first draft of such a Comprehensive Convention on International Terrorism (CCIT) in 1996. The CCIT would oblige member-states to implement the legal principle of 'prosecute or extradite' to deal with terrorism through international cooperation. For India, which has attempted since the 26 November 2008 Mumbai terror attacks to bring the perpetrators based in Pakistan to justice, the importance of the CCIT cannot be over-emphasised.

As with other legal instruments of the United Nations, which form the corpus of international law, the implementation of the obligations imposed by the CCIT is on UNGA member-states. In cases of disputes over implementation, the International Court of Justice (ICJ) has jurisdiction. In July 2016, the United Nations and the African Union worked in close collaboration to implement the principle of 'prosecute or extradite' by setting up a Hybrid Court in Senegal to prosecute and convict former president Hissene Habre of Chad for 'crimes against humanity.' The sentence of the Hybrid Court was endorsed by the ICJ, making the principle an integral part of international law.

Despite popular perceptions that the gridlock is due to lack of consensus on the 'definition' of terrorism in the draft of the CCIT, the reality is that UNGA member-states have already accepted the definition of terrorism in the sectoral conventions adopted by the UNGA between 1997 and 2005 referred to earlier. The current draft on the table prepared by the chairman of the Ad Hoc Working Group, Ambassador Rohan Perera of Sri Lanka (who was the chair of the groups that drafted the three sectoral conventions adopted by the UNGA so far), has cross-referenced this definition. The way forward is for the UNGA to meet and adopt the legal instrument of the CCIT with the political interpretations of terrorism being reflected in an accompanying UNGA resolution to be adopted when the CCIT is tabled.

The UN Global Counter-Terrorism Strategy

Following the historic 60th anniversary World Summit of the United Nations in 2005, member-states of the UNGA adopted a Global Counter Terrorism Strategy (GCTS) in 2006 to provide an operational framework for international cooperation on countering terrorism. The GCTS has four pillars, which are as under:

1. Addressing conditions conducive to the spread of terrorism;
2. Preventing and combating terrorism;
3. Building national capacities to counter-terrorism; and
4. Ensuring human rights and the rule of law in countering terrorism.

There is a specific requirement under the fourth pillar, relating the rule of law to the principle of 'extradite or prosecute,' which is at the heart of the CCIT. Effective implementation of the GCTS has been left to periodic reviews every two years by the UNGA. The reviews revealed that more than 30 UN bodies have some role to play in countering terrorism within the framework of the GCTS. During these reviews, several countries, including India, have raised the need for the UN to have a Coordinator for Counter-Terrorism, whose office would help member-states to implement the provisions of the GCTS. This issue was addressed during the recent elections of the new UN Secretary-

General, who has announced that his priority is to nominate a UN Coordinator for Counter-Terrorism to work under him.

The first and second pillars of the GCTS, which deal with addressing conditions conducive to the spread of terrorism and preventing and combating terrorism, have not seen any major impact on the ground so far. In response to proposals to create a platform for dialogue to prevent the spread of terrorism, the UN Secretary-General launched an Alliance of Civilisations in 2005. The Alliance has a focus on four areas: education, youth, migration and media. Similarly, the urgent need to eradicate poverty and catalyse development to prevent the growth of terrorism, which is today the core of Agenda 2030 for Sustainable Development, has not received adequate priority in the GCTS so far.

The second pillar of the GCTS contained a proposal for an international centre for countering terrorism. A United Nations Counter Terrorism Centre (CTC), anchored in the Counter Terrorism Implementation Task Force of the UN's Department of Political Affairs of the United Nations, was established in November 2011. The UN CTC has a 22-member Advisory Board, which includes India. The Board is chaired by Saudi Arabia, which contributed USD 100 million to finance the activities of the CTC in 2014. However, the utilisation of these funds by the CTC has been below optimal, mainly because of the uncoordinated nature of counter-terrorism activities by UN entities in the field.

Many member states experiencing the impact of terrorism have looked to the third pillar of the GCTS to help them strengthen national capacities to counter-terrorism. The biggest constraint in this area has been on harmonising national institutions and capacities to respond in a coherent manner to the challenges posed by terrorism. In addition, the issue of drawing upon financial resources from the UN's general budget has prevented meaningful action on the ground for capacity building.

The UN Security Council and Countering Terrorism

The direct impact of terrorism on international peace and security, especially after the 11 September 2001 attacks on the United States, galvanised the UN Security Council (UNSC) to assume an active role to counter-terrorism as a threat to international peace and security. By an internal arrangement between the five permanent members of the UNSC, the United States is the 'pen-holder,' or the lead country on any decisions of the Council on countering terrorism. The UNSC has adopted more than 30 resolutions to counter-terrorism so far. However, the ineffectiveness of the UNSC, due to its non-democratic structure and method of decision-making, has reduced the impact of these resolutions on the ground with countries flouting their obligations to enforce UNSC decisions with impunity.

The omnibus UNSC resolution 1373 adopted unanimously after the 11 September 2001 attacks on the United States is the flagship platform of the Council to encourage international cooperation on countering terrorism. Under this resolution, a Counter Terrorism Committee of the UNSC (which restricts itself to the current 15 members of the Security Council alone) is in operation. The Committee's main outcome so far has been to collect data from UN member-states on their legislation and policies to counter-terrorism. The Committee has also upheld 'zero tolerance' for terrorism during India's chairmanship in the period 2011-2012. Beyond collating data, the CTC is not effective in enforcing international cooperation to counter-terrorism, even by pursuing cases where the UN itself has been attacked, for investigation and prosecution. The best examples of this in recent years are the terrorist attacks on UN peacekeepers deployed by the UNSC in the Golan Heights of Syria and Mali where the perpetrators of these acts have yet to be brought to justice.

The way the UNSC has adopted double standards in implementing international cooperation to counter-terrorism is well illustrated by its sanctions-listing procedures. While in 2006, the United States as a permanent member could overcome these procedures by tabling a resolution in the Council for a vote, other countries which are not permanent members have been unable to achieve comparable results. India's case in attempting to include Masood Azhar in the sanctions list of UNSC resolution 1267 against al-Qaida/Taliban is well known. Unless India is permanently represented in the Council as an equal member, such double standards will continue to be applied.

Considering this pessimistic survey, what is the future of international cooperation on countering terrorism? One indicator could be the emergence of plurilateral arrangements which could eventually provide the norms for UNSC resolutions to turn to. Two such groupings have in fact already been referenced in UNSC resolutions. These are the 37-country Financial Action Task Force (FATF), established in 1989, to counter money-laundering which has given a focus on counter-terrorism since 2001; and the 30-country Global

Counter Terrorism Forum or GCTF established in 2011. All the five permanent members of the UNSC are members of these groupings, as is India.

The best example of the impact of the FATF on international cooperation in countering terrorism is the universal application of the Know-Your-Customer or KYC norms of the FATF by financial institutions. The GCTF's major contribution so far has been the development of norms contained in its Rabat Memorandum for applying the rule of law while countering terrorism. Both these norms have been integrated into UNSC counter-terrorism resolutions recently.

To conclude, the current reality of ineffective international cooperation on countering terrorism cannot be hidden. Three urgent steps are required to change this reality. These are the adoption of the CCIT by the UNGA, the use of the GCTS in a holistic and output-oriented manner by the UNGA and the amendment of the UN Charter by the UNGA to reform the UNSC, implementing the unanimous mandate of world leaders in 2005 to "make it more broadly representative, efficient and transparent and thus to further enhance its effectiveness and the legitimacy and implementation of its decisions."

42

An Action Plan to Combat Terrorism

Sir Aneerod Jugnauth

The IOR handles 30 percent of global trade and almost half of the global traffic of containers passes through Indian Ocean waters. Our region, therefore, holds strong strategic significance and keeping it safe is critical to our economy and prosperity. In early March 2017, the countries of the Indian Ocean Region (IOR) met in Jakarta, Indonesia and adopted a stand alone declaration strongly condemning terrorism. During the course of the conference, the leaders unequivocally recognised the need for information-sharing and close cooperation to defeat terrorism. This marks an important intervention to enhance the response mechanisms against terrorism and also acts to convey a strong signal to those who want to harm us, that we are united and totally determined in our battle against terror.

We are aware that terrorists often show ingenuity in their tactics to cause harm. Hence, it is imperative that we are ten steps ahead of them to undo their plots and win. Let me make it clear, that no cause, either political or otherwise, can justify the killing of innocent people in any society. India has faced several terror attacks in the past and continues to be the target of violent terrorist groups. Thousands of citizens of this country have lost their lives in terror attacks. One of our nationals was a victim of terrorist attacks in Mumbai in 2008. He was the CEO of the State Bank of Mauritius and was on an official mission here. He was, like thousands of others, an innocent bystander, caught in a senseless acts of violence. Such heart-breaking events torment us and we will react firmly to condemn them without any reserve. However,

I want to stress that the violent terrorist ideology should by no means be associated with any specific religion, nationality or ethnic group.

Terrorism today poses the greatest threat to mankind. It is a global problem requiring universal action, starting with coordination in and between regions. The global terrorism data base indicates that from 1970 to 2015, more than 150,000 domestic and international terrorist incidents have been registered. In 2010, there were 4782 cases registered, the number almost quadrupled in 2014, with 16,818 incidents. Terrorism did not start with 9/11 or with the hostage-taking in the Munich Olympics. It outdates these tragic events in our history. However, since the unprecedented 9/11 attack, there has been a growing determination to fight terrorism through the UN and an intensification of cooperation between nations. We already have 19 UN instruments and Security Council resolutions which form the basis for enhancing international cooperation to fight terrorist activities. The UN global counter-terrorism strategy, with its four pillars adopted by the United Nations in 2006, remains a unique instrument that enjoys worldwide consensus on the need for joint action against terrorism.

Mauritius was a founder member of the UN Counter-terrorism Committee in 2001. It is committed to the global counter-terrorism strategy and joined the global initiative to combat nuclear terrorism. My country welcomes the initiative of the Secretary-General of the United Nations to create a new counter-terrorism office to be headed by a new Under-Secretary General, to ensure that due priority is given to counter-terrorism across the UN system. Now I will highlight some areas where I believe we can do better and which deserve attention.

One, we need to elaborate a concerted plan of action that will bring all Indian Ocean countries on a single platform that will have an accrued repository in respect of potential threats before they spiral into uncontrollable happenings.

Two, we must develop an ad hoc task force to deliver capacity building assistance and share counter-terrorism experience among states. Terrorist groups are now using new covert methods such as encryption, dark web and messengers to conduct terrorist activities as well as for recruitment purposes. Radicalisation through the internet is a real issue in every country. Therefore, our intelligence units should have the necessary capacity to detect and neutralise these kinds of operations. Capacity building, real-time information sharing and usage of more sophisticated technology should be the focus of our collaborative efforts.

Three, it is important to put in place national counter-terrorism strategies to address the root causes of terrorism. Moreover, countries should ensure that their laws and regulations to counter-terrorism are aligned with the guidelines published by the UN. Mauritius is collaborating with the African Union to further strengthen its legislation on terrorism.

Four, fighting radicalism, violent extremism and terrorism by developing effective counter narratives against extremist propaganda should be high on the agenda of our national strategies. For that, we have to use all available means including social media, the Internet and electronic and print media.

Five, we should also enlist the cooperation of civil societies, NGOs, parents and teachers to identify and deter home-grown violent extremists who seek to disrupt social harmony. Civil societies create the space for dialogue and alternatives to violence. In this respect, the value of education, which promotes tolerance and mutual respect for others and inclusiveness, cannot be underestimated. We firmly believe that fostering dialogue within society must be part of a participatory strategy that protects communities from recruitment for extremist groups.

Six, religious leaders should be our privileged partners in the fight against terrorism. Engaging these leaders is crucial to promote inter-faith dialogue, tolerance and rejection of the doctrine of violence.

Seven, we must establish legal systems that criminalise the movement of foreign terrorists, their logistical support and the networks that facilitate their movements, departure and return, as well as the standardisation of punishment procedures. In the same context, the African Union Peace and Security Council emphasised the need for concerted efforts towards drying up the funding sources of terrorists and neutralising their modus operandi.

Eight, respect for human rights and the rule of law are critical when countries develop legislation and national strategies to counter violent terrorism. Mauritius is ready to share its experience and participate in training law enforcement officers on integrating law enforcement standards into their daily practices.

Nine, in a concerted manner, we must also address the issue of the cost of security which is very important for small island developing states like Mauritius.

I have mentioned earlier, the need for a human-centred approach in addressing the issue of terrorism. It is true that we are dealing with individuals and organisations that breed on hatred and violent killings. We cannot spare them as they are a threat to humanity altogether. But we need to understand what triggers this sort of behaviour. What is wrong with the world that fuels so much violence? Can we be happy with the doctrine that 'might is always right'? How do we react when those who advocate the rule of law and justice in the world do exactly the contrary when confronted with issues regarding the interest of others? There is also talk of good and bad terrorists. Can we accept that some people use other people to spread terror for their own selfish interest? These questions are prominent and they need answers if we are to win the battle against terrorism.

My country, Mauritius, has a multi-cultural and multi-religious population and we believe in an equitable world. We believe in equal treatment and inclusiveness. We have made 'Unity and Diversity' our mantra for social cohesion and harmonious living. We are of the view that there are four requisites that are essential to shield society from hatred and its implications. First, no discrimination. Second, no double standards. Third, tolerance and mutual respect, and fourth, readiness to act decisively and effectively.

In our fight against terrorism there are three things that we must do. First, we need to be vigilant more than ever before and enhance intelligence gathering and exchange of information. Second, to address a man-made problem, we need a human touch to address the root causes of terrorism and act humanly. Third, we have to make the ballot of democracy and the rule of law prevail over the bullet of anarchy and hatred. Finally, we must never lose faith in humanity. In the words of Mahatma Gandhi:

> *"You must not lose faith in humanity. Humanity is an ocean. If a few drops of the ocean are dirty, the ocean does not become dirty."*

List of Contributors

M. Hamid Ansari is an Indian politician who started his career in the Indian Foreign Service in 1961. He served as the Vice President of India for 10 years from 2007 to 2017. He is a scholar on West Asia and has authored a number of books. He was awarded the Padma Shree in 1984.

Ranil Wickremesinghe was sworn in as the Prime Minister of Sri Lanka for the fourth time on 21 August 2015. He is the leader of the United National Party (UNP), Sri Lanka's largest political party, which is a constituent member of the National Unity Government.

Manohar Lal Khattar is a Bhartiya Janata Party politician and the current Chief Minister of Haryana state in India. He contested the assembly elections for the first time in Haryana in 2014 from Karnal constituency and won the same, thereafter becoming the Chief Minister of the state.

Bimalendra Nidhi is a Nepali politician and the current Deputy Prime Minister and Minister of Home Affairs of Nepal. He is also a central-level leader of the Nepali Congress, the largest political party of the nation.

M.J. Akbar is the Minister of State for External Affairs, Government of India, and a Member of Parliament in the Rajya Sabha, from Madhya Pradesh. He is a distinguished writer who has authored several internationally acclaimed books. He also serves as Director, India Foundation.

Wiranto is the Coordinating Minister for Political, Legal and Security Affairs, Government of Indonesia.

Hekmat Khalil Karzai is the Deputy Foreign Minister of Afghanistan. He is the founding director of Afghanistan's Centre for Conflict and Peace Studies.

He is a former RMS Fellow at the International Centre for Political Violence and Terrorism Research in Singapore.

Asaduzzaman Khan is a Bangladeshi politician from the Awami league. He is the current minister of Home Affairs in the Government of Bangladesh. A heroic freedom fighter, he participated in Bangladesh's War of Liberation in 1971.

Sagala Ratnayaka is a Member of Parliament and the current Minister of Youth & Southern Development of Sri Lanka. He is also the Prime Minister's Chief of Staff. From January 2015 to September 2015 he served as the Chief of Staff to the Prime Minister, until he was elected to parliament and appointed as a cabinet minister.

Kasiviswanathan Shanmugam is a Singaporean politician and lawyer. He is a member of the governing People's Action Party (PAP), he has been the Minister for Law since May 2008 and the Minister for Home Affairs since October 2015. He previously served as the Minister for Foreign Affairs from May 2011 to September 2015.

General Vijay Kumar Singh, PVSM, AVSM, YSM is an alumnus of Birla Public School, Pilani and National Defence Academy, Pune. He served as the 26th Chief of Army Staff of the Indian Army. Currently, he serves as the Minister of State for External Affairs, Government of India.

Avi Dichter is an Israeli politician and the current Chairman of the Foreign Affairs and Defense Committee. He is a former commando soldier, Minister of Internal Security, and director of the Shin Bet. During the start of the Second Intifada, Dichter restructured the mission of the Shin Bet to serve at the forefront of Israel's security and counter-terrorism efforts.

Rajiv Mehrishi is an IAS officer of the 1978 batch who retired as the Home Secretary on 30 August 1917. He has earlier served as the Finance Secretary and as the Chief Secretary, Government of Rajasthan. He is the current Comptroller and Auditor General of India (C&AG) and Chairman of United Nations Board of Auditors.

Hein Kiessling is a political scientist and historian (PhD, Ludwig Maximilian University) who lived from 1989 to 2002 in Pakistan, including four years in Quetta and nine in Islamabad, during which he forged close contacts among

Pakistan's political, military and intelligence elites. In 2002 he was awarded the Order of Merit of the Federal Republic of Germany.

Simon Allison is a senior reporter for the Daily Maverick, a South Africa based digital publication, and a consultant with the Institute for Security Studies. He specialises in African news and analysis with emphasis on conflict, security and counter-terrorism. He holds degrees from Rhodes University and the School of Oriental and African Studies, and has lived and worked across Africa and the Middle East.

Takeshi Kohno is Professor, Department of Social Sciences, Toyo Eiwa University, Japan

Bilveer Singh is an Adjunct Senior Fellow at the Centre of Excellence for National Security (CENS) at the S. Rajaratnam School of International Studies (RSIS) and Associate Professor at the Department of Political Science, National University of Singapore. He was Acting Head, CENS from January to December 2010. He graduated with Masters and PhD in International Relations from the Australian National University.

Dam Phu Cuong is Chief of Asia and Oceania Division, General Department of Security, Vietnam.

Hamidin is the Director for Prevention, National Counter Terrorism Agency, Indonesia. He is serving as director of prevention, since June 5, 2015. Hamidin is a graduate of the Police Academy, 1987 and is also an experienced detective.

Min Zaw Oo currently serves as the Team leader, Technical Secretariat, Center of Joint Ceasefire Monitoring Committee, Yangon. He completed his M.A. from Georgetown University in 2008, Security Studies focusing on security sector reform and M.S. in Conflict Analysis and Resolution, George Mason University, 2002. His Masters' thesis was Conflict Analysis on Potential Political Transition in Burma: Conflict Mapping and Reconciliation.

Daniel Pipes is an American historian, writer, and commentator. He is the President of the Middle East Forum, and publisher of its Middle East Quarterly journal. His writing focuses on the American foreign policy and the Middle East. He is also an Expert at Wikistrat. Pipes has written sixteen books, and served as an adviser to Rudolph Giuliani's 2008 presidential campaign.

Vladimir Evseev is Deputy Director of the Institute for Commonwealth of Independent States, Russia.

Ilan Berman is Senior Vice President of the American Foreign Policy Council in Washington, DC. An expert on regional security in the Middle East, Central Asia, and the Russian Federation, he has consulted for both the US Central Intelligence Agency and the US Department of Defense. Berman has a BA in Politics from Brandeis University, an MA in International Politics from American University, and a JD from Washington College of Law.

Lt Col Vivek Chadha served in the Indian Army for 22 years before taking premature retirement. He joined IDSA in November 2011. His research focus covers counter insurgency, counter terrorism and terrorism finance.

Group Capt Ajey Lele is a Senior Research Fellow at IDSA. His areas of expertise include Weapons of Mass Destructions with major emphasis on Biological Weapons, Space and National Security and Non Military Threats.

Natallia Khaniejo is a research intern at IDSA. She has completed her Bachelors from Lady Shri Ram College and her Masters from Miranda house Delhi University. She is currently working on issues of Cyber Security.

E.S.L. Narasimhan is a former bureaucrat who is currently serving as the Governor of Andhra Pradesh and Telangana. He is an IAS officer from Andhra Pradesh cadre. He also served for many years in the Intelligence Bureau, before becoming director of the bureau in December 2006.

Mehbooba Mufti Sayeed is the current Chief Minister of Jammu and Kashmir State and also the president of Jammu and Kashmir Peoples Democratic Party (PDP). Mehbooba Mufti was also a member of the 14th Lok Sabha (2004-2009).

NN Vohra is the current governor of the Indian state of Jammu and Kashmir. Vohra served as Defence Secretary, Principal Secretary to Prime Minister and was a member of the National Security Advisory Board. He also headed the National Task Force on internal security and co-chaired the India-European Union Round Table in 2001.

Kiren Rijiju is an Indian politician and member of the Bharatiya Janata Party. He is the current Union Minister of State for Home Affairs, Government of India. He served as a Member of Khadi and Village Industries Commission from 2000 to 2005. Kiren Rijiju is arguably the most iconic political leader from Arunachal Pradesh in recent times; he is often being referred to as the "voice of North East India". He occasionally writes articles on security & socio-economic issues.

Baburam Bhattarai is a former Prime Minister of Nepal. He was a senior Standing Committee Member and vice chairperson of Unified Communist Party of Nepal (Maoist). He is now Coordinator of Naya Shakti a newly founded Party. His former party started People's War in Nepal (as self-proclaimed by Unified Communist Party of Nepal (Maoist)) in 1996 that had huge impact for the change of the political system in Nepal.

Rajavarothiam Sampanthan is a Sri Lankan Tamil politician and lawyer who has led the Tamil National Alliance since 2001. He has also been a Member of Parliament since 2001, and previously served as a Member of Parliament from 1977 to 1983 and from 1997 to 2000. Currently he is the Leader of the Opposition in Sri Lankan parliament.

Sajad Lone currently serves as the Minister of Social Welfare, ARI & Trainings and Science & Technology in the Government of Jammu and Kashmir, India. He is the chairman of the Jammu and Kashmir Peoples Conference.

Hagrama Mohilary alias Hagrama Basumatary is the Chief Executive Member of Bodoland Territorial Council. He was previously the chief of BLTF.

Muriel Domenach is the Secretary General of the Intelligence Committee for the Prevention of Crime and Radicalization in France. Prior to this, she has also served as the Deputy Director of the Policy Planning Staff in the Ministry of Foreign and European Affairs and as the Defence Advisor to the Permanent Delegation of France to NATO in Brussels.

Prof. Boaz Ganor is the Dean and the Ronald Lauder Chair for Counter-Terrorism at the Lauder School of Government, Diplomacy & Strategy, as well as the Founder and Executive Director of the International Institute for Counter-Terrorism (ICT), at the Interdisciplinary Center (IDC), Herzliya, Israel. Prof. Ganor serves as the Founding President of the International Academic Counter-Terrorism Community (ICTAC), an international association of academic institutions, experts, and researchers in fields related to the study of terrorism and counter-terrorism.

Vice Admiral G Ashok Kumar AVSM, VSM is an Indian Navy officer, currently serving as Deputy Chief of Naval Staff. An alumnus of National Defence Academy, Khadakvasla, Pune. He was commissioned into the Executive Branch of the Indian Navy on 01 Jul 1982.

Vladimir Milovidov is the Deputy Director, Russian Institute for Strategic Studies; Head of the Centre for Research Coordination and Public Relations, RISS, Russia.

Martin Kimani is the Director, National Counter Terrorism Centre, Kenya.

K.V. Bhagirath is the Secretary General of Indian Ocean Rim Association (IORA) since January 1, 2012. He was re-elected by the IORA Council of Ministers held in Perth, Australia, 9 October 2014 for a second term which commenced on January 1, 2015. Ambassador Bhagirath is from the Indian Foreign Service, which he joined in 1979.

Elizabeth Joyce works as the Section Chief-Asia Pacific and the Americas Counter-Terrorism Committee Executive Directorate (CTED) of the United Nations Security Council. Before the current post she was the Section Chief–Europe. She has worked for the UN since 1999, where she started as a Money Laundering Advisor to the UNODC. From there she moved into counter-terrorism via her work on countering terrorist financing.

Asoke Kumar Mukerji is an Indian diplomat and writer. He was Permanent Representative of India to the United Nations from April 2013 to December 2015. He worked as a trade negotiator in the newly formed World Trade Organization between 1995-98 and was among the first Indian officials tasked with representing India in trade disputes involving India brought before the WTO Dispute Settlement Mechanism.

Sir Anerood Jugnauth GCSK, KCMG, QC, MP, PC is a Mauritian politician who served as both President and Prime Minister of Mauritius. He is Member of Parliament for Piton & Riviere Du Rempart. Since 2017 he has been Minister Mentor, Minister of Rodrigues and Defence in the cabinet of his son, Prime Minister Pravind Jugnauth. A central figure of Mauritian politics in the 1980s and 1990s, he has continuously (except for the periods 1995–2000 and 2012–2014) held a constitutional office since 1976.

Index